THE
EVERYTHING®
GUIDE TO WRITING
YOUR FIRST NOVEL

Dear Reader,

I was one of those people who was sure that I'd never write a novel. Not clever enough. Not creative enough. No unique life experiences. I'd never come up with a good enough idea, and even if I did, I'd never have the stamina to wrestle it through 300 pages to a satisfying ending.

Then, one day, a wonderful story idea came to me and I decided to try writing it. I opened a new file, fingers poised over the keyboard, and right away I was stymied. Would it be "I" or "she," past tense or present, and where oh where to begin?

Writing those first pages was like squeezing blood out of a turnip. A writer friend who critiqued my fledgling effort wanted to know: From which character's viewpoint did I think I was writing that opening scene?

Viewpoint? Scene? Were those things that I needed to know about?

It was news to me that I couldn't simply plunge into writing fiction using all the techniques I'd mastered over years of writing nonfiction. More bad news: All these years that I'd been reading novels, I hadn't paid much attention to how it's done. That was understandable because, as I would later come to realize, only bad writing draws attention to itself.

So, gentle writer, I hope this book spares you the kind of ugly trial and error that I went through in order to write that novel that you know you've got in you.

Sincerely,

Hallie Ephron

Welcome to the EVERYTHING® Series!

These handy, accessible books give you all you need to tackle a difficult project, gain a new hobby, comprehend a fascinating topic, prepare for an exam, or even brush up on something you learned back in school but have since forgotten.

You can choose to read an *Everything®* book from cover to cover or just pick out the information you want from our four useful boxes: e-questions, e-facts, e-alerts, and e-ssentials.

We give you everything you need to know on the subject, but throw in a lot of fun stuff along the way, too.

We now have more than 400 *Everything®* books in print, spanning such wide-ranging categories as weddings, pregnancy, cooking, music instruction, foreign language, crafts, pets, New Age, and so much more. When you're done reading them all, you can finally say you know *Everything®*!

QUESTION

Answers to
common questions

FACT

Important snippets
of information

ALERT

Urgent
warnings

ESSENTIAL

Quick
handy tips

PUBLISHER Karen Cooper

DIRECTOR OF ACQUISITIONS AND INNOVATION Paula Munier

MANAGING EDITOR, EVERYTHING® SERIES Lisa Laing

COPY CHIEF Casey Ebert

ASSISTANT PRODUCTION EDITOR Jacob Erickson

ACQUISITIONS EDITOR Lisa Laing

SENIOR DEVELOPMENT EDITOR Brett Palana-Shanahan

ASSOCIATE DEVELOPMENT EDITOR Hillary Thompson

EDITORIAL ASSISTANT Ross Weisman

EVERYTHING® SERIES COVER DESIGNER Erin Alexander

LAYOUT DESIGNERS Colleen Cunningham, Elisabeth Lariviere, Ashley Vierra, Denise Wallace

Visit the entire Everything® series at *www.everything.com*

THE
EVERYTHING®
GUIDE TO WRITING YOUR FIRST NOVEL

All the tools you need to write
and sell your first novel

Hallie Ephron, book reviewer for the *Boston Globe*
and author of *Never Tell a Lie*

Avon, Massachusetts

An Everything® Series Book.
Everything® and everything.com® are registered trademarks of F+W Media, Inc.

Published by Adams Media, a division of F+W Media, Inc.
57 Littlefield Street, Avon, MA 02322 U.S.A.
www.adamsmedia.com

Contains material adapted and abridged from *The Everything® Guide to
Writing a Novel* by Joyce and Jim Lavene, copyright © 2004 by F+W Media, Inc.,
ISBN 10: 1-59337-132-2, ISBN 13: 978-1-59337-132-6.

ISBN 10: 1-4405-0957-3
ISBN 13: 978-1-4405-0957-5
eISBN 10: 1-4405-1063-6
eISBN 13: 978-1-4405-1063-2

Printed in the United States of America.

10 9 8 7 6 5

Library of Congress Cataloging-in-Publication Data
Ephron, Hallie.
The everything guide to writing your first novel / Hallie Ephron.
p. cm.
Includes index.
ISBN-13: 978-1-4405-0957-5
ISBN-10: 1-4405-0957-3
ISBN-13: 978-1-4405-1063-2
ISBN-10: 1-4405-1063-6
1. Authorship—Marketing. I. Title.
PN3365.E45   2010
808.3—dc22   2010038493

This publication is designed to provide accurate and authoritative information with regard to the subject matter covered. It is sold with the understanding that the publisher is not engaged in rendering legal, accounting, or other professional advice. If legal advice or other expert assistance is required, the services of a competent professional person should be sought.

—From a *Declaration of Principles* jointly adopted by a Committee of the American Bar Association and a Committee of Publishers and Associations

This book is available at quantity discounts for bulk purchases.
For information, please call 1-800-289-0963.

Contents

Acknowledgments

I'd like to thank Paula Munier, who made this project possible, and editor Lisa Laing, and all my writing friends who, over the years, have labored through my dreadful first drafts.

Top 10 Reasons to Write a Novel

1. You have a story you're bursting to tell.

2. You love reading novels and want to try your hand at writing one.

3. You have a passion for words and you love to write.

4. You've experienced something that you want to communicate to others.

5. The story you want to tell is too long and complex to fit into a short-story format.

6. You want to have the satisfaction of knowing you've completed a manuscript.

7. You want to try your hand at getting a novel published.

8. You're looking for a career that will last a lifetime.

9. You're looking for a career that can travel with you, no matter where you go.

10. You want to see if you can experience some of the fame, fortune, and prestige that successful novelists enjoy.

Introduction

IN 2008, MORE THAN 53,000 works of fiction were published in the United States according to Bowker, which analyzes data for the book business. Most of them were novels, and together they comprised more than one sixth of all the books published that year (including traditional print as well as on-demand titles but excluding audio and e-book titles).

That's more than a hundred novels published each day! And while there's no easy way to figure out how many of them were debut novels, it's safe to say that thousands of first novels are published in the course of the year.

Are novels big business? Take the #1 bestselling novel of 2009, Dan Brown's thriller *The Lost Symbol*. It sold 5.5 million copies. The #3 bestseller, Kathryn Stockett's mainstream fiction *The Help*, was a first novel by a previously unknown writer. Its sales broke the one million mark.

The profits publishers earn from books by brand-name authors like Dan Brown help to underwrite the risk of bringing to market novels by unpublished writers. Publishers and agents alike are looking for the next Dan Brown (thriller), the next Janet Evanovich (mystery), the next Danielle Steele (romance), or the next Barbara Kingsolver (mainstream). It can't be you if you never write that novel that you've got bottled up inside of you.

This book is designed to help you get that novel written.

No, there are no shortcuts or magic formulas, and it can't be done in a week. But writing a novel is not rocket science, nor is it some mysterious art form that only the most brilliant among us can master. It's challenging, but what is there in life worth doing that isn't?

The Everything® Guide to Writing Your First Novel will explain mainstream and genre fiction categories of novels, and take you through the process of coming up with an idea for a novel and transforming it into a premise. It will guide you through the process of conjuring your novel's main plot and subplots, its cast of characters, setting, context, and time frame.

No planning method is a one-size-fits-all. Because each writer has different strengths, a range of different planning methods is presented so you can choose the ones that suit your temperament and work style.

This book discusses research, how to learn what you need in order to write page one, and that additional ongoing research that you may need to do to nourish your story. Then it provides guidance for writing the novel, from the first scene to the final one. The basics of writing dialogue, writing action, and writing conflict are discussed with tips and insights for getting it right, and pitfalls to be avoided.

With guidance and diligence, and by using the material provided in this book, you should be able to complete a first draft, from writing the first scene to typing "The End," in six months. From there, you will be ready to revise and polish your novel until it is just as good as you can make it, and formatted so that literary agents and editors will take you seriously.

Then, maybe the next breakout bestselling novel will have your name on its cover.

CHAPTER 1

Defining the Novel

A novel is a work of fiction that tells of a series of connected events and the characters who experience them. A novel may be literary or genre fiction. There are few rules or conventions about what constitutes a literary novel, but the genres of fiction are very much defined by reader (and publisher) expectations.

A Definition

If you have an idea for a work of fiction that can be narrated in 50,000 words or more, then you are noodling around with an idea for a novel. Your story and characters may be completely of your own invention. Or perhaps your story is based on events that actually happened to real people. But as a novelist you have to be prepared to take "the fiction leap" and transform those real events and people into a compelling story. The story in every good novel has a shape and meaning often lacking in the characteristically chaotic unfolding of real events.

Types of Novels

Generally, novels fall into two types: literary fiction and genre fiction. The differences between literary and genre fiction can be quite subjective. Literary fiction is serious stuff that aspires to higher literary standards and often defies easy categorization. Genre fiction falls into specific categories and generally is written to conform to the conventions of a particular genre such as romance or mystery.

You may hear the term "mainstream" or "general" fiction, too. These are fuzzy terms often used to refer to novels that are more accessible to the average reader than a literary work, but that cannot be readily categorized into a genre. Some pundits joke that a "mainstream" novel is nothing more than a literary novel that finds a wide audience.

Each year Bowker analyzes data for publishers and booksellers. The list below shows their accounting of the percentage of fiction titles among all books sold in 2009.

- General Fiction (7%)
- Romance (7%)
- Mystery/Detective (5%)
- Fantasy (3%)
- Young adult (3%)
- Literary/Classics (2%)

Despite the fact that authors of "general" fiction and genre fiction such as romance, mystery, sci-fi, and fantasy don't get taken as seriously as authors of literary novels, their works dominate the fiction market.

Literary Fiction

There are no hard and fast rules defining a literary novel. A literary novel can tell the story of one day in a single character's life, as James Joyce did following Leopold Bloom through the streets of Dublin in *Ulysses*, or it can tell the stories of generations of characters over a century as Gabriel Garcia Marquez did following the villagers of Macondo in *One Hundred Years of Solitude*. The writing may be evocative and poetic as in Virginia Woolf's *Mrs. Dalloway*, raw and biting as in Chuck Palahniuk's *Fight Club*, complex and intellectually challenging as in Umberto Eco's *Foucault's Pendulum*, or vividly sensual as in Laura Esquivel's *Like Water for Chocolate*.

FACT

To find outstanding literary and genre novels from the present and recent past, lists of prizewinners are available on the Internet. The website of the Sacramento State Library (*http://library.csus.edu*) is an excellent source.

Literary novels are often rich in language and imagery and typically deal with transcendent themes. In most literary novels, character and technique may be even more important than plot, and often the author's goal is to say something profound, and in a new way, about the human condition.

General or Mainstream Fiction

A novel is considered "general" or "mainstream" if it is written for the average reader, cannot be categorized into a specific genre, or is so well written that it can be said to "exceed" its would-be genre. In addition, loosely defined subcategories like "men's fiction," "women's fiction," and "chick lit" can all be considered mainstream fiction.

Some bestselling novels that would be considered mainstream include *The Lovely Bones* by Alice Sebold, *The Girl with the Dragon Tattoo* by Stieg Larsson, *Message in a Bottle* by Nicholas Sparks, and *Water for Elephants* by Sarah Gruen.

Mainstream fiction usually has a strong hook or premise that is intriguing to a wide range of readers. The novel can be either plot driven or character driven, but usually the plot conforms to a traditional rather than a more experimental structure. The writing usually doesn't draw attention to itself, but serves the story.

Genre Fiction

Many novels fall into genre categories. Readers expect these novels to respect the conventions of the genre. If you are writing a genre novel, you should read them. Get to know the rules of that genre even if you plan to break every one of them. The main genre categories for fiction are mystery, thriller, romance, science fiction, and fantasy.

Mystery

A mystery novel is about a crime, often a murder, and the story involves a fictional sleuth solving the puzzle, or whodunnit. Sleuths come in all shapes and sizes. A sleuth can be a pro whose job is solving crimes, like a police officer or a private investigator. Alternately, a sleuth can be an amateur such as a teacher, librarian, or caterer who gets inadvertently drawn into solving a crime. Delightful mystery novels have even featured a dog or cat or sheep as sleuths.

Mystery novels come in series and as standalones. In a series, the same sleuth continues from one book to the next, each time out solving a new crime. Some bestselling series include Sue Grafton's *Kinsey Millhone* series, Michael Connelly's *Harry Bosch* series, Janet Evanovich's *Stephanie Plum* series, and even after all these years, Agatha Christie's *Hercule Poirot* or her *Miss Marple* series.

The conventions of the mystery genre include:

- Much of the story is narrated by a sleuth/protagonist
- Bad things happen; there's at least one murder
- There are multiple suspects
- There's a central puzzle for the reader (and the fictional sleuth) to solve

- The author plays fair with the reader, revealing everything the sleuth knows
- The reader feels satisfied at the end that justice has been served

In the best mystery novels, the solution delivers credible surprise; something that the reader didn't see coming but that, in retrospect, seems inevitable. Mystery novels that fall short rely on coincidence—some essential part of the solution depends on contrivance and chance—or have an obvious solution that readers get, long before the sleuth. A passive sleuths makes for a weak mystery. The sleuth needs to actively solve the crime rather than have the solution fall in his lap.

Finally, mystery writers cheat their readers when they don't "play fair." Readers expect to know everything the sleuth knows, when he knows it, not to have essential clues withheld by the author.

Thrillers

The main ingredient of a thriller is suspense. The reader stays on the edge of his seat turning the pages, feeling both anxious and afraid to discover what happens next. The stakes are as high as they can be, and evil itself is often what the protagonist is up against.

Thrillers often have multiple narrators, plus plenty of action and violence. Their stories move swiftly. Thrillers tend to be longer than mystery novels (400-plus pages is not uncommon) and the story often involves threats such as bio-terrorism, nuclear bombs, or political upheavals.

Some classic thrillers include Robert Ludlum's *The Bourne Supremacy*, Daniel Brown's *The Da Vinci Code*, Tom Clancy's *Patriot Games*, and *The Last Spymaster* by Gayle Lynds.

Here are some of the genre conventions of a thriller novel:

- The pace is fast, often unrelenting
- There's tension from page one
- There are lots of exciting, surprising plot twists
- A "ticking clock" ratchets the tension as it counts down to disaster
- The stakes are high
- The story often takes place in an exotic location
- The hero tends to be a maverick who follow his own moral compass

- The story often revolves around a "high concept" (like impending environmental disaster or terrorist threats to humanity)
- In the final climactic scenes the protagonist triumphs over ostensibly insurmountable odds

Thrillers are often written using a broad canvas, but sometimes the author falls in love with multiple viewpoints and the reader loses track of the plot. Another typical shortcoming is inadequate characterization; the author lavishes all his attention on the story and fails to develop believable, three-dimensional characters. Sometimes, too, the plots of thrillers stretch credibility past the breaking point. Too much high-tech and gee-whiz gimmickry also can keep the reader from suspending disbelief. Another common failing is the hero or villain who is all-powerful. Main characters need flaws in order to be interesting.

Action in a thriller is a requisite; but nonstop action with characters that never slow down keeps the reader from absorbing the magnitude of what has happened and caring about what's going to happen next.

Romance

Romance novels are about a romantic relationship (usually) between two people, and about overcoming the obstacles that keep them apart. These days there are plenty of the familiar heterosexual romance novels as well as gay and lesbian romance novels.

There are two general types of romance novels: category romance and single titles.

Single-title romance novels tend to be longer and have fewer constraints. Category-romance novels are shorter; they follow specific publisher's guidelines about aspects like historical backdrop and the level of sensuality.

For many years, so-called "Regency romance" (set in nineteenth-century England) by authors like Georgette Heyer and Barbara Cartland were wildly popular; more recently paranormal romance has surged to the forefront led by the surprising success of Stephenie Meyer's *Twilight* series that became breakout adult bestsellers.

Romance readers expect:

- A love story
- A central obstacle or conflict that keeps the lovers apart and must be overcome
- Erotic scenes and often hot and steamy sex
- Main characters who grow and change over the course of the novel
- An emotionally satisfying and upbeat ending

Writing a romance novel is demanding, and exotic settings and historical time frames require a sense of authenticity. A romance novel that is insufficiently researched will disappoint readers. Another typical shortcoming in a romance novel is the clichéd character—the evil mother, the shrinking violet, the profligate rake, and the other stock characters of romance novels that have been written a million times. The challenge for the writer is to come up with new twists on old clichés. Clichéd plot twists can also weaken the novel. Estrangement driven by a misunderstanding, for example, has been used and overused. Sex is an important ingredient in romance fiction, sex scenes written with purple prose and flowery euphemisms will generate more laughter than heat.

Science Fiction and Fantasy

Science fiction and fantasy are sometimes lumped together as "speculative fiction."

A science fiction novel envisions a scientifically plausible world in the future, in some alternative past, or in an alternate timeline. Sci-fi heroes may be scientists, or starship captains, or computer geeks. Classic sci-fi novels include Frank Herbert's *Dune*, Robert Heinlein's *Stranger in a Strange Land*, and William Gibson's *Neuromancer*.

Fantasy novels take the reader to an imaginary, fantastic world that might be deep in the earth's core, in the heavens, or in a setting from mythology. Characters that may or may not be human typically have extraordinary powers or the ability to work magic.

J. K. Rowling's *Harry Potter* novels, Madeleine L'Engle's *A Swiftly Tilting Planet*, and Diana Gabaldon's *Outlander* novels are stellar examples of the genre.

Here are some conventions that make both science fiction and fantasy novels work:

- The protagonist takes a hero's journey to reach some powerful goal
- Their fantastic or future worlds are utterly believable and internally consistent
- The hero is often the only person who can stop a powerful villain or evil force
- Heroes typically have someone or a special force that helps them and explains what challenges they face
- By the end, most of the main characters survive, having been transformed

A particular challenge for the fantasy and science fiction writer is to build a believable alternate reality that is consistent from the beginning of the novel to the end. Another challenge is to create a story that is not merely a series of episodes, stopping points in a journey. The story has to build, and the characters change as a result of what's happened to them.

Formats

Today's books come in a wide range of formats. The traditional book, printed on paper between hard or soft covers, is still the most common format. But audio books are popular, and electronic books are growing quickly in market share. Authors have more formats in which their books can be published than ever before.

Hardbacks

Books published between hard covers are the oldest format available. This format is the most expensive, and a hard-soft deal in which a book first comes out in hard cover and later in soft cover, is still the goal of many literary agents and their writers. Although the price of hardbacks puts them out of the reach of many readers, this is the basic format libraries stock on their shelves, so a single hardback often reaches multiple readers.

Mass-Market Paperbacks

These are the small paperback novels that have been popular since the "dime novels" (aka "pulp novels" that were first published in the late 1930s) became popular. Mass-market paperbacks are cheaper, easier to carry, and more likely to be readily available in airports and supermarkets than the larger trade paperbacks.

Trade Paperbacks

Trade paperbacks are published in a larger format than mass market and tend to use somewhat better quality paper and a larger typeface. These large soft covers are priced between mass-market and hardbacks. Literary and mainstream novels, later editions of bestsellers, as well as original editions of books from small presses often come out in this more prestigious format.

FACT

Bowker reported that of all books sold in the United States in 2009, 34.9% were hardbacks, 35.2% were trade paperbacks; 21.4% were mass market paperbacks, 1.6% were audio titles, and 1.6% were e-books. E-books were the single most rapidly growing category.

Electronic Books (E-books)

With the growing popularity of electronic devices like Amazon's Kindle, Barnes & Nobles's Nook, Apple's iPad, and the Sony Reader, the market for books delivered in electronic format is exploding. Books in this format are less expensive to publish because shipping, inventorying, and manufacturing costs are eliminated. Early on, these books are being priced about the same as a trade paperback, but only time will tell where those price points settle.

Audio Books

What we used to call "books on tape" have become very popular, especially for readers who like to listen to a lively narrator read the story. Audio books can be rented or purchased on CD or downloaded from the Internet (like e-books) as MP3 files and put onto players like the iPod.

CHAPTER 2

Getting Started

Your first task as a novelist is to take yourself seriously. You need a place to write your novel, the tools to write it with, and the time to get the job done. The good news is that these are probably gifts that you can give yourself. Read on for tips and advice on getting yourself into the mindset of a novelist.

Get Serious

It takes time, determination, and persistence to write a novel. If you take your writing seriously, the other people in your life will take your writing seriously, too. Setting aside time and space to write are first and foremost.

Here's some basic advice for getting started:

- Schedule time to write: Set yourself a schedule and set aside at least two hours, preferably more, each day to write.
- Write when you're at your best: Are you a lark or a night owl? Set aside that part of each day when you are at your sharpest.
- Create a dedicated space: Set up a place where you can write, uninterrupted by the ebb and flow of your home life; if not a separate room, then at the very least block off a corner of a room.
- Get disconnected: When you start writing each day, turn off the phone and your e-mail; you might even disconnect your computer from the Internet so you are less likely to get sidetracked.

And a final piece of advice: Don't quit your day job: Learning to write fiction well takes time; selling your work takes even longer; so unless you have an independent source of income, it's wise to keep your regular financial lifeline flowing.

ESSENTIAL

Virginia Woolf said it most eloquently: "A woman must have money and a room of her own if she is going to write." In today's equal opportunity environment, that often-quoted adage applies to men as well as to women.

Your "Office"

Even if it's just a corner of your bedroom, blocked off from the rest of the house by a bookcase or by a screen, set up your writing space like a professional. Though you may be one of those people who need to write the first draft longhand, these days publishers require manuscripts to be delivered electronically. You'll need access to a computer with basic word processing software and e-mail.

Don't wait until you lose a day's or a week's work to get serious about backing up your files. Back your files up regularly—some writers save their novels to a thumb drive or e-mail files to themselves several times a day. An automated backup system is an even better idea. A printer is essential, too, because there will be times that you'll need the distance that the printed page creates in assessing your own work.

Here is a summary of the essential elements of the novelist's office:

- A computer connected to the Internet
- Basic word processing software (like Microsoft Word)
- A comfortable desk chair with good back support
- A generous, well-lit work surface
- Paper and a reliable printer
- A file cabinet or two
- A "Keep Out" sign to stick on the *inside* of your office door

The Internet has pretty much eliminated the need for reference books that were once indispensable, not to mention most trips to the library. Encyclopedias, dictionaries, multiple versions of the Bible, a thesaurus, *Bartlett's Familiar Quotations*, and *The Elements of Style* by William Strunk and E. B. White, not to mention references and all manner of books and images, including photographs of just about any location where you might want to set your novel, are easily accessible on the Internet.

Create a Support System

Writing is a solitary endeavor—there's no water cooler or coffee machine where you can take breaks and reconnect with humanity. So it's important to create a support system to give you the perspective that you need and to keep you from going stir crazy.

There are hundreds of wonderful communities of writers, and it's easy to connect with them on the Internet. It's well worth the yearly dues to join an existing organization and grow a network of writer friends. Many of these groups have local chapters that meet regularly, publish newsletters and handbooks for writers, sponsor chat rooms and forums and conferences, and even provide expert staff who can answer the questions that arise when you are wondering whether to accept your first contract.

You may want to join a writers critique group or create your own group of like-minded writers with whom you can share the pains and pleasures of writing.

Organizations for Writers

There are hundreds of organizations that provide an easy way for writers to connect with other writers. Here are some of the major organizations for mainstream fiction and genre writers:

- Poets & Writers, Inc. (*www.pw.org*) provides information, support, and guidance for creative writers. Poets & Writers, headquartered in New York City, is the nation's largest nonprofit literary organization, serving poets, fiction writers, and creative nonfiction writers. Their Directory of Writers and message forum help their members connect with one other. Their literary events calendar posts events by city and state, and their online grants and awards database includes an inventory of writing contests. They also publish *Poets & Writers* magazine.
- Science Fiction and Fantasy Writers of America (SFWA) (*www.sfwa .org*) is a professional organization for authors of fantasy and science fiction. Unpublished writers can become affiliate members. SFWA sponsors member forums and provides a member directory. They host the Nebula Awards, provide an Information Center for novice authors, and the Writer Beware area of their website is one of the best clearinghouses for information educating writers about schemes, scams, and pitfalls to avoid.
- Romance Writers of America (RWA) (*www.rwanational.org*) is the premier organization for writers pursuing a career in romance writing. RWA hosts an annual conference and sponsors awards including the RITA Awards for published romance novels and the Golden Heart Awards for unpublished manuscripts. Regional chapters of the RWA host regular meetings as well as regional conferences.

- Mystery Writers of America (MWA) (*www.mysterywriters.org*) is an organization for professional crime fiction writers. Writers who are not yet published can become affiliate members. MWA sponsors an online forum and gives the prestigious Edgar Awards at an annual Edgar Weekend in New York City, where their main office is located. There are active regional chapters throughout the United States, many of which host regional conferences and keep up a lively calendar of meetings.
- Sisters in Crime (SinC) (*www.sistersincrime.org*) is an organization that supports the professional development and advancement of women crime writers in their effort to achieve equality in the industry. They have a lively online forum and newsletter. There are many active local chapters throughout the United States, and their on-line Guppies ("the great unpublished") chapter is one of the best mutual support organizations for unpublished writers.

Writers really do help other writers, and joining an organization like one of these can help keep you informed about the latest trends in publishing as well as provide you with an extended support group.

Connecting Through Social Media

Readers and writers hang out online and social networking sites like Facebook, MySpace, and LinkedIn allow you to set up a profile for yourself. Think of it as your own web page, and use it to connect with other writers and readers.

Join GoodReads (*www.goodreads.com*), Writerface (*www.writerface. com*), or WritingRoom (*www.writingroom.com*), for example, or one of the many other online groups, and stay in touch with likeminded people who share your passion and enthusiasm for reading and writing. If you post regularly in public forums and develop a wide network of "friends," you'll have a leg up on getting known even before your book is published.

Readers use social media: According to Bowker, 47 percent of women book buyers are on Facebook and 9 percent are on Twitter. Genre readers are most likely to be on social networks.

The unpublished writer who creates a presence online and connects with a network of writers and readers can harness those resources while writing. Post questions and find experts with the answers. Discuss writing issues with other writers. Find readers willing to critique early drafts. And once the novel is published, those connections become invaluable, too, for publicizing and marketing the book.

Working with a Writers Critique Group

Some writers get together regularly with a group of other writers to critique each other's work in progress. Some meet in person; others exchange manuscripts electronically and meet online or by phone.

Here are some guidelines, should you decide that a writers critique group might work for you:

- Form a group of between four and seven writers.
- Collaborate with others whose writing is at about the level of yours or somewhat better.
- Establish rules for critiquing and the minimal level of commitment required for participants.
- Develop a regular meeting schedule.
- Set a deadline for sending work to each other; be sure that the schedule gives everyone enough time to read and comment before you meet.
- When you give criticism, be as specific as possible, explaining what you believe are the strengths and weaknesses; critique the work, not the writer.
- When you receive criticism, listen and take notes; ask clarifying questions but do not defend your writing.
- Keep in mind that you don't have to do anything that anyone suggests, but you owe it to yourself and the group to listen and try your best to understand the substance of the critique of your writing.
- Agree to maintain mutual respect and confidentiality: what goes on in the group should stay in the group.

Whether or not you'll benefit from belonging to a writers critique group depends on your personality and work style. Some writers find it extremely helpful to get feedback while they are writing. Others find it distracting and feel that it actually gets in the way of finishing their manuscript.

Tune Your Ear: Read!

As a novelist, you should be an informed reader. Reading current novels can give you an intuitive feel for the current market and for what readers are responding to.

Reading critically acclaimed novels will tune you into what constitutes good storytelling, compelling characterization, and effective use of language and imagery. Reading in your own genre will sensitize you to the clichés of that genre so that you can studiously avoid them in your own writing.

ESSENTIAL

"Read, read, read. Read everything—trash, classics, good and bad, and see how they do it. Just like a carpenter who works as an apprentice and studies the master. Read! You'll absorb it. Then write. If it is good, you'll find it. If it's not, throw it out the window."—William Faulkner

When you finish reading a novel, try to figure out what you liked and disliked about it. If you loved it, go back and reread it to analyze what it was about this novel that made it sing. If you hated it, take the time to figure out why. It's often easier to see the flaws than it is to see strengths.

For added perspective, find reviews of the novel and visit online booksellers' sites to see what average readers have to say about the book. A single reader review won't tell you much, but when a book has twenty or more reader reviews, the comments taken together can be quite illuminating.

Finally, spend time with readers and people who make their living reading and recommending books. Hang out in bookstores and get to know the staff. Let yourself be hand-sold, and listen to how booksellers talk about their favorites. Chat with librarians. Dip into some of the online forums where avid readers are talking about books. By regularly participating at sites like Shelfari (*www.shelfari.com*), Goodreads (*www.goodreads.com*), or LibraryThing (*www.librarything.com*), you can develop a good understanding of the market for novels and begin to connect with and cultivate readers.

Do your research and by the time you are ready to pitch your manuscript to a literary agent, you should have no problem answering these questions: Where does your book fit in today's market? Fans of which best-selling writers will want to read your novel? How is your book unique?

Reading Lists

A good place to begin looking at books like the one you aspire to write is among recent award winners.

LITERARY NOVELS: NATIONAL BOOK AWARD WINNERS (THE NATIONAL BOOK FOUNDATION GIVES THIS AWARD ANNUALLY FOR THE BEST FICTION)

- *Let the Great World Spin* by Colum McCann
- *The Echo Maker* by Richard Powers
- *The Great Fire* by Shirley Hazzard
- *Three Junes* by Julia Glass
- *Cold Mountain* by Charles Frazier
- *The Corrections* by Jonathan Franzen

MAINSTREAM NOVELS: PUDDLY AWARD (POWELL'S BOOKS IN OREGON POLLS ITS CUSTOMERS AND AWARDS "GOLDEN GALOSHES" TO READERS' FAVORITES)

- *The Time Traveler's Wife* by Audrey Niffenegger
- *The Amazing Adventures of Kavalier and Clay* by Michael Chabon
- *Life of Pi* by Yann Martel
- *Twilight* by Stephenie Meyer
- *The Girl with the Dragon Tattoo* by Stieg Larsson
- *The Help* by Kathryn Stockett
- *Water for Elephants* by Sara Gruen

MYSTERY NOVELS: EDGAR AWARD WINNERS (MYSTERY WRITERS OF AMERICA AWARDS AN EDGAR EACH YEAR TO THE BEST NOVEL AND THE BEST DEBUT NOVEL)

- *Bootlegger's Daughter* by Margaret Maron
- *Citizen Vince* by Jess Walter
- *Winter and Night* by S. J. Rozan
- *A Dark-Adapted Eye* by Barbara Vine
- *LaBrava* by Elmore Leonard
- *Promised Land* by Robert B. Parker

THRILLERS: EDGAR AWARD NOMINEES AND WINNERS (EDGAR AWARDS HAVE GONE TO SOME OUTSTANDING THRILLERS AS WELL AS MYSTERIES)

- *Eye of the Needle* by Ken Follett
- *Day of the Jackal* by Frederick Forsyth
- *The Spy Who Came In from the Cold* John Le Carré
- *The Faithful Spy* by Alex Berenson
- *A Conspiracy of Paper* by David Liss
- *Vanish* by Tess Gerritsen

ROMANCE: RITA WINNERS (ROMANCE WRITERS OF AMERICA GIVES THESE AWARDS ANNUALLY IN A WIDE RANGE OF CATEGORIES)

- *Not Another Bad Date* by Rachel Gibson
- *Snowbound* by Janice Kay Johnson
- *Lessons of Desire* by Madeline Hunter
- *Ice Blue* by Anne Stuart
- *The Husband Trap* by Tracy Anne Warren
- *Revealed* by Tamera Alexander

SCIENCE FICTION: NEBULA AWARD WINNERS (CHOSEN BY THE MEMBERS OF THE SCIENCE FICTION AND FANTASY WRITERS OF AMERICA)

- *Powers* by Ursula K. Le Guin
- *American Gods* by Neil Gaiman
- *The Speed of Dark* by Elizabeth Moon
- *Dune* by Frank Herbert
- *Neuromancer* by William Gibson
- *Ender's Game* by Orson Scott Card

FANTASY: HUGO AWARD WINNERS (AWARDED BY THE CURRENT MEMBERS OF THE WORLD SCIENCE FICTION CONVENTION AND GIVEN IN NUMEROUS CATEGORIES)

- *Jonathan Strange & Mr Norrell* by Susanna Clarke
- *Blue Mars* by Kim Stanley Robinson
- *Hominids* by Robert J. Sawyer
- *Harry Potter and the Goblet of Fire* by J. K. Rowling
- *To Say Nothing of the Dog* by Connie Willis
- *The Diamond Age* by Neal Stephenson

Beyond these lists, look at the recent lists of bestselling fiction. Books that top the list in New York City will not be the top sellers in Salt Lake City, Utah, or in Pittsburgh, Pennsylvania, so look at the lists that reflect the readers you are targeting.

The more you write, the more you will recognize good writing and bad. Be sure to take notes, and use your observations to inform your own work.

Story Ideas

One of the questions most frequently asked of published writers is: "Where do you get your ideas?" The answer is that ideas are everywhere. What interests you is likely to interest others. Turning an idea into a premise can be your first step in preparing to write your novel.

Most writers don't have a problem coming up with story ideas. More often, there are too many ideas competing for attention. It's too hard and it takes too long to write a novel, so why waste your time developing an idea you don't care passionately about? Pick the idea that is clamoring the loudest to be told—that's the idea to run with.

Most likely, you will come up with multiple ideas for a novel. Here are some questions to ask yourself to help you narrow the field.

- Which ideas lend themselves to the novel form?
- Which ideas intrigue me most?
- Which ideas will I most enjoy researching?
- Which ideas will generate the kinds of characters and situations that I am most interested in writing about?
- Which ideas could be turned into a novel that I would love to read?

QUOTE

"You get ideas from daydreaming. You get ideas from being bored. You get ideas all the time. The only difference between writers and other people is we notice when we're doing it."—Neil Gaiman

As ideas strike you and spark your interest, write them down and save them in a file folder. It may be days, weeks, or even years before you go back and pull that idea out and start to build it into a novel.

Ideas from Personal Experience

Novelists often transform their own real experiences into novels. Personal experiences that are fodder for novels can range from the heroic to the commonplace.

Ernest Hemingway drew from personal experience as a young soldier in World War I and his love affair with an American nurse for *A Farewell to Arms*. The 2002 novel *The Nanny Diaries*, with its satirical take on wealthy Manhattan families, was drawn from the experiences of Emma McLaughlin and Nicola Kraus who worked as nannies to about thirty different families on Manhattan's Upper East Side.

Your experiences have the great advantage of being uniquely your own. No one else has gone through them in quite the same way, and no one else can transform them into fiction the way you can.

QUOTE

"If the story interests you enough to provoke you into temporarily withdrawing from society long enough to tell it, there is at least a fair possibility that when you are finished, it will interest other people enough to prompt them to forgo companionship long enough to read it. If that proves to be the case, and one of those people is an editor, he or she may actually give you some money in order to make the opportunity available to a whole lot of other people, which is presumably what you had in mind as your ultimate objective when you began spoiling the paper."—George V. Higgins

Ideas from Others and Their Experiences

You can also find inspiration in what happens to friends, relatives, the people you work with, or in events you witness firsthand. For instance, Sapphire's novel *Push* tells the story of a dark-skinned, heavyset, illiterate African-American girl who has survived multiple pregnancies by her father. Sapphire found the idea for this powerful, gritty novel when she was teaching girls like Precious in a remedial reading program in Harlem. As Sapphire told an NPR interviewer, "I had the intense feeling that if I didn't write this book no one else would."

Even when the idea for your novel is based on the personal experiences of others, you will find yourself mining the details of your own life, digging back to recall your emotional reactions in similar situations, and embellishing characters with details from your own experience. But be careful about creating fictional situations that are recognizable. If you don't disguise the characters and the situation sufficiently, you could invite a lawsuit.

FACT

A Virginia family sued Patricia Cornwell in 1992 for revealing factual details in her book, *All That Remains*. They argued that the information was privileged and part of a real murder investigation that Cornwell worked on as part of her job in a medical examiner's office.

Ideas from News

News stories, large and small, are excellent jumping-off points for works of fiction. Once a story appears in a newspaper it is considered in the public domain and fair game for you to borrow from as a novelist.

Some news stories, like the 1999 Columbine High School shootings or the September 11 terrorist attacks, have inspired numerous novels. Wally Lamb's *The Hour I First Believed* follows the life of a fictional Columbine High School nurse, and her teacher husband, as they deal with posttraumatic stress disorder after she survived the library massacre. Don DeLillo's *Falling Man* tells the story of a man who survived the terrorist attack on the World Trade Center. Both authors drew from news stories as well as their own imaginations to craft their novels

Small stories from the news may spark ideas as well. Cemetery vandalism in your hometown, an idiosyncratic string of burglaries, or a local beauty pageant might intrigue you enough to develop into a novel.

Ideas from Dreams

Your dreams are fertile ground for ideas as well, growing as they do out of your own needs and anxieties. Though dreams are often disjointed and rarely have the storytelling logic that a novel requires, they can provide ideas or images that spark a novel.

Jacquelyn Mitchard says that the story idea for *The Deep End of the Ocean*, her debut novel that became the first Oprah Book in 1996, came to her in a dream. She wrote down the plot, saved it, and three years later after the death of her husband, recovered it from a drawer and started writing. *The Deep End of the Ocean* went on to be named the second most influential book of the past twenty years by *USA Today*.

Keep a pen and paper by your bed so that when you wake up from a particularly compelling and vivid dream, you can write it down. The details of even the most disturbing or exciting dream will soon fade from your consciousness the minute you wake up.

QUOTE

"When an idea comes, spend silent time with it. Remember Keats's idea of Negative Capability and Kipling's advice to 'drift, wait and obey.' Along with your gathering of hard data, allow yourself also to dream your idea into being."—Rose Tremain

Formulating a Premise

A premise is the basic proposition behind a book. Transforming an idea into a well-articulated premise can be the first step you take in writing your novel.

Here are three premises that most readers can easily recognize:

- Suppose a miserly, greedy, petty tyrant is murdered, and what if each of his four sons has good reasons for wanting him dead. (*The Brothers Karamazov* by Fyodor Dostoevsky)
- Suppose a girl who wants to run away from home is whisked away in a tornado, and what if she lands in a magic land and must find her way home. (*The Wizard of Oz* by L. Frank Baum)
- Suppose an incurable epidemic of blindness strikes a city without warning, and what if all but one of the city's residents goes blind. (*Blindness* by Jose Saramago)

Once a premise has been articulated, it suggests all kinds of plot possibilities. You can tack on additional ideas for how a story might unfold with the words "and what if . . . and what if . . . and what if." By transforming an idea into a premise and putting it into this format, you can start to see where you're going with your novel.

What's Hot (and Should It Matter?)

Many writers wonder if they should pick the trendiest ideas to write about in order to game the market. Vampire romance novels may be hotter than hot at the moment, but does that mean you should write one? If the best-seller list is full of thrillers about decoding ciphers and mystery novels about female serial killers, are you making your novel more saleable by adding secret codes and villainous women to your story?

The answer is a qualified "maybe but probably not." Remember, from the time you come up with an idea, at the very least it will be two years before it hits bookstore shelves—and that's a best-case scenario. By then, vampires and secret codes and female serial killers may be as passé as yesterday's news. On top of that, agents and editors aren't looking for the next *Da Vinci Code*; they're really looking for the next book to break out of the pack and define its own category.

So trust your own instincts. Write what you care most about and forget about trying to game the market. It's hard enough to write a novel, so why not write one that comes from your heart?

CHAPTER 3

Elements of a Novel:
An Overview

Novels can be 250 or 600 pages long; they can be stories of love, adventure, or horror. They can span a day or a century. A core of elements distinguishes novels from memoirs and from nonfiction. These elements include character, plot, setting, narrative voice, and theme.

The Origins of the Novel

People have been making up stories for centuries. In the early 1600s, what many consider literature's first modern novel was published with Miguel De Cervantes's *Don Quixote*. Its hero, Alonso Quijano, is an Everyman who reinvents himself as knight errant Don Quixote de la Mancha and sets off to redress "all manner of wrongs." Battered by reality, finally (after 900-plus pages) he gives up, returns to being Alonso Quijano, and dies. Most modern novelists give their readers more upbeat endings, but they are still giving readers the quest, the hero's journey, and the obstacles along the way.

The format of *Don Quixote* and of other early novels like *Gulliver's Travels*, *Tom Jones*, and *Moll Flanders* is a picaresque. That format is used only rarely today.

QUESTION

What is a picaresque?
A picaresque is the episodic tale of a knavish protagonist's often humorous experiences as he travels from place to place along a journey.

Another popular early form, used occasionally today, is the epistolary novel. In what some claim is the first English novel, Samuel Richardson's *Pamela: Or Virtue Rewarded* (1740), the entire story is presented through letters the protagonist Pamela writes to her parents. *Bridget Jones's Diary* is a modern epistolary novel written entirely in diary entries. The popular *The Guernsey Literary and Potato Peel Pie Society* by Mary Ann Shaffer and Annie Barrows, another modern bestseller, is told entirely through letters.

Over time, the style of novels has changed. For instance, today's novels are narrated from the viewpoints of characters rather than from the viewpoint of an omniscient narrator. In addition, modern novels are typically broken up into a series of dramatic scenes.

But despite how much novels have changed, each is still composed of five basic elements:

1. Character
2. Plot

3. Setting
4. Narrative voice
5. Theme

    Each element is essential, and they work together to support the novel. In different genres, one of these elements takes a stronger position than the others. For instance, if you are writing a thriller, plot will tend to move to the forefront. On the other hand, if you are writing a romance novel, character may take a more dominant role.

    Let's look, in a bit more depth, at each of these elements of a novel.

Character

Your story unfolds through the characters in your novel. Who can forget the tyrannical and increasingly erratic Captain Ahab, captain of the *Pequod* in Herman Melville's *Moby Dick*, and his obsession with killing one special white whale, the one that took his leg? Or the beautiful Sophie Zawistowska, a Roman Catholic immigrant who is haunted by a decision she had to make in order to survive Auschwitz in William Styron's *Sophie's Choice*? Or Stephanie Plum, the Jersey girl, lingerie buyer turned bail bondsman, who tracks down criminals but never quite snares her man in Janet Evanovich's blockbuster mystery series that began with *One for the Money*?

    Every novel needs a full cast of characters—protagonists like these, plus other main characters, supporting characters, minor characters, and walk-ons—to tell their story. More important characters require more planning; they get described more vividly and should leave a distinct impression on the reader from the first moment they appear on the page.

The Protagonist

    The protagonist is the one character with the most at stake, the one who takes a virtual if not literal journey. The protagonist's goal, what she wants and needs, is the driving force behind the novel; the obstacles and setbacks the protagonist encounters in the struggle to reach that goal form the backbone of the plot.

By the ending, the protagonist is the character that has been transformed. The author wants readers to identify with the protagonist and to root for her success.

Other Main Characters

Every novel requires a range of main characters, central to the plot, in addition to the protagonist. Some main characters fill standard roles in relationship to the protagonist. Here are just a few examples of these standard roles:

- A close family member such as a mother or father, sister or brother, daughter or son, husband or wife
- A coworker such as the boss or colleague or assistant
- A neighbor
- A lover
- A friend

One of these characters may fill one of these essential roles vis-à-vis the protagonist:

- **Villain:** The "bad guy" (or gal) who bears the protagonist ill will; this character tries to stop the protagonist from reaching her goal.
- **Antagonist:** This character is not evil; he just has a different agenda from the protagonist and generally obstructs and gets in her way.
- **Sidekick:** This character helps the protagonist reach her goal.
- **Sounding board:** This character listens and reflects his perspective, arguing or sympathizing, allowing the protagonist to process the events that have transpired.
- **Mentor:** This is the character whom your protagonist goes to for advice, particularly when she feels as if she's hit the wall and is out of options.

For example, in Sir Arthur Conan Doyle's *Sherlock Holmes* novels, Inspector Lestrade, a Scotland Yard detective, plays the role of the antagonist who often obstructs Holmes's inquiries, while the villain is the evil Professor James Moriarty who pushes Holmes to his death from atop

Reichenbach Falls. Dr. Watson plays the roles of both sidekick and sounding board, his blockheadedness providing the perfect foil for Holmes's brilliance. Holmes rarely needs a mentor, but occasionally his brother Mycroft steps into that role for him.

Any well-defined main character walks and talks and dresses in a special, unique way. Most authors develop back-stories for each of their main characters, including a past history and a life story that they may or may not share with the reader. The backstory helps the author create a consistent pattern of behavior for that character.

Supporting Characters

Supporting characters are characters that are essential to the plot, but may only appear in a single or a few parts of the book.

Supporting characters usually are given names and personalities. They each have a unique appearance and a way or presenting themselves. But authors don't usually spend a lot of time developing back-stories for a supporting character unless that character plays a pivotal role in the story.

Walk-on Characters

Walk-ons are characters that interact only briefly with main or supporting characters, or are simply there to create a sense of place and authenticity. For instance, a walk-on might be the street vendor from whom the protagonist buys the newspaper that contains a secret message from an informant, or the babysitter in the house where she visits her ex-husband.

Walk-ons usually appear only once or twice and are rarely given names, full descriptions, or backstories. They appear on the page, perform their function, and then vanish.

Plot

A plot, as E. M. Forster pointed out in his landmark book *Aspects of a Novel*, is not merely a sequence of events: "'The king died and then the queen died' is a story. 'The king died and then the queen died of grief' is a plot." Plot is a "narrative of events, the emphasis falling on causality." In other words, a plot is a series of interconnected, not random events. Forster went on, "If it is in a story we say 'and then?' If it is in a plot we say 'why?'"

In every plot, there are three key elements:

1. A goal
2. Obstacles to be overcome
3. An outcome

Different genres of fiction have their own plot elements, as well. For example, in a mystery novel the plot moves the main character from puzzle (like *Who Killed Roger Ackroyd?*) to solution, taking him (and the reader) from confusion to knowledge. The main question driving the plot is usually something such as: Will the sleuth identify the killer before he can kill again?

FACT

Plot is what characters do to adapt to whatever situation they are in. Just like real people, characters react when something happens that alters their status quo.

Compare this to the basic elements of plot in a romance novel. In a romance, the plot drives two characters apart and then brings them together, taking them from unhappiness to happiness. The main question driving the plot of a romance novel is usually something such as: Will Bill and Mary find true love together before it's too late?

The Main Plot

The main plot is the story that forms the backbone of a novel. It starts at the beginning of the book and is finished by the end.

In a fantasy novel, it could be the story of a character's quest to recover some sacred object. In a thriller novel, it could be the story of how a character infiltrates al Qaeda and prevents a massive terrorist attack. In a literary novel, it could be the story of how a character runs away from an abusive home and finds the strength to return and face her abuser. Regardless of the type of novel, the main plot concerns the protagonist's struggle to reach a goal.

Subplots

Subplots are the smaller series of interconnected events that run through a novel, often interwoven with the main plot. These may be plots that belong to secondary characters, or simply smaller stories unfolding at the same time as the larger one.

For example, while tracking down a killer, your protagonist's apartment might get infested with bedbugs so she's forced to move in with her sister whom she detests. Tracking down the killer remains the main plot, but the battle of the bedbugs and sibling rivalry are subplots that provide comic relief.

Subplots work best when they're connected to the main plot. So, for example, a subplot that involved the sisters finally resolving past issues would be particularly effective if that resolution helps the protagonist gain some insight into the identity of the murderer.

Setting

The setting of your novel encompasses more than the physical locations where the scenes are set. The time when your novel takes place—the days of the week, the season, the century—is an essential aspect of its setting. Another aspect of setting is its context, including the cultural backdrop and organizational structures that surround the characters.

The physical locations in your novel can be as real and authentic as the gritty Charlestown of Dennis Lehane's Boston in *Mystic River*. Or, like Madeline L'Engle's classic science fantasy *A Wrinkle in Time*, it may take place in a fantasy world on another planet. A novel may be anchored in some nebulous future time, or the present, or sometime in the historical past. For context, your story might be set in the world of high-stakes gambling, or fashion modeling, or extreme sports, or inner-city gangs.

But whether realistic or fantastic, past or present or future, and regardless of the context, the setting of your novel should feel utterly believable and provide a backdrop against which your characters can act out the dramas that you have in store for them.

Time

Your novel's time frame is a basic element of your setting. What you pick—the past, the present, the future, a particular historical time period, an alternative timeline—will affect everything from how your characters speak, to what they wear, to how they behave and interact with one another, to how they get around.

The season matters, too. Spring in Alaska. Winter on Miami Beach. Fall in New England. What you choose will shape and constrain your storytelling.

Another aspect of time is how long your story spans—is it a day, a year, a decade, or several centuries? The duration will determine whether you will be able to tell your story as a continuous timeline or in separate episodes. It will also determine whether you will need to jump ahead or back in time.

Place

Where will the scenes in your novel be set? Does the drama take place in a small town, in a big city, or on a farm? In Paris, in the middle of the Mojave Desert, or on Mars?

An exotic location, like the heart of the Amazon jungle, will appeal to readers who love to read books that take them where they might never otherwise go. A familiar location like downtown Los Angeles will have a special appeal to readers who have lived or visited there.

Context

The context of a novel—an industry, or a culture, or an institution—is also part of its setting. Will you set it in the banking industry with characters who are titans of big business and their minions? Or in a traveling circus with characters who are clowns and acrobats, elephant tamers and equestrians? Or perhaps in a research lab where dangerous pathogens are not guarded closely enough.

The context is an integral part of the story you want to tell. Pick a context that intrigues you, one that you know well, or one that interests you sufficiently that you will like doing the research necessary to render it credibly.

Narrative Voice

A strong narrative voice is critical to any work of fiction. In most modern novels, each scene is narrated by a character who tells the reader what's going on, narrating through the lens of his own personality and perspective. A strong narrative voice reflects the attitude of that character.

Here's an example of a strong narrative voice in the opening from Meg Cabot's *Queen of Babble*:

I can't believe this. I can't believe I don't remember what he looks like! How can I not remember what he looks like? I mean, his tongue has been in my mouth. How could I forget what someone whose tongue has been in my mouth looks like? It's not like there've been that many guys who've had their tongues in my mouth. Only, like, three.

An equally strong, but very different kind of narrative voice opens Amy Ephron's *A Cup of Tea*:

A young woman stood under a street lamp. It was difficult to make her out at first because she was standing almost in shadow and the mist from the ground, the rain, and approaching night made the air and the street seem similarly gray and damp. It was dusk. A light rain was falling.

For each scene, it's up to you to decide the narrative voice. Will it be the voice of a character or of a more omniscient observer? Will your narrator say "*I* watched Bill get of the car," using the first-person viewpoint, or "*She* watched Bill get out of the car," using a third-person viewpoint?

Many novels are narrated throughout by a single character. For instance, Harper Lee's *To Kill a Mockingbird* is narrated by the young girl in the story, Scout, but from her perspective years later as an adult.

Other novels have multiple narrators. For instance, about half of the scenes in Audrey Niffenegger's *The Time Traveler's Wife* are narrated in the first person by Clare (the wife), as in this example:

It's hard being left behind. I wait for Henry, not knowing where he is, wondering if he's okay. It's hard to be the one who stays.

Other scenes in the novel are narrated by Henry (her time-traveling husband), also in the first person, as in this example:

I hate to be where she is not, when she is not. And yet, I am always going, and she cannot follow.

A pair of narrators, male and female, narrating alternating scenes, is a common technique used in many romance novels.

Many thrillers like Dan Brown's *The Da Vinci Code* have multiple third-person narrators. Writing from multiple viewpoints enables the writer to generate tension by showing the reader several events going on simultaneously.

It's usually not a good idea to have a minor character narrate. Each time a character narrates a scene, the reader not only learns what's happening, but sees it from a specific character's viewpoint. So most writers bestow the power of narration only on main characters.

Theme

Every novel tells a story, but good novels have a deeper underlying meaning, more than "this happened and then this happened and then this happened." The theme of a novel answers the question, "Okay, I get what happened, but so what?"

A theme might be the resilience of the human spirit, as in Alice Walker's *The Color Purple*. Or a novel might explore the toxic power of prejudice, as in *To Kill a Mockingbird*. Or, as in the J. K. Rowling's Harry Potter books, a novel might explore the difference between good and evil and the power of love and friendship.

Some authors set out to write a story that enables them to examine a specific theme. Others find themes in their novels as they write. Theme is what gives a novel deeper meaning and elevates a work from a story to a meaningful work of fiction. Themes give great works of literature their lasting power.

CHAPTER 4

Creating the Protagonist

The protagonist is your main character. This is the character whose goals drive the main plot of your novel. He is the one character you want your readers to bond with emotionally. Because readers care, they'll keep turning the pages to find out what happens to him. Your protagonist is the character you should take the most time inventing.

The Protagonist

Characters make the book. Of all the characters, the protagonist is the single most important one for you to flesh out and understand. Your job as a novelist is to bring the protagonist vividly to the page and make the reader care, really care about what happens to him.

Does that mean the protagonist needs to be perfect? Absolutely not! A nice, pleasant bloke makes for a boring protagonist. Characters who are flawed can be much more appealing and interesting to readers. But even the snottiest, most self-absorbed protagonist has to be fundamentally likeable, or readers simply won't want to hang around with him for 300 pages.

Details that define your protagonist include name, physical presence, wardrobe, the vehicle (or lack thereof) that he drives, the words he chooses, and most importantly his dreams and ambitions, fears and desires, and those past experiences that have made him who he is.

Can your novel have more than one protagonist? It's not unheard of, and authors have made it work. But usually a novel is the story of a single character's journey, struggle, or quest. From a practical point of view, it's difficult enough trying to write a novel with a single protagonist; with two protagonists you run the risk of splitting the focus and losing your readers.

The most important things to know about your protagonist are: what he wants above all else, and what stands in the way.

What Does Your Protagonist Want?

Your protagonist's goals and aspirations provide the driving force behind your plot. Goals come in all shapes and sizes. Here are just a few of the many goals that have driven protagonists:

- To get the girl
- To stop the killer
- To win the prize
- To prove someone's innocence
- To be forgiven
- To preserve a family legacy

- To wreak vengeance
- To make amends
- To find true love
- To preserve a way of life

Do protagonists always know what they want? Absolutely not. Like the rest of us, a protagonist may want several different things at the same time. He may be unsure of what's important. And his experiences through the course of the novel may change his understanding of what matters most.

ALERT

What your character wants and needs should grow organically from personality and life experience. Goals can't be thrown in randomly to achieve conflict; they have to grow out of character.

For example, a character might think that what she wants most is to marry a rich man; by the end of the novel, she may have learned that what she really wants is to marry the man she loves. Another character might yearn to climb to the top of the corporate ladder, but by the end of the novel discover that what he cares most about is spending time with his family.

The Worthy Goal

Whatever your protagonist's goal, it has to be a worth all the trouble he's going to have to go through in order to reach it. This might be worthy in a real-world sense—like recovering a priceless treasure or preventing an assassination. Or it might be worthy in a personal sense—like saving a reputation or preserving a family legacy.

Often the goal is represented by something tangible—like a priceless painting or a family farm—but always that thing should be symbolic of something larger, something that really matters to the protagonist and meets a fundamental underlying emotional need. Whatever the goal, the plot has to involve the protagonist actively seeking it.

What Obstacles Are in the Way?

Your protagonist will encounter obstacles, from within and from without, that will make it difficult, at times seemingly impossible, to reach the goal. By dealing with obstacles and conflict, your protagonist shows the reader what she's made of. Your protagonist may possess strengths like cunning, or physical strength, courage, or intellect that she marshals in order to reach the goal. Likewise, your characters will have a weakness such as a physical disability or an overweening ego or prejudice that gets in the way.

An obstacle can be as subtle as shyness and low self-image that hinder a woman in her quest for love and power, as in Barbara Taylor Bradford's *A Woman of Substance*. Or it can be a terrifying, powerful force like viruses that rage out of control and threaten to wipe out humanity in novels like Stephen King's *The Stand* or Michael Crichton's *The Andromeda Strain*.

No matter how great or how small, obstacles must engage not only the protagonist but also the reader. They must seem real and powerful so that the reader can empathize with the character's struggles to overcome them.

Internal Obstacles

All kinds of internal emotions can cause obstacles for characters. Fear can prevent a character from acting heroically. Shyness may keep a character from speaking up for herself. Overcoming internal emotions can make what might be an everyday act for one character an act of heroism for another.

In women's fiction and romance, for example, internal conflicts are typically more salient than external conflict. That's because these books are about relationships.

External Obstacles

External obstacles show how the character deals with the world around her. External obstacles don't have to be huge; there is no need for an earthquake or plane crash or bomb explosion in a novel. A car breakdown, a thunderstorm, or even a simple misunderstanding can work well, as long as the obstacle keeps the character from getting what she wants. In Charles Frazier's *Cold Mountain*, for example, the Civil War separates W. P. Inman from his beloved Ada Monroe; then, he must cross a mountain to get back to her. In

Larry McMurtry's *Lonesome Dove,* forces from a swarm of locusts to an evil Comanche chief conspired to keep Captain Call and Gus McCrae from completing their cattle drive.

ALERT

Beware of throwing so many obstacles at your protagonist that you turn her into a victim; a protagonist who continues to appear passive or weak or merely bumbling will lose your reader's sympathy.

In thrillers or adventure novels, external obstacles tend to play a bigger role than internal obstacles. These books don't require the hero to go through a great deal of soul searching because their protagonists thrive on action.

A Mix of Obstacles

Most novels plague their protagonists with both external and internal obstacles. In romance novels, for example, an internal obstacle might be the heroine's changing feelings, while an external conflict may be that her house is being torn down (contemporary) or her father is pressuring her to marry a suitor she doesn't love (historical). In a mystery novel, typically the sleuth's efforts to overcome inner obstacles (like fear or self-doubt or alcoholism) are balanced by her efforts to overcome external obstacles and find the killer.

A Breakdown of Your Protagonist

The protagonist in your novel should be complex. Like a real person, he should have strengths and weaknesses, skills and blind spots. He should have a unique physical appearance—hair, clothes, and complexion, for example—that expresses who he is and how he wants others to perceive him. He should have an attitude that governs how he responds to babies, stray dogs, beautiful women, and authority figures. There should be music and food and cars that he likes and dislikes, and a backstory that explains how he came to be the way he is.

Your Protagonist's Strengths

Is your hero a superhero who can pick up cars in one hand and save a busload of children with the other? Maybe not. Maybe your hero is just an ordinary mom who manages to raise a crippled son and a rebellious teenage daughter. Or maybe it's a little girl whose astronaut father disappears and she has to stow away on a shuttle craft and travel into outer space to find him.

Every character is endowed with certain character strengths. Even though Frodo in Tolkien's *Lord of the Rings* trilogy has no great physical or mental prowess, his strength is his inner goodness. It's enough to carry him to victory against the forces of darkness.

Here are just a few personal strengths with which you might endow your protagonist:

- A great sense of humor
- Fearlessness in the face of danger
- A cool head
- An analytic mind
- Acute empathy
- Honesty
- Loyalty

Remember, strengths can also grow out of skills and abilities. To find these, ask yourself: What does your character know how to do? What are her skills? What does she excel at? It doesn't have to be anything dramatic. She might only be the very best cherry pie maker in the county. Or she might be the family storyteller. It doesn't take a great deal of thought to consider what might make a character special to others.

ESSENTIAL

Readers prefer protagonists who have human failings and flaws, so if you heap your character with strengths, be sure to give her a flaw or two as well.

Whatever your characters' special skills and abilities, they should be used to help those characters solve the problems you create for them.

Your Protagonist's Weaknesses

What makes a protagonist even more interesting than her strengths and skills are her weaknesses, especially when you can use those weaknesses in your plot as obstacles to be overcome.

Here are some examples of weaknesses you might give your protagonist:

- A physical handicap (blind, hearing impaired, injured)
- An emotional handicap (shyness, impulsivity, depression)
- An addiction (to alcohol, gambling, drugs)
- An illness (narcolepsy, epilepsy, brain tumor)
- A lack of resources (impoverished, uneducated)

Flawed protagonists abound in great novels. For example, Amir in *The Kite Runner* by Khaled Hosseini is a liar and a coward. Humbert Humbert in *Lolita* by Vladimir Nabokov is a pedophile and a murderer.

Flaws are important in creating a protagonist. This is because a primary purpose of the plot is to force the protagonist to change, usually by recognizing and overcoming some internal conflict. Flaws provide a source of internal conflict.

Your Protagonist's Appearance

How your protagonist appears to the world—his physical presence, his clothing, his car, his physical beauty or lack thereof—determines how the other characters respond to him. A shambling, poorly dressed, unkempt individual will be quickly dismissed and often underestimated by others. A tall, handsome, vigorous fellow in a fancy suit may engender either respect or distrust, depending on who's looking at him. A voluptuous blonde may look to some men as if she's giving them the come-on, or be perceived as a threat to other women.

Does your protagonist's appearance camouflage her true self? That's up to you. You may choose to make appearance consistent with or at odds with the inner persona.

Going for a disconnect can make life interesting for your protagonist. For example, that tall vigorous guy in the suit might turn out to be meek and unassuming. That shambling derelict might be a brilliant scientist.

It's a good idea to envision what your protagonist looks like early on. Some authors search for images on the web and find a photograph of a stranger who becomes their protagonist. Others envision a particular actor or actress in the role.

Here are some aspects of your main character's appearance to consider:

- Age, and whether the character looks that age
- Build
- Most striking feature
- Hair color (and is it natural)
- Hairstyle
- What she wears to work
- What she wears to sleep
- Idiosyncrasies (facial hair, tattoos, body piercings, scars)
- Ethnicity, and how her appearance hides or betrays it
- Trademark mannerisms and gestures

Finally, consider whether the character's appearance shows or hides who that character really is. When Agatha Christie created Miss Marple, she had a wonderful time playing with the disconnect between Miss Marple's dithering appearance and her incisive powers of observation and intellect. Miss Marple looks like she's tending to her knitting, but watching and eavesdropping, she misses nothing. Official investigators and villains alike underestimate her.

Your Protagonist's Attitude

Interesting characters have attitude. Think about what kind of attitude you want your protagonist to convey to the world. Is she polite or demanding to waiters? Is she respectful of authority figures or resistant to taking orders? Is she patient or curt and annoyed when someone asks directions? Does your character feel one way but behave another?

Before you even start to write, try to imagine how your character would behave in various situations. At a cocktail party, for instance, would she readily introduce herself to others or hang back, checking her watch every five minutes, wishing she were home? If she accidentally walked into a lamppost would she laugh at herself or punch the post?

Think about what would make your protagonist laugh, argue, cry, tremble, or smile. Is she fearless when climbing mountains but terrified by cockroaches? Does she think puns are hilarious but hates practical jokes?

Understanding your character's emotional core and how it's reflected in the way she interacts with the world will help prepare you to unleash her in the many difficult situations you're going to put her.

Your Protagonist's Likes and Dislikes

Part of your protagonist's personality is expressed by what she likes and dislikes. Consider a character who is perfectly content with a can of tomato soup for dinner, night after night, as opposed to a character who detests packaged food and whips up a gourmet meal from leftovers in the fridge. Consider a character who orders a Bud at her local bar as opposed to a character who orders her martinis dry with Tanqueray and extra olives. Consider a character who likes to shop for her clothes at Bloomingdales, as opposed to a character who shops secondhand stores.

What your character dislikes can be equally telling and useful. Something that a character intensely dislikes may represent something she fears, something painful in her past, or a secret she wants to hide. Maybe she dislikes wearing low-cut blouses because they reveal a scar. Maybe she can't abide dogs because she was once attacked by a neighbor's pit bull.

Details about your character's likes and dislikes may or may not enhance your plot. But they give your character more depth and provide a window into her personality.

Your Protagonist's Backstory

Ultimately, no matter how much thought you've given to your protagonist's strengths and weakness, her skills, her attitude toward the world, and her likes and dislikes, once you start writing the novel your protagonist becomes what she does, and every move she makes should make sense in light of her past life experiences.

A character's backstory is composed of the experiences and the circumstances of that character's life prior to the novel's time frame. If your protagonist came from a broken home, or was abused as a child, or saw her younger brother drown, that experience will affect her behavior in the novel. If she went to a fancy girls' school and had every wish granted by doting parents who died when she was twelve, leaving her destitute, those experiences will affect her behavior in the novel.

ESSENTIAL

Characters *are* what they *do*. It's up to the author to imagine a backstory that explains behavior and makes it into a coherent, consistent whole.

So as a novelist, you must not only create the characters for your story, but also create their backstories that explain why they behave the way they do. Here are some questions to ask yourself as you come up with your protagonist's backstory.

Did your protagonist:

- Grow up in a happy home?
- Grow up with older/younger siblings?
- Complete educational degrees?
- Get along with her parents?
- Experience any significant trauma or loss or illness?
- Grow up to have the career she always dreamed of having?

Finally, try to imagine the single most important formative event in your character's life. This could be the loss of a loved one, or divorce, or illness, or some profound disappointment.

What to do with all this material? Write it down. Save it. And keep it in mind as you write the novel. Every time your character does something that surprises you, return to the backstory and add something in the past that explains that behavior.

Only bits and pieces of the backstory that you invent for your protagonist will actually appear in the novel, but you need to know your character's past in order to make her consistent and believable in the present.

Pitfall: Character Clichés

A clichéd character is one your readers have seen before. Many times.

Literature is full of character clichés—in fact, that's where they come from. Way back when, someone wrote a great character like that, and then other people copied it until it became a cliché. Clichés are particularly lethal in your protagonist.

Some of literature's character clichés include:

- The sleazy attorney
- The psychiatrist who's sleeping with his patients
- The prostitute with a heart of gold
- The alcoholic cop
- The handsome but corrupt politician
- The absent-minded professor
- The clueless blond

Clichés are a problem because they're predictable. No reader enjoys a novel that's full of characters who do exactly what is expected of them.

Smart writers twist familiar clichés into something fresh and different that the reader isn't expecting. For example, Michael Connelly's protagonist Mickey Haller in *The Lincoln Lawyer* may be a sleazy defense attorney, but he's unlike any that most readers have encountered before. His office is his Lincoln Town Car, his ex-wife still likes him well enough to pretend to be his secretary and answer his "office phone," and he's a devoted father. Connelly takes a familiar character cliché and twists it into a pretzel to make a satisfyingly complex protagonist.

Naming the Protagonist

Think about some of the enduring protagonist names from fiction: Atticus Finch (*To Kill a Mockingbird*), Scarlett O'Hara (*Gone with the Wind*), and Holden Caulfield (*The Catcher in the Rye*). From more recent fare, there's Susie Salmon (*The Lovely Bones*), Jacob Jankowski (*Water for Elephants*), Dirk Pitt (Clive Cussler's adventure novels), Bella Swan (*Twilight*), and Stephanie Plum (from Janet Evanovich's mystery series). Their names are unique, catchy, easy to remember, and most of all they express something essential about the characters themselves.

Janet Evanovich says she picked the name Stephanie Plum for her bounty hunter protagonist because of the way "Stephanie" rolls off the tongue, and because she likes the juicy ripeness of "Plum." And besides, Evanovich says, there were lots of Stephanies when she was growing up in blue-collar New Jersey, and Stephanie Plum is the quintessential "Jersey girl."

For some authors, their protagonist arrives in their heads, full blown, with a name attached. For others, finding the right name takes time and care. So what's a good name for your protagonist?

Choose a name that fits the character you have in your mind. If you're writing a historical novel, take care that the name you choose is appropriate for the era you're writing about.

Later, as your character comes into his own on the pages of your novel, you can revisit the name question. Perhaps you'll find that the character who started out as "Edward" when you began writing the novel turns out to be more of a "Gunner" or "Peyton" or even "Ebenezer." The good news is that word processors come with a "Find/Replace" feature!

Writing a Character Sketch

A useful way to pull together your ideas for your protagonist (or any other character in your novel) is to write a character sketch. This is a way to gather insights into that character's presence and personality before you start writing the book.

Here are some of the things you might consider including in the sketch:

❒ The character's name and gender, job or profession
❒ A description of the character's physical appearance

- ❏ A summary of what happens the first time the character appears in the novel
- ❏ The character's best friend
- ❏ The character's family
- ❏ A conversation you might have with the character
- ❏ A description of the character's most treasured possessions and keepsakes
- ❏ The character's favorite book, flower, tree, food, drink, way of spending free time
- ❏ The character's habits, good and bad
- ❏ A description of the character's home or bedroom

Here's an example of a brief character sketch:

Ivy Rose is a thirty-one-year-old woman about to have her first child. She's married to her high school sweetheart, David. She's been married for six years and has suffered multiple miscarriages. She desperately wants this baby to be born healthy. She has no siblings, and her father died when she was young; her mother, who is also dead, was an alcoholic. Ivy was always closer to her grandmother than to either of her parents, and her grandmother's death a few years ago left her feeling very much alone. Her treasured keepsake is a charm in the shape of a hand, a good luck charm given to her by her grandmother. Ivy is tall and athletic. She moves like an antelope. She is dark-haired and interesting looking rather than beautiful. Her Victorian house, which she and David bought as a handyman's special, is filled with special vintage furniture that she has picked up at yard sales. Her favorite book growing up was *Madeline*—she loves the little girl's plucky courage.

As you can see, a character sketch rambles all over the place, inventorying the character and her past but not really telling a story. It's a working document, for your eyes only, and provides a place to dump all of the miscellaneous thoughts you have about your character and what happened to her before the novel opens. Add more information to your character sketches as new ideas strike you, and as your character does things that surprise you.

CHAPTER 5

Creating the Supporting Cast and Settings

Your protagonist will be surrounded by a cast of supporting characters in various settings. A few of the supporting cast will be main characters, each one nearly as important to the plot as the protagonist himself. Other characters will have a smaller role to play. Still others will be walk-ons, put on the page to make the setting feel authentic. You'll need to think about creating a worthy cast and setting to support your plot and your protagonist. Can you imagine *Gone with the Wind* without Atlanta under siege during the Civil War? Or *Dune* without the desolate desert sands of the planet Arakis? Or *Wuthering Heights* without the moor? In novels like these, the setting (time, place, context) is like another main character.

Creating Main Characters

Of course you need more than a protagonist to tell your story. There will be other main characters, and each has to be able to hold his own against the protagonist.

Here are some examples from literature of protagonists and other main characters:

- In *The Wizard of Oz*, Dorothy had the scarecrow, the tin woodman, and the cowardly lion.
- In *Gone with the Wind*, Scarlett O'Hara had the dashing Rhett Butler, the gallant Ashley Wilkes, and loyal Melanie Hamilton.
- In the *Sherlock Holmes* novels, the brilliant, coolly analytic Sherlock Holmes had the more mercurial, impulsive (and usually wrong) Dr. Watson.
- In *Jane Eyre*, plucky young Jane had the moody, broody, and much older Mr. Rochester.

In all of these cases, the protagonist finds a foil by being paired with the other main character or characters, and is enhanced by the contrast.

QUOTE

"In every novel, the character is a collage: a collage of different characters that you've known or heard about or read about."—Gabriel Garcia Marquez

Where do characters come from? Some characters arrive apparently out of nowhere in a dream or offer themselves up, and it is a wonderful gift when that happens. More often, writers create a pastiche from real people whom they know. Once you start putting a character on the page, you want that character to grow and change into someone who exists only in your novel.

Using Differences

When creating main characters, pay attention to how they contrast with the protagonist. Make each main character as distinct as possible from your protagonist, yin to the protagonist's yang, and use those differences to drive the plot and foment conflict.

Use the same techniques to create other main characters as you would to create the protagonist—character traits, character sketches, and so on are useful. As you develop main characters, pay attention to their strengths and weaknesses, appearance and attitude, and create backstories that explain why they are that way.

Help your readers by making your characters as distinctive as you can from one another. A fast-talking, manic protagonist needs a laconic friend with a Southern drawl.

A Special Case: The Villain

In many novels, one of the main characters plays the special role of the villain, or antagonist, obstructing the protagonist in reaching the goal. In *Jane Eyre*, the mysterious Bertha Mason stands between Jane and happiness. In *Dracula*, Count Dracula wants Jonathan Harker's beloved Mina for his own. In *The Wizard of Oz*, the Wicked Witch of the West tries her best to keep Dorothy from finding her way home.

The villain in your novel may be pure evil, but more likely not. Even Sherlock Holmes's arch-antagonist Professor James Moriarty is described as having redeeming features: "He is a man of good birth and excellent education, endowed by nature with a phenomenal mathematical faculty." Doyle goes on to say, "But the man had hereditary tendencies of the most diabolical kind. A criminal strain ran in his blood, which, instead of being modified, was increased and rendered infinitely more dangerous by his extraordinary mental powers" (*The Final Problem*).

Must a villain be loathsome? Not at all. He can be chilling but charming, like Hannibal Lecter. Thoroughly evil? It's better when the reader can muster a little sympathy for a complex, realistic character who feels he's right to obstruct the protagonist.

So, in planning, try to understand why your villain does what he does. Consider the standard motivations like greed, jealousy, or hatred. Then go a step further. Get inside your antagonist's head and see the protagonist's goal from his perspective.

Here's how a villain might rationalize his actions:

- Righting a prior wrong
- Wreaking revenge
- Reaching a competing goal (like protecting a loved one)
- Doing God's work
- Restoring order to the world

Finally, think about what happened to make that villain the way he is. Was he born bad, or did he sour as a result of some traumatic event? If your villain has a grudge against society, why? If he can't tolerate being jilted, why? You may never share your villain's life story with your reader, but to make a complex, interesting villain, you need to know what drives him to do what he does.

QUOTE

"That is the power of a three-dimensional antagonist: the power to sway our hearts in directions we would not expect them to be swayed. To get us to see, even accept, the antagonist's point of view."—Donald Maass, *The Fire in Fiction*

Just as you drew a character sketch of your protagonist, take the time to sketch out the villain. Think about what the pivotal moments have been in your antagonist's life. Was his brother unfairly convicted of a crime he didn't commit? Did his family go bankrupt? Did his wife leave him for his best friend? Did his mother disappear? Was he abused as a child?

To develop a credible villain, here are some questions to ask yourself:

- What does the villain want?
- How does the villain see the protagonist obstructing him in reaching his goal?
- How does the villain explain his own motivations to himself?

Villains are much more interesting when they are believable. Just as it's important for you to understand what motivates your protagonist to strive to reach his goal, you need to understand what motivates your villain to keep getting in the way. Creating a backstory for the villain will help you to understand that character as a three-dimensional human being with as many complexities as any of your other main characters. Characters who are simply monstrously evil can come off as old-fashioned clichés.

Creating Supporting Characters

Novels have a range of supporting characters, and every one of them should be there because they are necessary to tell the story. If a supporting player has no role in the story, then you should consider dropping that character from your novel.

Supporting characters are less important than the main characters, and they require much less planning. Often it's their relationship to the protagonist that defines them.

Some of the typical roles that supporting characters play in novels include:

- Mentor
- Sounding board
- Caretaker
- Love interest
- Chum
- Assistant
- Colleague
- Expert
- Family member

You will be able to plan for some of these characters in advance. Others will just show up, initially intended to be a minor character or a walk-on. Then they'll act up, or do pirouettes on the page, and you'll find yourself promoting them to supporting status.

Creating Minor Characters and Walk-ons

You don't need to have planned in advance for the minor characters and walk-ons who will inevitably show up in your novel. The waitress who serves scrambled eggs to your protagonist at a restaurant where he meets his lover can be conjured on the spot. The mail carrier who brings a long awaited letter to your protagonist's sister can be invented when the time comes to write him.

QUOTE

> "Respect your characters, even the minor ones. In art, as in life, everyone is the hero of their own particular story; it is worth thinking about what your minor characters' stories are, even though they may intersect only slightly with your protagonist's."—Sarah Waters

Some minor characters will have names and all will have at least some sense of physical presence. How much attention you pay to bringing them to the page will depend on how important the character is to the story and to the protagonist.

Naming Characters

Just as with naming your protagonist, you need to provide each supporting character a name that in some way fits that character's persona. As you consider names, think about how you can help your readers keep them all straight. Pick names that make it as easy as possible for readers to remember who's who.

Nicknames are easy for readers to remember, especially when they provide a snapshot reminder of the character's personality. You might name a tough guy Spike or a character with red hair Red. Opposites work, too—a character who is bald might be named Curly. Throwing in some ethnicity (Zito, Sasha, Kwan) makes a name easier to remember,.

Avoid the dull, boring, generic names (Bob Miller) since these names are easily forgotten. Avoid the weirdly exotic name (Dacron) that draws attention to itself and doesn't feel credible.

Finding Names

Names are hard to come up with when you need them. An obvious source of inspiration is a telephone directory. Census lists from the present and past yield a trove of names to match time periods. There are also books of baby names.

Another resource is the Internet. You'll find websites with lists of surnames and first names from Aaron to Zinnia, in every ethnicity and culture. Search for "dictionary names" and you'll find lots of information sources waiting to be exploited.

Create a list of names that you consider "keepers," and add to it whenever you find a new one you like.

Pitfalls: Character Names

It's not easy for readers to keep all of the characters in a novel straight, so help them out by giving them distinctive names. Here are some tips:

- Avoid giving characters names that start with the same letter, like Jack and Josh and Janet.
- Don't give a character two first names like William Thomas, Stanley Raymond, or Susan Frances.
- Pick a name appropriate to the historical time frame or setting—Neville Longbottom is a perfect name for a student at Hogwarts, but it wouldn't feel so much at home for a crusty character in a novel set in the old West.
- Vary the number of syllables in character names—it's harder to confuse a Jane with a Stephanie than it is to confuse a Jane with a Meg.
- Don't pick names that sound similar, like Leanna and Dana.

It's a good idea to keep an inventory of your characters and their names along with any features you give them. This is especially important for characters that make only sporadic appearances in the book.

Physical Locations

Your novel will be set in many locations, both interiors and exteriors. Perhaps your novel begins in an open marketplace in Algiers, or in the attic of a Victorian house, or in the cockpit of a jet fighter, or in your protagonist's home office. You'll have many other interiors and exteriors to create, and some of them may be so rich and intriguing that they reach "virtual character."

Some settings will be particularly important to your plot: the bar where your romantic couple meets, where they later break up, and at the end of the novel where he asks her hand in marriage. Or the cliff where your protagonist nearly falls to her death.

Other settings are opportunities to further define your characters. For instance, the details of your protagonist's office, or her boyfriend's bedroom, or her mother's kitchen are extended ways of showing the reader those characters.

ALERT

Your novel needs a variety of settings unless you want to deliberately create a feeling of claustrophobia.

It's a good idea to start an inventory of all the places where you'll set scenes in your novel, listing the details of each place. As you write, update the inventory so you can keep track of all the details you've added and make the place consistent each time you reprise it.

Geographic Locations

Readers enjoy novels that are set in real places, but if you use a real location you'd better get the details right. If your character is driving around South Beach, readers will howl in disgust if you have him turn off Washington onto Collins. The streets don't intersect. You'd figure that out from a good map, and fortunately good maps abound on the Internet.

Developing a location requires more than getting the landscape, streets, and buildings correct. The weather, the sounds, the smell, the color of the sky—get these details right and your reader will be transported.

Let the geographic locale shape your characters' behavior. For example, pedestrians on the busy streets of New York or in the subway avoid eye contact with strangers; Texans tip their hats and say "howdy" to everyone. A Milwaukee police officer might have a passion for bratwurst; one of Chicago's finest might be an aficionado of Red Hots.

Below, Stephenie Meyer talks (on her website) about how she used Google to find the setting for her vampire-infested blockbuster novel, *Twilight*.

> For my setting, I knew I needed someplace ridiculously rainy. I turned to Google, as I do for all my research needs, and looked for the place with the most rainfall in the U.S. This turned out to be the Olympic Peninsula in Washington State. I pulled up maps of the area and studied them, looking for something small, out of the way, surrounded by forest . . . . And there, right where I wanted it to be, was a tiny town called "Forks." It couldn't have been more perfect if I had named it myself.

Here are some ways your novel might reflect the geographic locale you pick:

- How characters talk—word choice, speech patterns, and dialect
- What characters wear
- What is considered "good" and "bad" behavior
- What characters eat and drink
- How characters travel from place to place
- How strangers are treated

Be sure to take advantage of either the fit or misfit of your characters and the setting. Glamorous bohemian Holly Golightly in Truman Capote's 1958 novella *Breakfast at Tiffany's* is a creature who yearns to belong in the novel's Upper East Side of Manhattan setting. Dorothy Gale in L. Frank Baum's *The Wizard of Oz*, a girl who has lived all her live on a barren "great gray prairie," is filled with awe when she is transported to Oz with its "lovely patches of green sward all about, with stately trees bearing rich and luscious fruit." The contrast of a character and her setting enhance both.

Indoor Spaces

Your novel may have as many as a dozen interior settings. A recurring interior might be your protagonist's home, or the office where she works, or the interior of her car. Create interiors that reflect the characters that inhabit them. If a character is neat and methodical, his office might be furnished with steel and glass and a geometric Mondrian print might hang on the wall. The floor and desk of an absent-minded character's office might be covered with drifts of papers and books. A cheerful, optimistic character's office might be freshly painted with gingham curtains in the windows. The windows of a morose and brooding character might be shrouded with dusty velvet drapes.

ESSENTIAL

Draw floor plans of the rooms and buildings where you set scenes of your novel; this will help you create a consistent sense of place for your readers.

When you sit down to describe a setting, close your eyes and, in your mind, try to transport yourself there. See what your character would see. Hear what your character would hear.

Is it a mansion, apartment, mountaintop cabin, or homeless shelter? Conjure the details. Maybe it is filled with fine antiques, or battered items picked from yard sales and thrift stores, or minimalist designer furniture, or unopened storage boxes. Is there a large-screen TV or a vintage radio? Does the kitchen have all the latest gadgets or just a microwave for reheating takeout?

And don't forget about smell. Smells are so evocative of place. Cookies baking or mildew or car exhaust or rotting fish—use these kinds of smells to put your reader there.

Using Real Places

As a writer, it's easier to write about a place where you've actually been. Many authors, following the old adage to "write what you know," set their novels in the town where they live or where they grew up. Then they disguise the place with a different name.

For instance, Grace Metalious, whose shocking 1956 *Peyton Place* sold in *Da Vinci Code* numbers, insisted that the town was fictional. But her neighbors disagreed. It felt a whole lot like a barely disguised version of Gilmanton, New Hampshire, where Metalious lived. The disguise fooled no one, her neighbors were outraged, and Metalious's husband lost his job as school principal just before the book hit the bookstores.

It's fun to use real interiors to set scenes, too. Local readers enjoy finding familiar bars or movie theaters or factory complexes in the pages of a novel. Use a real restaurant if your characters go there and have a wonderful meal; use a made-up restaurant if your character is going to get food poisoning after eating there. You don't want to make enemies out of restaurant owners, and you certainly don't want to get sued.

ALERT

Use caution in creating settings based on real places. A good rule of thumb: Use a real place if nothing terrible happens there in your novel.

To research a location, nothing beats going there. You can't smell a picture of a street market, or hear traffic on a roadmap, or feel the surge of a crowded busy street from its description, or fully appreciate the beauty of a mountaintop view from a video. Firsthand research can take the setting in your novel from accurate to visceral. By visiting the settings you write about, you'll find the telling details that make each place unique.

When you go places, take notes or bring a tape recorder and describe what you hear, smell, and see. Record the sounds of that place. These are the kinds of details that you could never make up. Later, you will be able to use those details that you have since forgotten and create a setting for a scene in your novel.

Using Weather

Wherever you set the novel, there will be weather. Ordinary weather, like cloudy skies or rain or snow, or extreme weather like hurricanes, blizzards, and torrential rain can be exploited to create a backdrop for your story.

Beware the potential nuisance factor in the season and setting that you pick. Set your story in winter in Maine and your characters can't just jump in their cars and go; they'll be scraping and de-icing and pulling on snow boots and parkas every time they go out.

Use weather to enhance your storytelling. For instance, a character who has just suffered a miscarriage would ache as she watches new shoots emerge from the ground in spring. An ice storm can keep a character from traveling somewhere, or it can hold him captive with a group of people he detests.

While it may not be consequential, weather is a given. Even if it doesn't impact your story, don't neglect it. Weather gives a setting authenticity, so even if you don't dwell on it, be sure to at least make the reader aware of what the weather is.

Creating an Authentic Time Period

It's so much easier for authors these days to correctly portray the details of past time periods. With so much historical material available on the Internet, including historical photos and period documents, research that used to require trips to special libraries can now be done from your computer.

Historical Settings

If you decide that the perfect setting for your novel is Venice in the 1400s, expect to do a lot of research. But don't let that put you off if this is when and where your story needs to be set. Certainly, if your main character is an Italian priest who knows Christopher Columbus, Italy in the 1400s would have to serve as your setting.

FACT

While there are legal issues involved in using real living people as characters in your book, there are no issues with using dead historical figures.

Setting your story in a particular historical time frame allows you to intertwine your story with concurrent events. Virtually any historical time and place can provide a rich backdrop with real events (The Civil War, The Great Depression, the Crusades) that can become part of your story. You can even have well-known historical figures take part in your drama, as

E. L. Doctorow does in his novel *Ragtime*. Set in New York at the dawn of the twentieth century, one hilarious scene in that book features Carl Jung and Sigmund Freud taking a boat ride through the Tunnel of Love at Coney Island.

Contemporary Settings

Set your story in the present and you can include current events. Sometimes this works well, but use current events sparingly. What may seem like a major news story when you're writing your novel may have turned into big yawn a year later. So only include current events that matter to your story.

ALERT

Including current events in a novel can quickly make your story seem dated; remember, even for established authors, it usually takes at least two years between when a book is started and when it's published.

Some current events feel too big to be left out. The 9/11 terrorist attacks are a case in point. Many authors were in the middle of writing set-in-the-present novels when the terrorists struck. Some rewrote their novels to include the attacks. Others felt the event was so big, so disturbing, and so recent that they lacked the perspective needed to include it in their books. As time has passed, more and more authors have used the events of 9/11 as key events in novels.

Fictional Fantasy Settings

Jules Verne looked into the future and saw men in flying machines, living and traveling underwater, and walking on the moon. In 1931, Aldous Huxley looked ahead and saw a stark, frightening vision of a new world order, its utopia ruled by hedonism, its population genetically engineered humans. Diana Gabaldon creates a fictional past in *Outlander*, taking its protagonist from 1945 to 1743 Scotland by time travel.

Creating a fantasy world, or setting your story ten or a hundred years in the future, requires a leap of imagination. How will things be the same and how will they be different? Will it be a utopia or a dystopia, or just a grittier or more glamorous version of today's world?

When you write a fantasy past or future, remember it's your world to conjure. Create it in as much rich detail as a setting drawn from a real place, only you get to make it all up. What matters is that the place feels authentic and consistent, enabling your readers to suspend disbelief and go there with you.

Creating an Authentic Context

There's more to setting than the time and the place. A novel set in the world of high finance will be very different from one set in the world of high fashion.

It helps if you know the context you're writing about, but it's not essential. Though Sara Gruen had never been to the circus as a child, and she'd certainly not grown up as part of one, her interest in circus life was piqued by a vintage circus photograph and she spent four months researching what would become her bestseller, *Water for Elephants*. But she had the advantage of being an experienced horsewoman, so she was well equipped to create the character of Marlena, the circus star with a special empathy for animals and for the horses she trains.

Think about the activities and institutions that will provide a backdrop for your novel. Pick ones that interest you enough to research thoroughly, or one that you already know intimately from first-hand experience.

Here are some contexts you might choose for your novel's settings:

- **Finance:** banks, the stock market, investment firms
- **Gambling:** casinos, racetracks, lottery management
- **Art collecting:** museums, auction houses, art galleries
- **Journalism:** the newsroom, the TV studio, crime scenes
- **Medical research:** hospitals, universities, research labs

Whatever context you pick, it's important to learn everything you can about how that context would affect the characters in your novel. For instance, context affects what your characters wear, what jargon they use, what special equipment or skills they need to do their jobs, how their days and nights are scheduled, and whether there's a hierarchy that determines how people relate to one another.

Sweat the Small Stuff

When it comes to creating a believable setting, pay attention to the details. Even small tears in the believability of your setting will stop readers in their tracks.

So once you've picked a time, a place, and a context, you should pay attention to details like these:

- What time of day would the sun rise and set? If you need your character to stand in a pool of light under a street lamp, be sure that it would be dark at that hour.
- How would people communicate with one another? If it's 1965, no one would be using a cell phone.
- How would people get around—short distances and long? If your story is set in downtown Peking, the traffic would be impossible.
- What wildlife would inhabit your setting? Get the birds and the bugs and the critters right for the place and the time.
- Would houses have window screens, basements, tin roofs; would buildings have multiple floors or only one? Earthquake danger, the water table, and climate affect what buildings are like in different parts of the world.

Pay attention to the details of the setting you create and your readers will go there with you. But put a condor in the Everglades or an alligator in Australia (their native species are crocodiles) and you risk losing your reader's trust.

CHAPTER 6

Building the Plot

Scenes are the most fundamental building blocks of plot. Scenes are grouped together into chapters, which are in turn grouped together into acts, each with a rising story arc as the protagonist seeks a goal and is ultimately transformed by her journey. This chapter helps you begin to organize the building blocks of your plot and plan out the scenes of your novel.

What Is Plot?

Plot is, simply speaking, the story that you are going to tell in your novel. It consists of all the things that happen between page one and the end of the book.

Some of the terms you may have heard used to describe different elements of plot are:

- **Exposition:** Introduction and establishment of the characters, setting, and situation; exposition includes the narrative that gets the story moving forward; authors use exposition to set up the main character and his problem or goal.
- **Complications and conflict:** The events and characters that thwart your protagonist and prevent him from solving his problem or reaching his goal.
- **Crisis:** Complications and conflict hit their highest point.
- **Climax:** Crisis builds to a dramatic, do-or-die moment.
- **Resolution:** The problem is resolved and the protagonist has either reached his goal or failed to reach it
- **Reflection:** A change that the main character undergoes as a result of learning something important about himself or the situation he's in; he experiences an epiphany about life and the great scheme of things.

Like all kinds of drama since the earliest Greek play, the plot of a novel is divided into a beginning, middle, and end, parts that can be thought of as comprising three acts.

▼ **THE THREE-ACT STRUCTURE OF A NOVEL**

Act	Approximate Length	Contents
Act I (the beginning)	The first quarter of the novel	Exposition: introduces characters, setting, situation goal; complications and conflict begin
Act II (the middle)	Half of the novel (the longest act)	More exposition as characters and story are developed; complications and conflicts escalate and the act ends with the crisis
Act III (the end)	The final quarter of the novel	The crisis reaches its highest point and finally is resolved and characters reflect on the resolution

This structure is often referred to as the "story arc." That's because the tension in the story gradually builds to a crisis and then, much more quickly, falls with resolution and reflection.

Coming Up with a Plot

A good plot keeps readers interested and turning the pages because they need to find out what's going to happen next. To design a plot, the author must continually ask: "What happens next?" followed closely by the all-important question: "Why?"

At every turning point in your story, there will be multiple possibilities for what might happen next. Readers especially enjoy plot twists that surprise them and take them to unexpected places. It's up to you to decide where your plot goes and which obstacles you place in your protagonist's way as she struggles to reach her goal.

QUOTE

"I start with a tingle, a kind of feeling of the story I will write. Then come the characters, and they take over, make the story. But all this ends up by being a plot."—Isak Dinesen

The key to making your plot feel compelling is finding that worthy goal for your protagonist to pursue, something that's worth all the complications and conflict you're going to put her through.

The Worthy Goal

It is essential in every novel that the protagonist has a goal. As an author, you need to find that goal for your character, and it has to be worth fighting for. Is achieving a career change a worthy goal? By itself, not so much. But if making that career change means that the character can prove to herself and to her family that she's not a loser, then it becomes worthy.

A goal is worthy if the stakes are high and the consequences of failing are catastrophic, either in material or emotional terms. Stakes and consequences. Those are the things to keep in mind when you assess your main character's goal.

Here are some more examples:

- In Madeleine L'Engle's *A Wrinkle in Time*, Meg Cabot must travel through time and space and journey to the "dark planet" to find her missing father.
- In Joseph Heller's *Catch-22* Captain Yossarian, a bombardier, strives to stay alive, retain his humanity, and get the hell out of the war.
- In Jane Austen's *Pride and Prejudice* Elizabeth Bennett wants nothing more than to be well married.

The Journey and Setbacks

A journey is interesting only if it is difficult, so setbacks along the way are essential. There are many potential sources of setbacks. Here are a few examples:

- A weakness in the character like cowardice or prejudice or impulsivity.
- An external event like a war, a plague, or a traffic accident, or a tear in the space-time continuum.
- An opposing character—like her lover's ex-girlfriend or her controlling mother or her mercenary boss—who tries to keep the protagonist from reaching her goal.
- A misunderstanding in which the character misinterprets something she hears or witnesses.
- An injury like a broken leg, a gunshot wound, or temporary blindness.

The more your character must struggle to reach the goal, the more heroic the journey seems to the reader. But be sure to modulate the misery, and beware that readers have little patience with a protagonist who whines.

The Transformation

Characters, like real people, are transformed by their experiences. They often are wiser having gone through the struggle of reaching their goal. For instance, they realign their priorities, or lose their innocence, or accept responsibility.

A character may realize, as the novel progresses and the character gains knowledge and self-knowledge, that she was wrong about what was truly important to her. In Lauren Weisberger's *The Devil Wears Prada*, for example, Andrea Sachs yearns for a job on a high-fashion magazine, only to find that she's not willing to sell her soul to succeed.

Scenes

Modern novels, like movies and television shows, are usually broken up into scenes. A scene is action that takes place at a particular time in a particular setting. The average novel consists of anywhere between thirty to seventy scenes.

In a novel, a scene is bound in time and place, though characters can enter and exit. Writing your novel in dramatic scenes, and resisting the urge to summarize the events, has the added benefit of anchoring your novel in drama (showing) instead of synopsis (telling).

In every scene in a novel, something should happen, and by the end something should have changed. For instance, the change may be emotional: the character starts the scene happy and by the end is grieving. Or an unexpected revelation may occur: the character is looking for her sister in a bar and by the end discovers her sister's boyfriend in a dark booth, cuddling with another woman. Or a peril emerges: the character comes home from work exhausted and by the end of the scene finds an intruder in her apartment.

Scenes end when the setting or time changes, or when the narrator changes. Readers are accustomed to the convention of a doublespace to indicate a break between scenes. Using scene breaks allows you to jump from one bit of compelling drama to the next, skipping over the boring in-betweens that don't produce any drama.

QUOTE

> "Usually, when people get to the end of a chapter, they close the book and go to sleep. I deliberately write a book so when the reader gets to the end of the chapter, he or she must turn one more page. When people tell me I've kept them up all night, I feel like I've succeeded."—Sidney Sheldon

Readers are also accustomed to reading books that are broken up into chapters. In a novel, a chapter can be composed of a single scene, or several scenes, or even part of a particularly long scene. While scene breaks always come between scenes, or between narrator shifts, chapter breaks can come anywhere. The author can even insert a chapter break into the middle of a scene at a logical resting point to give the reader a break, or at a cliffhanger moment, deliberately accelerating the pace.

Planning Strategies: The Method for Your Madness

Some writers need to know before they start writing, scene by scene, the progression of the plot for their entire novel. Others need to have some idea of what's going to happen in the beginning, in the middle, and at the end, but are happy to start writing and discover how the parts connect. Still others start with a vague idea of where they're going, a main character, and an opening scene, but they like to be surprised as their characters take over, moving their story hither and yon.

There simply is no single method that works for every writer or for every book, so you have to try different approaches until you find one that suits your strengths and style. Some authors write a detailed outline of every scene in the novel; others only feel as if they need to outline the first scene, the major turning points, and the ending. Others tell the story from start to finish in a detailed synopsis. Still others are content to just take lots of notes and write character sketches before jumping into writing page one.

Writers disagree on whether and how much planning is needed:

"If I didn't know the ending of a story, I wouldn't begin."—KATHERINE ANNE PORTER

"The novelist should, I think, always settle when he starts what is going to happen, what his major event is to be."—E. M. FORSTER

"I work away, a chapter at a time, finding my way as I go. . . . Things come to me in driblets, and when the driblets come I have to work hard to make them into something coherent."—ALDOUS HUXLEY

Interestingly, though authors disagree widely about whether to outline first, most authors agree on the necessity of creating an outline *after* writing. An outline of what you've written gives you an overview of your story thus far, and will provide a perfect starting point for revision—a topic that will be discussed in detail later on.

Scene-by-Scene Outline

Many authors like to write a scene-by-scene outline of their book before they start writing. A basic outline gives a brief description of what happens in each scene.

Here's an example of the outline of the first four scenes in a novel:

Scene 1: Tuesday, 6 PM, Gary Brewster arrives at his girlfriend Madison Gavin's apartment. He's looking forward to their date. He rings her bell; no answer. He waits for another tenant, an old woman who is carrying groceries, to go in and follows her, offering to help carry them and sneaks past the doorman and into the elevator.

Scene 2: Continued, Gary rides up in the elevator to Madison's apartment, wonders why she isn't answering her bell. He gets to her apartment door, listens, hears music and shouting inside. He knocks. A man comes to the door who says he's never heard of Madison.

Scene 3: Tuesday, 8 PM, Gary drives home. Tries to figure out what's going on. Madison is waiting in front of his house, furious and insisting that she was supposed to meet him there; they argue; she leaves in a rage.

Scene 4: Continued, Gary goes inside and finds that his house has been burgled.

In a scene-by-scene outline like this, the author sketches out the basics of each scene, including these elements:

- When it happens
- Where it happens

- Which characters are in the scene
- What happens

Jump Start Your Planning: Find the "Tent Poles" of Your Plot

The prospect of sketching out, even in a high-level outline, all forty to seventy scenes of your novel can be daunting. You may be able to envision the scenes at the beginning and how your story is going to end. But laying out the middle in detail may seem impossible.

So, a useful alternative approach to outlining is to begin by staking out what can be thought of as "tent-pole" scenes—these are the key turning points in your book, those scenes that are most essential to your story.

Here are five key scenes you might want to stake out in advance:

1. The opening scene
2. The scene that marks a major turning point at the end of Act I
3. The scene that marks a major turning point at the end of Act II
4. The scene where the plot climaxes near the end of Act III
5. The scene that provides resolution at the end of Act III

Taking *The Wizard of Oz* as an example, here are one-sentence descriptions of the tent-pole scenes in that novel:

1. Dorothy and Toto are swept away in a cyclone and land in Oz (opening).
2. The Wizard meets Dorothy and her friends and tells them that before he'll grant their wishes they must bring him the broomstick of the Wicked Witch of the West (reversal at the end of Act I).
3. Dorothy is captured by the winged monkeys and carried off to the witch's castle (reversal at the end of Act II).
4. Dorothy melts the witch (climax in Act III).
5. Dorothy's returns to Oz with the witch's broomstick and uses the silver slippers to carry her home (resolution at the end of Act III).

Of course, much more happens in this novel, but nailing four key plot points like these is a good way to jump-start your planning process.

Filling in the Scenes Between the Tent Poles

The next step is to write a short description of every scene you can envision between these tent-pole scenes. For instance, after Dorothy arrives in Oz, an additional scene description might be: *Dorothy meets the Munchkins and Glinda the Good Witch of the South who send her off on the Yellow Brick Road to meet the Wizard of Oz.*

You will probably find it easier to envision in detail, scenes that take place early in your novel, say between the opening and the end of Act I, and also the scenes that will come in and around the climax at the end. Do the best you can, outlining as many of the scenes as you can envision, but don't be dismayed if there are gaps. The scenes that take place in the middle of your novel will start to take shape by the time you reach that point.

ALERT

Though outlining takes time and can seem difficult, authors who don't take the time to think through their plot before they start writing can end up spending far more time revising or may even abandon their novel because they write themselves into corners or run out of steam.

Early on, there's no need to worry about how to group the scenes into chapters. Just think in terms of scenes. Chapter breaks can easily be inserted later.

An outline is a wonderful planning tool, and can make writing flow much more quickly. But don't get so wedded to your outline that you become afraid to deviate from it. Be prepared for inspiration to strike as you write a scene—it may turn out entirely differently from what you originally planned.

Writing Notes and Sketches

A more informal approach works for some writers. They begin by quickly jotting down ideas for characters, setting, and plot on index cards. Then they apply some organizational structure to the chaos. For instance, they might take all the character cards and group together ideas about each character. They might organize plot cards by plot and subplot, and sort them all chronologically, and finally separate them into three acts.

If your character is taking an actual journey in the book, you might go a step further and draw a map on a big piece of paper. Stick event Post-it notes at different points along the journey.

If your story takes place over an extended time period, you might draw a timeline on a big piece of paper and stick Post-it notes with the events when they occur at different points along the timeline.

Writing a Detailed Synopsis

Writing out the plot of the novel, in synopsis form, is another way that many authors get ready to write. They "tell" their story, fast-forward, getting down the main story line without trying to dramatize every scene.

To give you the flavor of a synopsis, here's how a synopsis of *The Wizard of Oz* might begin:

Dorothy Gale is an orphan living with her Aunt Em and Uncle Henry on a farm in Kansas. One day, a tornado tears through the farm. Her aunt and uncle make it safely into the storm cellar, but Dorothy and her dog Toto are trapped in the house, and when the house is carried up into the sky, they are carried with it. The house crashes to the ground in a place Dorothy does not recognize. . . .

This kind of synopsis tells the story, from start to finish, in sufficient detail to show how all the plots and subplots articulate and how all the characters and settings fit together. A synopsis for what will be a 300-page manuscript can be as short as ten pages or as long as sixty pages.

Novelists who create a detailed synopsis often find that, having nailed down the details of their story, once they sit down to write the actual novel they can concentrate on the details, the dialogue, and the action, and they don't get stuck worrying about where the story is going next.

You can share a synopsis with your writers critique group to get feedback on your overall story before you start writing. You can share it with an editor or agent. In fact, some publishers require authors to submit a synopsis as the first deliverable of a book contract.

As a working document, a synopsis is very different from an outline. It is not broken down into scenes, does not spell out viewpoint changes or time shifts, but it shows how the pieces of the plot articulate with one another. The great advantage of writing a detailed synopsis is that it requires you to think through all the plot twists and turns and fully understand how each part of the story connects to the next.

Storyboarding

Storyboarding is another plot development process, one that novel writers have borrowed from screenwriters. Traditionally, storyboarding involves arranging a series of images for a film, showing visually how the plot will progress.

Novelists have adapted this process, drawing or writing the basics of each scene on index cards. Answers to these key questions go on each card:

- When and where does the scene take place?
- Which characters are in the scene?
- How does the scene open?
- What is the main thing that happens/changes?

When all the scenes have cards, they get arranged in storytelling order. Retracing the cards, you will find gaps that need to be filled, including those places where your story jumps and needs some connective tissue. You may find some spots where you need to insert a blank card to hold the place, hoping that by the time you get to writing that part of the novel, inspiration will have struck and you'll know what scene or scenes should fill the gap.

Using Software Tools to Plan

Whether you would benefit from using software to help you plan depends on your own work style. If you like being organized and are comfortable with electronic tools, then you might want to explore basic options and more.

Word processing software like Microsoft Word and spreadsheet software like Microsoft Excel make it easy to create tables, allocating each row to the description of a single scene. It's easy to shift, insert, or delete rows as your plot grows and changes. You can even print out the table later and cut it apart, moving around the pieces to see how shifting plot elements affect the overall story. Or use the outlining tool in Word to create an outline.

There are many special software programs available, designed specifically for writers in general and fiction writers in particular. Most offer a free demo, or can be downloaded and used for a trial period so you can see if it helps you or slows you down.

Here are just a few examples of the tools available:

- Dramatica Pro (*www.dramatica.com*): Calls itself the "ultimate creative writing partner"; through a slew of questions about plot and character it helps a novelist construct a story and then stay organized (for PC and Mac).
- NewNovelist (*www.newnovelist.com*): Helps structure a novel using the "hero's journey" paradigm; it includes a word processor, tools for storing notes and outlines, and story prompts (for PC).
- Scrivener (*www.literatureandlatte.com/scrivener*): Contains both a word processor for writing, and management tools to help track ideas, take notes, storyboard, outline, store all kinds of research material, and write (for Mac).
- Storyist (*http://storyist.com*): Includes word processing software tools with a range of planning and outlining tools and project views to help an author stay organized (for Mac).
- StoryWeaver (*www.storymind.com/storyweaver*): Uses interactive "Story Cards" to help an author generate ideas and a plot for a novel (for PC and Mac).

Remember, how you plan and what tools you use are your choice. It's fine if you are most comfortable with a yellow pad and a sharpened pencil. The tools you use and processes you follow should help you write the novel, not get in your way.

CHAPTER 7

Research

But it's fiction! Can't I make it all up? The answer is: yes, and no. Sure, you make some things up. But the time period and locations of your story, the way your characters dress and talk, and how they relate to one another have to feel utterly credible. That's where research comes in. You need to know when to research, and how to go about it.

Bridging the Credibility Gap

For some writers, research is nirvana. For others it's another form of purgatory or worse. But research is absolutely essential for making your characters and plot pass the credibility test, enabling your readers to suspend disbelief and go wherever you want to lead them.

Some kinds of novels—historical novels, thrillers, novels set in exotic settings—will require more research than others. Research helps you find the details that make your setting ring true.

Research can also help you make your characters feel believable. It can inform their wardrobe, how they talk, what they eat. Suppose you're writing about engineers who work in high tech, or teenagers who are constantly text-messaging one other. A little research will help you make their routines, appearance, and dialogue pass muster.

But research can go deeper, still. For instance, suppose you're writing about a character who is paranoid. Research into paranoia can help you understand how that character would behave differently from the average person in various situations in your novel.

ESSENTIAL

Prioritize your research. Make a list of the specific topics you need to research for this manuscript. Separate information you will need early from what you will need later on. Then, sort within each category, from most to least important.

Research and Story: The Feedback Loop

The wonderful thing about research is that it not only *informs* your writing, it *propels* your story in interesting directions that you couldn't have imagined if you hadn't done the research.

For example, suppose that you are writing a novel set during Mardi Gras in New Orleans. Going online, you will discover photos and firsthand accounts of what it's like to be there. Better yet, travel to Mardi Gras and you will not only experience the sounds and smells and sensations that will make your story pop off the page, you will also encounter people who can become the basis for colorful, believable characters in your book.

A case in point: Arthur Golden's tour de force novel, *Memoirs of a Geisha*, grew out of years of academic training, travel, and a chance encounter in Japan with a man whose mother was a Geisha. Ironically, knowledge of real life is what enables writers to take the fiction leap.

QUOTE

"I had to do a lot of research to put myself in a position where I could begin to know enough about that imagined other to make that leap. But the leap, I think, is the same, whatever kind of fiction you're writing."—Arthur Golden

Of course, if you're basing your story on your own personal experiences, then you'll have far less to research. For instance, Dori Sanders knew firsthand the rural world of tractors, yellow jackets, lightning bugs, and mason jars filled with fresh cut flowers that she describes in her novel *Clover* because she grew up on a South Carolina peach farm.

When to Do Research

Should you research before, during, or after you write the first draft? Yes, yes, and yes. There may be some research you'll need to do before you start writing. Research while you're planning will not only help you flesh out your story up front, it will give you ideas that you never would have come up with on your own.

More questions will inevitably come up while you're writing the first draft. While it's true that researching questions that arise while you're writing can slow you down, taking short forays to the library or onto the Internet to find answers often gives you tidbits of information that will enrich your story and provide you with new ideas. When you feel stuck while writing or planning a scene, that's often a tipoff that you need more information; a little research can get you unstuck.

Finally, some unanswered questions can be left to research after you finish writing the first draft. Nits like dates or the spelling of the names of historical figures, can be left flagged in the manuscript and researched later so you don't lose momentum you've gained writing.

Where to Do Research

The good news (and the bad) is that all kinds of research tools are right at your fingertips or within easy driving distance.

It's easier than ever to do research from your computer with all of the resources now available on the Internet. Libraries, newspapers, magazines, historical societies, and many more information sources are getting into the act, making readily available documents that once could only be viewed in person. Blogs, chat rooms, and interest groups make it possible to read about or reach out to just about anyone you might need to complete your research.

But not all your research can or should be done from your home office. There are still special collections that can only be accessed in person, places to go, and people to meet, yielding the kind of source material that can give your novel that special quality that sets it apart from the pack.

Libraries and Historical Societies

University, public, and private libraries are full of source materials for writers. Lists of the documents in their archives may be online, some of it may have been scanned in as images that you can access from your own computer, and often all you have to do is go there to see the materials themselves.

For instance, a public library in a Boston suburb, Danvers, has one of the richest archives in the country of primary source materials about the Salem Witch Trials. The Los Angeles Public Library has a treasure trove of photographs of historic Southern California, many of them easily accessible in an online database. Your source for precisely the materials you need may be only a few clicks away.

Virtually every good-sized town and city also has its own historical society. These are often run by volunteers, but provide a rich source of historical documents like letters and diaries, as well as artifacts, photographs, and old maps.

Online Resources

Online resources enable you to search for material electronically. Some of the basic search engines are Google (*www.google.com*), Ask Jeeves (*www.askjeeves.com*), Bing (*www.bing.com*) and Yahoo! (*www.yahoo.com*).

Here are just a few other resources. Many of these are free to all and the others can be accessed through your local public or college library.

- Bartleby (*www.bartleby.com*): Classics from literature, dictionary, *Bartlett's Quotations*, *Roget's Thesaurus*, and much more.
- Google Books (*http://books.google.com*): Gives you access to the full text or portions of text for some books in print and many more that are out of print.
- Project Gutenberg (*www.gutenberg.org*): This was the first and largest collection of free electronic books; at last count there were over 33,000 titles that could be downloaded, including the works of Lewis Carroll, Sir Arthur Conan Doyle, Jane Austen, and James Joyce.
- Wikipedia (*www.wikipedia.com*): Launched in 2001, this collaboratively produced, user-created source of information can be edited by any visitor; double check anything you pull from here, but it makes a great starting point.

Here are some online resources that require subscriptions. Many university and public libraries subscribe and offer their patrons access through their computer systems.

- LexisNexis (*www.nexis.com*): Searchable content from newspapers, magazines, legal documents, and more; LexisNexis calls itself the "world's largest collection of public records, unpublished opinions, forms, legal, news, and business information."
- Oxford Reference Online (*www.oxfordreference.com*): Combines nearly 200 Oxford reference titles in a single searchable website.
- Encyclopedia Britannica (*www.britannica.com*): Yes, the one you probably grew up with still lives, but now it's online.

These are just the tip of the iceberg when it comes to available sources. Librarians remain one of the best resources to guide you to finding information in a specialized area.

Researching Places

Every day there are more and more ways to check out places anywhere in the world from your own computer. Google Earth, for instance, is a free program that allows you to view satellite images of many places on the surface of the earth. You can see cities and houses, as they look from above or at an oblique angle. "Street View," a feature of Google Maps, gives you a panoramic, three-dimensional view of many streets in the world. These are views assembled from images taken by a fleet of specially equipped cars, bikes, and even snowmobiles.

How did a city street look twenty years ago? Fifty years ago? A hundred years ago? Every day more and more old photographs are being made available on the Internet as well as in archives in libraries and historical societies.

Visiting Places

If you are setting a scene for your book in an oil field, you should visit one. If your protagonist is a chef at a diner, sweet talk your way into spending an afternoon hanging out behind the counter at one. And of course, if your novel takes your protagonist on a wild ride through the streets of Paris, there's no better way to research the scene than to go there and drive around (at the speed limit of course) so you'll know just what she's up against.

ESSENTIAL

When you research a setting for your novel, bring a camera and tape recorder to capture the sights and sounds of the place, and to record your observations about what you see.

Inventory the places in your novel. Check off the ones you know already from firsthand experience. Then try to find out as much as you can about the other geographies and settings. Nothing beats going there, and when you go, take notes, take pictures, and record the sounds.

Researching People

If your protagonist is a high fashion model, or a high-stakes gambler, or a jockey, or a sports fishing enthusiast, you need to learn as much as you can about the kinds of people who inhabit that world. The quickest way to learn is to find an insider who's willing to talk to you, perhaps take you on a tour, give you the inside scoop about what it's like, and answer your questions.

Often an expert is happy to share expertise and experience with a novelist. All you have to do is call or e-mail and ask. Some will even be willing to read pages from your novel and offer you feedback on whether you got it right. Don't be afraid to ask.

There are hundreds of websites devoted to connecting experts with folks who need their expertise. Many experts have their own websites with e-mail links. If you need to find out how your local police department works, or how your state's House of Representatives operates, most organizations have a designated public relations person who may be more than happy to connect you with someone who can show you around.

ALERT

> When you ask for help, be specific about what you are looking for and be sure to say that you are writing a novel. People love to share their expertise, but they hate to have their time wasted.

Interest groups and forums on the Internet are a good place to find people who have the expertise and information you're looking for. Social media is another avenue for connecting with experts. Join Facebook interest groups, LinkedIn, or Yahoo! groups, for instance, and connect with people who can help you.

Don't forget to keep a list of everyone who takes the time to give you a hand. These are folks you'll want to thank in the acknowledgments section of your novel.

Staying Organized

As you continue to research, you will probably generate pages and pages of computer printouts, Xerox copies, and handwritten notes. As the material accumulates, you need to develop a system for keeping track. There's nothing worse than collecting lots of special information and then being unable to find it when you need it.

So get organized early on. You should:

- Create a special folder on your computer where you save all the content and notes and images that you collect.
- Bookmark and categorize the web pages that you know you're going to come back to.
- Highlight the material of particular interest to you in each source so you can locate it later, at a glance.
- Develop a system for filing the hard copies of materials you collect, and keep them close at hand so you can refer to them when you write.

Organization will pay off later. For every piece of information that you gather, be sure to note what research question you were trying to answer, and where you found the material. Later you'll be able to go back to the source and verify or find more.

Pitfalls: Knowing When to Stop

Writer beware! Research can be a little like playing that solitaire game on your computer. It can be the thing that keeps you from writing.

The key is to collect just enough information to give you a solid foundation. Some writers set aside a time period, a few weeks or a month, for instance, to devote to research. Then start writing.

Remember, you don't have to do it all up front. Research at least enough to develop a sufficient understanding of your characters, your setting, and the story.

Then start writing. When you need to, take a break for research. Especially early on in writing the novel, you may need to take frequent breaks as you discover information that you need to know. But don't get sidetracked for too long.

CHAPTER 8

Starting the Rough Draft

You've set aside a place where all you do is write. You have a good idea of your premise. You've conjured up the main characters, and the settings, and you've done your up-front research. You've outlined or storyboarded or summarized your plot. Now it's time to get started writing the rough draft.

Time to Start Writing

The rough draft of your manuscript should be exactly what it sounds like—rough. No smooth edges or rounded corners. It might bulge out in some places or sag in others. Maybe that's why some writers prefer to call it the discovery draft. It sounds so much neater.

Whatever you choose to call it, sit down and write all of your heaped-up ideas and pictures in your mind, as short scenes—whether or not they come in order. Play with words. Let all of the research you've done come together. It doesn't have to be coherent. Shift it around like a puzzle until you know exactly how everything goes.

This is where you have the chance for your writing to really be creative. Throw wild colors at your canvas. Don't be shy. Let it all come out and worry about it later. No one else has to see this version of your story.

Writers talk about "writer's trance," moments when the story seems to take over and the text begins to flow without the writer thinking about it. For most, this is the best writing they will ever do, and it usually occurs during the rough draft process.

Find a Working Title

Perhaps you already have a title in mind for your novel. If not, now is a good time to come up with at least a working title, one that you can live with until you come up with something better.

A good title is short and catchy, and it both says something about the novel and is appropriate to the genre. Having said that, now is not the time to agonize over what to call this work-in-progress. But do give it a name, because there is something emotionally satisfying about doing that, and because it will give you something to name your project files.

Set Up Your Files

Set up folders on your computer for working on your manuscript. You'll need a folder for your current draft, a folder for files containing outdated versions, research, interviews with subject-matter experts, reviewer comments, and whatever other categories of material you need to keep organized.

ALERT

> Keep the most current draft of your novel in a different folder from out-of-date drafts; it's too easy to click and start editing in the wrong file.

As you go along, from time to time you'll want to make a major change. For instance, you may want to alter your story, or give a character a different backstory. It's wise to archive a snapshot of your manuscript that shows what it was like before you embarked on that major revision. That way it will be easy for you to dial it back if you decide the earlier version is better.

It's also a good idea to set up a separate folder for your research and source material, and another one for your planning documents like an outline, character sketches, or notes on story ideas.

Here are four folders you might create:

1. Current folder for the draft you are working on
2. Archive folder for saving early drafts
3. Sources folder for research
4. Planning folder for planning documents like notes, storyboards, outlines, synopses, and character sketches

Start an Out File

It might seem premature, but the moment when you start writing the first page of your novel is the ideal time to create a safe place to put all the words and sentences and paragraphs and pages you will write and then, for various reasons, delete.

It's hard work, writing, and harder work still taking courage in hand and deleting what you've written. But as you work on your novel, you will add and take away, shape and shave. All those changes will be easier to stomach if you have a place to save what you cut.

So when you create a file for your manuscript, create an Out file for your discards, too. Suppose your novel is titled *Blue Shoes*. You would create a file Blueshoes1.doc in which you will begin to write the first working draft of your novel and save it in your Current folder. Then create a second empty file, Blueshoes-Out.doc and save it there, too.

Don't be dismayed as the Out file grows—it may end up being even longer than your manuscript. But having it readily accessible will give you the courage to cut. Later, if you decide you want any of those bits and pieces back, you will know exactly where to find them.

Turn Off Your Inner Editor

You won't be able to get that first draft written quickly unless you turn off your inner editor. Every writer has one, and you probably do, too. It probably pipes up in the back of your head whenever you hear a newscaster saying "who" instead of "whom," or mangling meaning with a double negative, or offending your delicate writer's sensibilities by using passive voice. You notice every time there is a question mark where there isn't a question. Grammatical and spelling errors that no one else notices seem to pop off signs and billboards.

It's that inner editor that makes writers their own toughest critics. They may not be able to see holes in their plots or character flaws because they're too intimately enmeshed in them. But the bloopers in spelling, grammar, and punctuation that they see in their work haunt them like an irritating jingle.

It's difficult, but to get that first draft written, you'll have to put your inner editor in a box and slam the lid. Don't let that whiney voice keep you from telling the story by making you picky-picky-picky about every word choice and semi-colon. That's what later revisions are for. Too much obsessing over details at this stage will distract you and you'll never get the novel written.

Learn to ignore these minor problems. Resist the urge to correct everything you see. Repeat to yourself: "Perfection is the enemy of a finished first draft." From a finished first draft you can revise your way to excellence.

Keep a Flexible Mindset

No matter how much research and planning and outlining you've done, once you put a character on the page you just never know what he's going to do. Of course you're in charge of the Delete key. But when you write something that surprises you, stop and look at it carefully before you wipe it out and return to the track you've set for yourself.

Surprise is one of the best gifts an author can give the reader, and if you're surprised by what happens in your novel, readers will be surprised, too. So, be prepared to jettison preconceptions and go with the flow. Practice saying this to yourself: "Nothing is set in stone." Say it over and over, believe it, and you'll have the flexible mindset you need to write your novel.

Important Decisions Before You Start

Sure, you've probably read hundreds of novels. But when it comes to writing the first page of your own, you are faced with a whole raft of decisions such as:

- Where to start?
- Present or past tense?
- Which point of view?

Let's look at these decisions and more, the choices you must make on the first page.

Where to Start

Your novel should open with something that piques the reader's interest and gets your plot rolling. It might be an interesting character, snappy dialogue, an intriguing situation, a dramatic description of a place, or a combination of elements. Remember, you want the reader to keep reading.

For example: A science-fiction novel about a submarine voyage through a rift in the space-time continuum might begin with the submarine captain and first mate, mapping their course and starting their voyage. This could work if the characters being introduced were compelling enough, and as long as the reader felt the promise of something exciting happening soon.

QUOTE

"Never begin the book when you feel you want to begin it, but hold off a while longer."—Rose Tremain

The same story could begin with the submarine drifting along and suddenly being sucked into the vortex. This would be a much more exciting, dramatic opening, ending at a cliffhanger moment that forces the reader to turn the page and find out what happens next.

Or the novel could just as easily begin with a prologue, a scene from outside of the frame of the novel's timeline: a century earlier when an earthquake created the temporal rift and a fishing boat and its crew disappeared into the past. That would be an exciting opening scene, too, and it would set up the story of the book with a dramatic punch.

There's no magic formula for how to start a novel, but whatever your opening, it should do three things: capture the reader's interest, set up your story, and make the reader want to keep reading.

Tense

As soon as you start to write your first scene, you will have to decide whether you are telling the story in the present or past tense. Most of today's novels are narrated in the past tense.

Here's an example, the first line of Philip Pullman's *The Golden Compass*.

Lyra and her daemon moved through the darkening hall, taking care to keep to one side, out of sight of the kitchen. The three great tables that ran the length of the hall were laid already, the silver and the glass catching what little light there was, and the long benches were pulled out ready for the guests.

Notice the past tense of the verbs (moved, ran, were laid, were pulled). From start to finish, this novel is written in the past tense.

Some writers prefer to tell the story using the present tense. This gives the storytelling a kind of immediacy, a feeling of reportage that is harder to achieve with the past tense. John Updike, one of the literary icons of the twentieth century, wrote one of the first novels in English to be narrated entirely in the present tense. Here's a short excerpt from that novel, *Rabbit, Run*.

Boys are playing basketball around a telephone pole with a backboard bolted to it. Legs, shouts. The scrape and snap of Keds on loose alley pebbles seems to catapult their voices high into the moist March air blue above the wires. Rabbit Angstrom, coming up the alley in a business suit, stops and watches, though he's twenty-six and six three.

Notice the present tense of the verbs (are playing, stops, watches). Nowadays, many novelists use the present tense to tell their stories.

Here's another example of a novel narrated in the present tense. This is the opening of the gritty noir mystery novel *Beat the Reaper* by Josh Bazell.

So I'm on my way to work and I stop to watch a pigeon fight a rat in the snow, and some [a**hole] tries to mug me! Naturally there's a gun. He comes up behind me and sticks it into the base of my skull. It's cold, and it actually feels sort of good, in an acupressure kind of way.

Whatever tense, past or present, that you choose for Chapter 1 of your novel, readers will expect you to stay with that tense throughout the book. There are exceptions. Sometimes an author will have one of the narrators tell his scenes in the present, for example, while another narrator narrates in the past tense. Or only the opening of the book might be narrated in the past tense, providing a sort of prequel or prologue to the rest, written in the present.

ALERT

Once you pick a tense to write in, stay there. Sliding between present and past tense within a scene is sloppy writing.

If you're not sure whether to write in present or past tense, just jump in and try it one way. You won't know for sure until you try writing a few pages, and if you don't like how it feels, revise.

Point of View

In the majority of modern novels, each scene is narrated by one of the characters. The protagonist narrates most of the scenes, but other characters may have scenes where they get to "hold the camera" and tell the story from their own perspective, showing what they see, think, feel, and experience.

When you sit down to write, you need to decide whether you will write in the first person or the third person, and whether you will have one character or more than one narrate. The answers to these questions may be crystal clear to you, even before you start writing. Or you may have to find your way, starting the novel in first person and partway through discovering it's too limiting, or starting the novel in the third person with multiple narrators and feeling dissatisfied because there's not a strong enough sense of the main character and his arc.

Here are your viewpoint choices:

- **First person:** One character holds the camera; the narrative is written in the first person.
- **Third person limited:** One character holds the camera; the narrative is written in the third person.
- **Multiple third person:** One character *at a time* holds the camera; the narrative is written in the third person.
- **Omniscient:** The camera can be anywhere; the narrative is written in the third person.

With each choice there are benefits and tradeoffs. Whichever you choose, viewpoint allows you to filter the story through the consciousness of one character at a time.

First Person

A single, first-person narrator is the simplest viewpoint choice for new writers to manage. It's hard enough to get a single point of view under control, and you only have to create one compelling narrator's voice.

Here's an example of a novel's opening lines written in the first person, anchored in the present, from Walker Percy's *The Moviegoer*.

This morning I got a note from my aunt asking me to come for lunch. I know what this means.

Those opening sentences are so simple, but they do double duty. They tell the reader about something that happened and hint at what this narrator thinks about it. We can almost see the character rolling his eyes.

You can also narrate in the first person and convey the sense that the narrator is looking back from some future vantage point. Authors often do this when writing a coming-of-age story. This example is from Philip Roth's *Portnoy's Complaint.*

> She was so deeply embedded in my consciousness that for the first year of school I seem to have believed that each of my teachers was my mother in disguise.

The big advantage of writing in the first person is that it enables you to bring the reader intimately close to your main character. It enables you to load the narrator's voice with attitude and feelings.

The big disadvantage to first person narrative is that it limits you to writing what one character experiences. Suppose that first-person narrator gets trapped in a cave? Your story gets trapped there, too. What if something very exciting happens while your character is trapped in that cave? The reader can't be on hand to experience the excitement.

Third Person Limited

The most commonly used viewpoint in novels is the third-person limited—a single character narrates throughout and the story is told in the third-person. With this viewpoint, the author can bring the reader close inside the characters head, or pull back and insert more distance, while still providing a single narrator's filter for the events of the novel.

ESSENTIAL

If you want to insert distance between a single point-of-view character and the narrative, write in the third person instead of in the first person. You'll be able to draw back the camera, from time to time, and show the reader a bigger picture that your point-of-view character may not be able to see.

Here is an example of a novel opening in third-person narrative from Larry McMurtry's *Lonesome Dove*.

When Augustus came out on the porch the blue pigs were eating a rattlesnake—not a very big one.

Notice how McMurtry drops the reader right into the middle of the scene. Augustus is the viewpoint character, but it feels as if we're watching him more from outside rather than inside.

Writing in the third-person limited viewpoint gives you more flexibility than writing in the first person. It allows you to pull the camera back at some times and bring it in close at others.

But third person is more difficult to control than first person. It's easy to find yourself slipping out of one character's head and into another. And you're still limited in what you can show the reader, since there's still just a single character that tells the story.

Multiple Third-Person

Allowing multiple characters to narrate a novel—writing in the third person with the camera close over the shoulder of one character at a time—enables you to tell a story on a much broader canvas. Different scenes can be narrated by different characters, and if one viewpoint character gets trapped in a cave, you simply switch to the viewpoint of another character. Multiple viewpoints give the author much more flexibility in telling the story.

FACT

Using multiple points of view can be liberating. You can dramatize virtually anything—just shift the point of view to a character who's there.

The great advantage of multiple viewpoints is that it enables you to create considerable dramatic tension and suspense because the reader is privy to much more information than any individual character.

But don't underestimate the skill it takes to create even one strong, distinct narrator's voice, never mind several of them. Too often, inexperienced writers attempt to write in multiple points of view and the book ends up feeling disjointed and lacking a strong coherent story line or a strong protagonist for the reader to root for.

Omniscient

Some authors use the voice of a god-like narrator who sees all and knows all, who hovers above the action and is simultaneously inside each character's head. Jane Austen used omniscient third person in *Pride and Prejudice*. She took the reader inside the heads of Jane, Mr. Darcy, Mr. Bingley, and all the rest of her characters, while at the same time providing her own satiric running commentary on the mores of the time.

You can easily see this omniscient narrator's voice from the novel's first line:

> It is a truth universally acknowledged, that a single man in possession of a good fortune, must be in want of a wife.

The omniscient narrator can go anywhere and see anything. But many modern authors shun the omniscient voice because it seems stilted and old-fashioned. It can also hold readers at a distance and prevent them from identifying with the protagonist.

Still, omniscient narration is often used at the beginning a novel, or in the first paragraphs of a scene or chapter. In this example from Tony Hillerman's *Listening Woman*, the story begins with an omniscient storyteller painting the setting for the reader.

> The southwest wind picked up turbulence around the San Francisco peaks, howled across the emptiness of the Moenkopi plateau, and made a thousand strange sounds in windows of the old Hopi villages of Shongopovi and Second Mesa. Two hundred vacant miles to the north and east, it sandblasted the stone sculptures of Monument Valley Navajo Tribal Park and whistled eastward across the maze of canyons on the Utah-Arizona border. Over the arid immensity of the Nokaito Bench it filled the blank blue sky with a rushing sound. At the hogan of Hosteen Tso, at 3:17 p.m., it gusted and eddied, and formed a dust devil, which crossed the wagon track and raced with a swirling roar across Margaret

Cigaret's old Dodge pickup truck and past the Tso brush arbor. The three people under the arbor huddled against the driven dust.

Did you notice how Hillerman draws the reader in—first from a vast distance, then to the hogan, then to the truck, then to characters huddled in a brush arbor? Hillerman continues this entire scene, writing in an omniscient viewpoint and relating a conversation among these three characters. But later chapters are narrated from viewpoints of his two main characters, Jim Chee and Joe Leaphorn.

Omniscience is particularly useful for showing a vast landscape or giving the perspective of a scene viewed from the future. It's best used sparingly, and for effect.

Anchoring the Sliding Viewpoint

A sliding viewpoint, slipping from one character's head into another and into another ("head hopping") within a single scene, is the mark of an inexperienced writer. To keep the point of view from sliding when you don't want it to, keep asking yourself: Who is narrating this scene? Then, as you write, keep the storytelling anchored in that character's head, too.

Write each scene as the viewpoint character experiences it, revealing his thoughts and feelings, what he can see and hear, his *observations* of other characters and his *interpretation* of what those characters might be thinking and feeling.

ALERT

Whether you tell your story in the first or third person, or have only one point-of-view character or several, it's best to anchor the narration in a single character's head within each scene. Insert a scene break, and you can shift to a new narrator.

Point-of-view differences can be subtle. In the brief example below, Friedkin is the third-person narrator.

Friedkin kept checking his watch. He was afraid that they wouldn't get there in time.

Suppose a different character, Myrna, is the third-person narrator instead of Friedkin. You might write that same idea differently.

Myrna noticed that Friedkin kept checking his watch, as if he were afraid they wouldn't get there in time.

The difference between these two examples is subtle. That's why you have to stay alert when you write so that you don't allow the viewpoint to slide.

Pitfalls in the Opening

It's critical that you write an opening that intrigues readers so that they want to continue reading. However, writing the opening of your novel is fraught with pitfalls. Here are a few:

- Taking too long to get the story moving: Something compelling has to happen in that first scene, something that makes the reader have to turn to the next page.
- Starting with backstory: Readers have to care about a character before they are interested in learning about that character's past.
- Sowing confusion by starting too many plots and subplots: Take your time and focus on a single plot strand at the beginning; get that one going before you start subplots spinning; and always show how the different characters and their stories connect.
- Overwhelming the reader by introducing too many characters at once: Just a few at a time is better.
- Leaving your characters floating in space: Be sure to give the opening a clear sense of time and place.
- Over-describing the setting: Write enough but not too much; a little weather goes a long way; layer in the details later.
- Under-describing the characters: Give at least some sense of a character's physical appearance when the character first appears; if you don't, readers will fill the void and create their own version of that character's physical presence.

- Stealing your novel's thunder: Don't open with a scene that is so exciting that nothing in the rest of the novel will match it; likewise, don't reveal a surprise that spoils what comes later.

Lastly, don't worry too much about making it perfect. Typically, new authors work and work and work that opening scene of the rough draft and stall out on moving ahead with the rest of the novel. Give yourself permission to write a lousy first draft and move on.

CHAPTER 9

Shaping Scenes

Every scene, from the opening of your novel to the final scene at the end, should move your story forward. Scenes may contain character introductions, descriptions of setting, dialogue, and action. In some scenes, characters reflect on what just happened or remember events that transpired far in the past. But fundamentally, each scene in your novel should result in some kind of change that pushes your story forward.

Little Story Arcs

Most novels have a three-act structure and the plot has an overall arc. Each of the scenes that makes up another of the building blocks of your novel should contain its own smaller story arc.

Here is an overview of the elements of the smaller story arc that may be contained within each scene:

1. Establishing narrative: Placing characters in a setting and a situation
2. Events: Characters acting and reacting to outside forces and to other characters around them
3. Change: An emotional change of tenor or a situational change
4. Reflection: Characters reacting to what just happened, trying to understand, think it through
5. Realization: Character grasping the implications of what has happened and drawing some kind of conclusion
6. Moving Forward: The conclusion that allows the characters to move forward in the same or a changed direction

Here's a simple example of a small story arc:

1. Establishing Narrative: Chet Anderson, a young businessman arrives home at his apartment building, parks his Porsche; he's exhausted and looking forward to a quiet dinner with his wife.
2. Events: He parks the car. Picks up the mail—he's surprised that his wife hasn't already collected it. Takes the elevator up. Walks down the hall. Notices that his apartment door is ajar.
3. Change: He pushes open the door and sees that all the furniture in the apartment is gone and a single red stiletto high heel is sitting in the middle of the floor. He hurries through the apartment and finds his wife's clothing is gone from the closets but his are still there.
4. Reflection: Chet calls the police and tries to explain the situation. While he waits for them to come he tries to puzzle out what in the heck is going on.
5. Realization: Chet realizes he's seen that shoe before; he remembers his wife's wardrobe (it wasn't her shoe); then he realizes where he saw the shoe before: his mistress was wearing it.

6. Moving forward: Chet picks up the shoe and tries to hide it, but before he can, the doorbell rings.

This could be written as a single scene. But that scene might end up being quite long, in which case it would be better broken into two scenes. Scene 1 starts: Chet arrives home. Scene 1 ends: Chet sees the empty apartment and the red stiletto. Scene 2 starts: Chet calls the police. Scene 2 ends: Chet realizes the shoe belongs to his mistress but before he can get rid of it the doorbell rings.

Your novel will be filled with little interconnected story arcs like these, each one propelling the story forward. Act I and Act II culminate with major changes, twists, or setbacks that propel your story forward into the next act.

Starting a Scene

It's important to give careful thought to the point, in the ongoing action, when you want to start writing a scene. A good rule of thumb: Start as *late* as possible. In other words, when things begin to happen. Often writers do this by jumping right into the middle of some ongoing action.

Suppose a scene involves a teenager getting arrested for shoplifting. Unless you're just introducing the characters, you wouldn't start this scene with the girl leaving home and walking to the store; you'd probably avoid a detailed description of the neighborhood she walks through. You'd probably want to start just before the arrest, when she's looking around and being tempted by what she sees and realizes that she has no money with her, and even if she did, it's all more expensive than what she can afford.

Even though you want to start late, don't forget to orient the reader at the start of each scene by establishing, right away, when and where the action is taking place and who is present.

Here's an example from *Olive Kitteridge* by Elizabeth Strout. Notice how artfully Strout orients her reader at the start of a scene without making it feel like a dry news bulletin.

At the marina on Sunday morning, Harmon had to work not to stare at the young couple. He had seen them before in town, walking along

Main Street: the girl's thin hand—cuffed at the wrist by fake fur on the end of her denim jacket sleeve—had been holding the boy's hand loosely as the two had looked in store windows with the same laconic, unqualified comfortableness they now had leaning against the railing by the stairs.

Strout sets this scene, which takes place in the middle of the novel, quickly and economically. We know when (Sunday), where (at the Marina), and who (Harmon and the young couple). She establishes all this and quickly follows up with dialogue and action as the characters interact.

Ending a Scene

Where to end a scene is also an important choice. A good rule of thumb: End as *early* as possible. In other words, don't let the scene dribble off, end it at a strong moment and leave out any unnecessary final bits. You might end the shoplifting scene with the girl feeling a heavy hand of the security guard on her shoulder, or with her being hustled into a back room for questioning. Then, you could start the next scene with the girl's mother coming to pick her up at the police station. Depending on the momentum you're trying to create, you can end a scene with a sense of finality or with something that propels the reader forward.

Here are two examples of scene endings from Yann Martel's *Life of Pi*. Read them and notice how one has a settled, finished feeling; the other is more of a cliffhanger that propels the reader forward.

Scene ending 1: I turned around, stepped over the zebra and threw myself overboard.

Scene ending 2: I crossed my arms on the lifebuoy around my waist, brought my head down and fell soundly asleep.

Obviously, the first ending is a cliffhanger. The second is a settled ending. Both kinds of scene endings have their place in a well-modulated novel.

The Essential Change in a Scene

In the course of each scene, some change should occur to move your story forward. It's not enough for a scene to just introduce a character or convey lots of fascinating information about the setting. In every scene something has to change. This means that something has to happen that changes the situation, or a character's perception of it, and that change propels the story forward.

The change might be a big change caused by some external cataclysmic event like a tsunami or a bomb blast, or it can be a subtle change caused by a small event like the discovery of a disturbing letter or the realization that a loved one is behaving oddly.

Kinds of Changes

The change that occurs in a scene can be a change in a character's emotional state, or a change in a relationship among the characters, or a change in a situation.

▼ **CHANGES IN EMOTIONAL STATE**

A character goes from feeling . . .	To feeling . . .
Safe	Unsafe
Contentment	Yearning
Laconic	Enraged
Loved	Hated
Frightened	Secure
Worried	Relieved

A scene can also contain a change in the relationship between two characters.

▼ **CHANGES IN RELATIONSHIP BETWEEN CHARACTERS**

A character goes from feeling . . .	To feeling . . .
Trust	Distrust
Admiration	Scorn
Certainty	Doubt
Unconditional Love	Uncertainty
Lust	Disgust

The change can also be situational. Here are some events that can radically change the situation for a character:

- He meets the "woman of his dreams"
- His apartment is burgled
- He loses his wedding ring
- His dog disappears
- His wife leaves him
- He has a premonition of his death
- He finds out that his best friend betrayed him
- He discovers that his e-mail account has been hacked
- He is stranded when his car breaks down on a dark road in the middle of nowhere

If a scene doesn't have some kind of fundamental change in it, then the scene is dramatically unproductive. Consider deleting it and incorporating any bits that you need into another scene that's working for you dramatically. Whatever parts you delete, be sure to paste them into your Out file for safekeeping in case you later decide you need them back.

Conflict in a Scene

Conflict for the reader is like salt and pepper for the chef. It's the thing that makes what's going on more interesting. Conflict allows your characters to show who they are.

Every scene in your novel should have at least some conflict in it. Does that mean that characters have to yell at each other and fight in every scene? Of course not. That would make for a strident and ultimately boring novel.

But look at what just a little bit of conflict does for what is otherwise a simple interaction between characters:

Example 1:
"Where are you going?"
"I need to find my brother."

Example 2:

"Where do you think you're going?"

"Get out of my way. I need to find my brother."

There are only a few words' difference between these two examples, but the second example is far more dynamic.

Sources of Conflict

Conflict happens when one of the characters meets an obstacle to getting something she wants. The following table shows examples of conflicts between characters.

▼ **EXAMPLES OF CONFLICT AS A RESULT OF CONFLICTING GOALS**

Character A	Character B
Wants a piece of information	Needs to keep that information secret
Is exhausted and wants to go home	Wants to stay and party and orders more drinks
Wants a promotion	Gives the promotion to someone well connected but unqualified
Wants the man to love her	Wants to get the woman into bed
Wants to prove himself by poisoning the water supply	Wants to prevent his family from being poisoned
Wants to protect her brother	Wants to prove that the brother is a thief

Conflict can be internal, as when one character seems to shut down and refuse to connect with another, or pretends that everything is fine when in reality it isn't. Or conflict can be external, as when two characters disagree or argue or engage in a chase or a physical fight. A scene is always more interesting and allows your characters to show who they are if you layer in some conflict.

Conflict Throws Characters Off Balance

Even the most subtle of conflicts has the effect of throwing a character out of equilibrium. Move a character out of her comfort zone and you have something interesting going on.

For example, a character arrives at a cocktail party in a fancy dress when everyone else is in shorts and sandals. A character is expected to give a eulogy for another person she secretly detested. A character has to be a bridesmaid at a wedding where her sister is marrying a man whom she herself is in love with. A character has been instructed to follow orders from the president but he isn't sure that those orders are legitimate or warranted.

In every scene that you write, there should be some source of conflict. It can be between characters, between a character and the elements, or even within a character. Find that source of conflict and heighten it, and the scene will become more interesting.

For Each Scene, Picking the Viewpoint Character

Each scene in your novel should be narrated throughout by a single character. If your novel is written throughout from a single viewpoint, either in first person or in third, then the same character narrates every scene. But if you are writing from multiple viewpoints, with different characters narrating different scenes, then there may be times when more than one of your narrators is present in a scene. Then, your challenge is to decide which of those characters is going to narrate the scene. Which one do you pick?

OPTIONS FOR PICKING A CHARACTER TO NARRATE A SCENE
- Pick the character with the major role in the scene, or
- Pick the character with most at stake in the scene, or
- Pick the character who is thrown most off balance by what happens in the scene, or
- Pick the character with the most interesting and complete vantage point

If you're not sure which character should narrate, then write two versions of the scene, one from each character's viewpoint. Decide for yourself which one works better. What is gained and lost by allowing a given character to narrate instead. Which version better holds your interest? Look at the big picture, too: Which version reveals to readers what you want them to know at this point in the novel and keeps hidden what you don't want them to know. Then be sure to save the version you like least in your Out file just in case you change your mind.

How Many Viewpoints Is Too Many?

It is possible to diffuse the emotional impact of your story with too many narrators. For readers to keep reading, they have to care about the protagonist as well as about the story you're telling. If you give them too many competing narrators, they won't know whose story to pay attention to. Readers who stop caring stop reading.

There is no maximum number of narrative viewpoints. You need as many viewpoints as are necessary to tell your story. The commercial blockbuster *The Da Vinci Code* has at least five viewpoint characters, including the villain. In Toni Morrison's Pulitzer-winning novel *Jazz*, about a half dozen characters take their turns narrating in what ends up feeling like the theme and improvisation of a jazz ensemble. William Faulkner's tour de force *As I Lay Dying* has fifteen narrators, the members of a family carrying Addie Bundren's coffin to where she wished to be buried. Even the dead Addie takes a turn as narrator.

Never add a viewpoint character just because you feel there's something important you have to tell the reader and none of your chosen viewpoint characters are privy to it. Find another way out of that dilemma. Viewpoint is too powerful to bestow for such an artless reason.

The only way to know if you have too many viewpoint characters is by gathering reader reaction. This is why having trusted readers give you feedback is so critical.

Connective Tissue Between Scenes

Sometimes you will simply jump from one dramatic scene to the next with a doublespace between them. At other times, you may want to write a bit of material that either loosely connects or separates the scenes. For instance, a scene might begin with a bit of omniscient scene setting from the author rather than in the voice of one of the characters. Be forewarned, that this bridge material can be boring, so try to keep it as short as you can and move as quickly as you can into the next scene.

Here are examples of some bridges and how they function between scenes; all of these examples are excerpted from Ron Carlson's novel *Five Skies*.

Purpose: Conveying background

When Gary and his wife Alicia had come to Southern California, Arthur knew it wasn't great news. Gary had folded many tents, staying with one public relations company for almost four years; that was his record. He was what? Too young.

Purpose: Summarizing events that are not important or interesting enough to dramatize

In town he went to the First Idaho Bank and deposited his check. He got another money order for his mother and he walked next door to the post office and mailed that.

Purpose: Creating a logical transition between one set of events and the next.

[Harry] learned long ago to tell just by the way Key walked onto the set whether to move fast or slow. He knew what to do now.

These connecting bits, like bridges between the dramatic scenes in your novel, usually come from the viewpoint of the narrating character, but might come from that character's perspective looking back from the future or from an omniscient viewpoint. Bridges don't feel as if they take place in real time like the dramatic elements of a scene.

Writing Flashbacks

There will be many times when you need to show the reader something that happened in the past. Sure, you could summarize the brief memory and move on. But if the past event is something very important and emotionally connected to your story—for instance, the protagonist's first meeting with her deceased husband, or the moment when she held their first child—then you might want to write it as an extended flashback.

An extended flashback is a dramatic way to tell the reader about past events, but it interrupts the narrative flow of your main story. Delivered at an inopportune time, a flashback can derail the current action and dissipate any momentum you've gathered. Delivered at the right dramatic moment, a flashback enhances and deepens your story.

ALERT

Keep any bridge material connecting scenes short. These passages will lack the drama and momentum of scenes; to a reader they feel like synopsis.

Transitioning Into a Flashback

The tricky thing about writing a flashback is transitioning into the past and then transitioning back to the present. You want to do so in a way that feels clear and effortless.

Following is an example showing you how to begin a flashback. This is the beginning of a four-page flashback in William G. Tapply's novel *Bitch Creek*.

An hour before sunup on a June morning almost exactly five years earlier, Calhoun had been creeping along the muddy bank of a little tidal creek that emptied into Casco Bay just north of Portland. A blush of pink had begun to bleed into the pewter sky toward the east. The tide was about halfway out, and the water against the banks lay as flat and dark as a mug of camp coffee.

Notice how Tapply handles the time and space shift:

- The time shift: "almost exactly five years earlier"
- The space shift: "along the muddy bank of a little tidal creek"

He also handles the tense shift. The rest of this novel is written in the past tense, but this flashback begins with the past perfect tense:

- "Calhoun had been creeping"
- "A bush of pink had begun to bleed"

Had, had, had . . . Past perfect quickly gets cumbersome, and so once the flashback is established, Tapply returns to the simple past tense: "The tide was about halfway out. . . ."

Transitioning Out of a Flashback

At the end of a flashback, the writer must once again cue the reader to the time and space shift back to the novel's primary timeline. To show the transition, insert the past perfect a time or two at the end of the flashback; when you're out of the flashback and back in the main story, revert to past tense. Here's an example of a sentence that signals a transition back.

She had never called him. At the time, he had thought it was odd. Now he wasn't so sure. He got up and headed . . .

Of course the tense you write in the flashback depends on the tense you are using for the main story.

▼ **TENSE TO USE FOR FLASHBACKS**

If the main story is written in . . .	Write the flashback in . . .
Present tense	**Past tense**
He runs	He ran
Past tense	**Past perfect tense**
He ran	He had run

Scene Checklist

After you write each scene, there are questions you can ask yourself to determine whether the scene is strong enough to stand on its own in your novel.

❐ Did you establish when, where, and who near the start of the scene?

❐ Is the scene narrated by a single character?

❐ Have you anchored the viewpoint in that one character's head through-out the scene, with the possible exception of any bridge material?

❐ When you introduced new characters or new settings, did you take enough time to describe them without overdoing it?

❐ Have you made it clear to the reader what these characters want?

❐ Does something change in the scene—emotional valance, character relationships, or situation?

❐ Is there some conflict?

❐ Did you start the scene as late as possible?

❐ Did you end the scene as early as possible?

❐ If there is any connecting material, is it short and focused?

Remember, scenes are the basic building blocks of your novel. Each one has to contribute dramatically to moving your story forward. Each one has to hold the reader's interest. Each one has to show the reader something that the reader didn't know before the scene began.

CHAPTER 10

Writing Characters

Now it's time to take all your ideas about your protagonist, your main characters, and your minor characters and channel them into the writing of your novel. You'll need to show your readers who your characters are and make room for those characters in the driver's seat so that they can help direct your plot.

First Impressions

Every character in your novel has that first appearance on the page. As in life, first impressions matter. You want to stamp into your reader's brain your own sense of who each character is—their emotional presence as much as the details of their appearance and wardrobe.

Whatever you decide your protagonist looks like, it's a good idea to communicate that to the reader within the first ten pages or so; otherwise readers will busily create their own image of your character and it may not be at all what you want them to see.

In this example from *Fantasy in Death*, Nora Roberts, writing as J. D. Robb, introduces Bart Minnock, who will soon be murdered by his holographic video game.

> While swords of lightning slashed and stabbed murderously across the scarred shield of sky, Bart Minnock whistled his way home for the last time. Despite the battering rain, Bart's mood bounced along with his cheerful tune as he shot his doorman a snappy salute.
>
> "Howzit going, Mr. Minnock?"
>
> "It's going up, Jackie. Going way uptown."
>
> "This rain could do the same, if you ask me."
>
> "What rain?" With a laugh, Bart sloshed his way in soaked skids to the elevator.

Notice how economically Roberts introduces this character with only a scant physical description. And yet, from his dialogue and behavior, the reader has a strong feeling for this upbeat, goofy guy who bounces along, whistling, completely oblivious to the storm raging around him. The little detail of a doorman shows us Bart Minnock is a wealthy city dweller. Notice, too, that the character's full name is right there, the moment he appears on the page.

Here is another example from the same novel. In a phrase, Roberts introduces a more minor character, an android.

> His in-house intercom greeted him with a cheery *Welcome home, Bart,* and his server droid—custom-made to replicate Princess Leia, classic Star Wars, slave-girl mode (he was a nerd, but he was still a guy)—strolled out to offer him his favorite orange fizzy with crushed ice.

Again, there's almost no description, and the "server droid" doesn't even merit a name. The shorthand of "Princess Leia" in "slave-girl mode" gives the reader the picture. Of course, this character is a cliché. But with a minor character like this one, you can get away with a cliché.

A little further on in the novel, there's another character introduction. We meet CeeCee. Think about how this one feels different from the previous two.

> Eve found CeeCee in the media room on the first level. A pretty blond with an explosion of curls, she sat in one of the roomy chairs. It dwarfed her, even with her legs tucked up, and her hands clasped in her lap. Her eyes—big, bright, and blue—were red-rimmed, puffy, and still carried the glassiness of shock.

Did you notice that this introduction of CeeCee contains much more physical detail? It's written so that the reader can really see CeeCee with her "explosion of curls" sitting in a chair that "dwarfed her," her eyes red-rimmed and glassy with shock (she's just learned of Bart's demise).

The surfeit of detail, and the explanation that she's in shock, make perfect sense because the viewpoint character observing her and narrating the description is Eve Dallas, a detective. Eve is a trained observer, so naturally she picks up on all that physical detail and nuance—it's part of her job and essential to who she is.

Showing the Reader a Viewpoint Character

One of the special challenges in writing a novel is giving the reader a sense of what your protagonist looks like, particularly when the whole novel is written from that character's viewpoint. With the viewpoint anchored in the character's head, it simply wouldn't feel natural for the character to say, "I have red hair and horn-rimmed glasses. . . ." The one time you can get away with this, however, is if your character speaks directly to the reader.

So how does a viewpoint character convey his own appearance to the reader? It's become a cliché to have the character look in a mirror, or notice his own reflection in a window and describe what he sees. However, many writers do just that and make it work. But there are other ways.

In this example from *How the Garcia Girls Lost Their Accents*, novelist Julia Alvarez manages to convey what her viewpoint character looks like without having Yolanda see her own reflection.

> Before anyone has turned to greet her in the entryway, Yolanda sees herself as they will, shabby in a black cotton skirt and jersey top, sandals on her feet, her wild black hair held back with a hairband. Like a missionary, her cousins will say, like one of those Peace Corps girls who have let themselves go so as to do dubious good in the world.

Here's another example of a viewpoint character conveying what she looks like to the reader. This comes from *Come and Find Me* by Hallie Ephron.

> He touched a long index finger to his cap. "You're lookin' spruce."

> Diana looked down, taking in her matted furry slippers, sweat pants, and an oversized Smashing Pumpkins T-shirt, black with a silver "ZERO" printed across the chest. Her face grew warm, and she tried to run her fingers through the tangles in her hair.

In that example, Diana is a viewpoint character who looks down at what she's wearing in response to another character's offhand remark about her appearance. Of course the reader has no idea what Diana's face looks like or her eye color, whether she's pretty or plain, tall or short, but we do get a sense of who she is from the few details provided.

Conveying a Character with Telling Details

In describing a character, think about the one or two key details that say it all. Normally trivia like height and hair color and shoe size fail miserably in expressing a character's appearance. Here's an example from Fern Michaels's *Weekend Warrior*. Notice the telling details Michaels picks to describe her character, Charles Martin. As you read the brief excerpt, think about which of the details are most striking.

> Charles Martin was a tall man with clear crystal blue eyes and a shock of white hair that was thick and full. Once he'd been heavier, but this past year had taken a toll on him, too. She noticed the tremor in his hand when he handed her a cup of coffee.

Though the "clear crystal blue eyes" and the "shock of white hair" give the reader a visual image of a vigorous man, the contrasting hand tremor conveys to the reader even more information: though he seems vigorous, he's been through some trauma or illness. This is a telling detail—it intrigues, and we'll have to read on to find out what it's all about.

Here are a few examples of telling details:

- The character wears an expensive suit with a button missing
- The character wears a tattered but once glorious bridal gown
- The character arrives at a cocktail party in jeans, cowboy boots, and a ZZ Top T-shirt
- The character is wearing wristwatches on both arms
- The character has beautifully manicured nails but her fingertips are calloused
- The character wears steel-toed construction boots and his fingernails are manicured

Try not to over-describe your characters or you'll bury the telling detail.

Here is another example. John Berendt introduces the character Chablis, when she appears for the first time in the novel *Midnight in the Garden of Good and Evil*. As you read it, think about how this description conveys so much more than Chablis's appearance.

She was wearing a loose white cotton blouse, jeans, and white tennis sneakers. Her hair was short, and her skin was a smooth milk chocolate. Her eyes were large and expressive, all the more because they were staring straight at mine. She had both hands on her hips and a sassy half-smile on her face as if she had been waiting for me.

Berendt has chosen the telling details carefully. His description is vivid and conveys not only Chablis's physical presence but also her attitude. Berendt piles on the detail to achieve this, and it could have read like a laundry list. Instead, the character nearly pops right off the page.

Characters Are What They Do

You've probably heard, over and over, that fiction writers need to "show not tell." One of the best ways to show a character to the reader is by putting her on the page and letting her perform, especially when the character does something that's surprising.

You can give your character gestures or habits that convey her inner character. A character's actions—what she does or doesn't do—also show your reader what the character is made of.

"Don't say the old lady screamed. Bring her on and let her scream."—attributed to Mark Twain

Telling Gestures and Habits

Characteristic gestures or habits, chosen carefully, can show the reader without having to explain. The gesture or habit will suggest several possible explanations. Through your storytelling, you'll show the reader which it is.

▼ **EXAMPLES OF TELLING GESTURES OR HABITS**

What to show the reader	What it might mean
The character covers her mouth when she talks	She's embarrassed by her crooked teeth or bad breath or painfully shy
The character avoids eye contact and answers a question with a question	The character is hiding something, is afraid, or is a compulsive liar
The character continually twists what looks like a wedding band on her right hand	The character is recently divorced or widowed, or not married at all but pretending to be

But beware of tells—gestures and habits that have been used a million times before by authors to telegraph information. For instance, the donut-eating cop (dumb) or the professor who keeps squinting or losing his way (absent-minded) or the mousy librarian who is revealed to be gorgeous when she takes off her glasses and lets down her hair (hot hot hot).

Overused habits or gestures can feel like annoying tics. A character who grins, or turtles his neck, or bulges his eyes, or cries "Ay, carumba!" every few pages feels like a two-dimensional cartoon.

Showing Character Through Behavior

Writing is all about making choices. On each page, you have to decide, "What is this character going to do now?" Suppose, for example, your character walks into a department store. What does she do?

- Head for the sales rack?
- Browse designer jewelry and slip on a ring that she forgets to take off?
- Mix a bunch of size-two dresses in with the size twelves?
- Try on every pair of Manolo Blahnik shoes in her size?
- Get weepy as she browses baby items?
- Plant a bomb?
- Set a fire?
- Crouch behind a potted plant and watch one particular sales person?

If you've thought through your plot and have an outline or synopsis written, then you'll have a pretty good idea what this character will do. But suppose you start writing the scene and the character does something that surprises you. Authors talk about a character who "takes over." When it happens to you, welcome it. Try to go with it, for at least a few more pages. It might turn out to be a terrific plot twist, and what surprises you will be sure to surprise your readers, too.

Characters and Their Voices

Another way to show your character is through voice. All characters have spoken dialogue; viewpoint characters have internal dialogue, too. Lace that dialogue with attitude and you can show your character's personality.

Take, for example, something as simple as the way that your character greets another character. Is it "Howdy," or "Yo," or "Pleased to make your acquaintance"? Is it stony silence when the other character is his wife?

You can show the relationship between characters, perhaps even unfinished business between them, by the way they greet one another. "Hi, there," conveys a whole different feeling from "So?"

Internal Dialogue

One of the strongest tools for showing character is internal dialogue. Only a point-of-view character gets to show the reader his thought process, communicating why he does what he does. Internal dialogue is what's going on in your point-of-view character's head as he muses, argues with himself, observes, makes decisions, and so on.

Here's an example of internal dialogue from Rebecca Wells's *Divine Secrets of the Ya-Ya Sisterhood*. In this short excerpt, main character Sidda opens her mother's scrapbook and, in the process, discovers the novel's eponymous "secrets."

The first thing Sidda did was to smell the leather. Then she held the album to her chest and hugged it. She wasn't sure exactly why, but it occurred to her that what she wanted to do, what she *needed* to do, was light a candle.

A few paragraphs later, after Sidda has looked at a few pages.

She wanted to devour the album, to crawl into it like a hungry child and take everything she needed. This raw desire made her feel dizzy.

Wells does so much more than merely show Sidda's thoughts. She shows the reader Sidda's overwhelming sensations, her reverence in this moment, as well as her confusion about what it all means.

Another example of internal dialogue comes from the opening paragraphs of a quirky novel *Dog On It* by Spencer Quinn. Notice how Quinn reveals to the reader the identity of his first-person narrator.

I could smell him—or rather the booze on his breath—before he even opened the door, but my sense of smell is pretty good, probably better than yours. The key scratched against the lock, finally found the slot. The door opened and in, with a little stumble, came Bernie Little, founder and part owner (his ex-wife, Leda, walked off with the rest) of the Little Detective Agency. I'd seen him look worse, but not often.

He mustered a weak smile. "Hey, Chet."

I raised my tail and let it thump down on the rug, just so, sending a message.

"I'm a little late, sorry. Need to go out?"

Why would that be? Just because my back teeth were floating? But then I thought, What the hell, the poor guy, and I went over and pressed my head against the side of his leg.

Through the internal dialogue, the reader gradually realizes that the narrator is a dog named Chet, and also comes to understand the relationship between Chet and his owner.

Finally, look at this example from Nancy Pickard's *The Scent of Rain and Lightning*. As you read it, think about how Pickard uses internal dialogue to show this character's yearning.

Her thoughts made her shiver.

In that overheated moment, she intensely felt her own raw, tingling nakedness under her sundress, longing for hands upon her skin that were not her husband's callused, fumbling, clumsy ones.

Showing Character by Revealing Backstory

Just as real people are shaped by past experiences, a character's fictional past (also known as backstory) influences how that character thinks, looks, and behaves in the present.

Suppose you are writing about a character who is terrified of snakes or unable to commit to a relationship, or is an obsessive workaholic. If you've done your homework and developed a backstory for that character, then you know exactly why she is the way she is. That snake phobia may have resulted when her brother put a pet boa constrictor in her bed when she was six. Maybe she can't commit because of how traumatic it was for her to watch her mother fall apart after her father abandoned the family. Or she may be a workaholic because she's afraid to slow down enough to grieve for her dead husband.

One of most frequent mistakes authors make is to lay out the character's backstory in the beginning of the novel. They go on and on, dumping the backstory in the reader's lap, telling how the character grew up in a broken home and how she was an alcoholic who inadvertently killed her child in a car accident, and, and, and . . . .

ESSENTIAL

How much backstory your reader will tolerate is in direct proportion to how much forward momentum your novel has achieved.

It turns out that the reader probably doesn't need to know any of this. At least not yet. Backstory about characters readers don't yet care about is boring. So, first you have to make the reader care about the character, then you can layer in all the backstory you want.

So when it's time to tell the backstory, how do you do it? Not all at once. There are many different ways to convey backstory without writing a clunky backstory dump. Bits and pieces can be layered in as the story moves forward; the more important chunks of backstory can be told in flashbacks.

Backstory Layered in Internal Dialogue

Internal dialogue is an effective technique for slipping the reader information about a character's backstory. Here are a few examples:

- There was Bruce. I hadn't seen him for months, not since his wife disappeared.
- The tiny gravestones reminded Sarah of her own stillborn child; her husband had insisted that they whisk his little body away before she even had a chance to say good-bye.
- Jane wanted to tell him she loved him. Really she did. But something about him reminded her of Daniel, and what had happened the last time she'd let down her guard.

In each of these examples, the viewpoint character conveys a little flash of memory, triggered by an object or event in the present. In the first little excerpt, for example, the trigger is seeing Bruce, and it reminds the narrator of his wife's disappearance.

Backstory is often best layered in. So you might write just a quick reference, like these, to some event in the past. And then later add more detail in another quick flashback, and later add in even more until the full story emerges.

Backstory Conveyed in Dialogue

Another simple way to convey information about your characters' pasts is through spoken dialogue. Here are a few simple examples.

- "Bruce! I haven't seen you in so long, not since the funeral." I paused, wondering why on earth I'd blurted that out. But he didn't seem bothered. "I'm sorry. I know should have called."

- "Yes, I had a child," Sarah said. "Once. She was two pounds, two ounces, and we named her Amanda." Her vision blurred. "I never even got to hold her."
- "I just couldn't say it," Jane said later to Miranda as they sat in Miranda's kitchen eating fresh-baked chocolate chip cookies. "I kept thinking about Daniel, and how he betrayed me the day after I told him I loved him."

When the opportunity arises in the story and dialogue like this feels natural, then it's an easy and straightforward way to convey backstory. But beware of overdoing it. For example:

"As you know, my sister Louise was married to Bartie, of course that was a long time ago, when they lived over on Fisher Lane and the baby next door got kidnapped and the police questioned Louise and Bartie for the longest time. . . ."

This dialogue sounds clumsy and contrived. Real people would never talk this way. Instead, it sounds like the author trying to shovel information into dialogue.

Backstory Conveyed with Props

Fill the fictional world your characters inhabit with props. Use them to suggest your characters' backstories. Consider a character's bedroom. Here are just a few items it might contain that will give you a chance to hint to the reader something about your character's past:

- A wedding picture with the glass broken
- A colorful but fraying afghan crocheted by the character's grandmother
- A bulletin board with curling yellowed clippings tacked to it
- A photo booth strip of pictures of the character mugging for the camera with a beautiful young woman
- Bookshelves loaded with self-help books like *When Am I Going to be Happy?* and *Women Who Love Too Much*
- A collection of guns in a wall-mounted display case with one of the guns missing

Each of these props suggests a backstory. When your character looks at that wedding picture, or adds another clipping to the bulletin board, you get a natural opportunity to convey backstory as the prop triggers a thought or a bit of dialogue about the past.

Backstory Conveyed with a Flashback

There will be big, important parts of the backstory that you may want to dramatize rather than relegate to internal or spoken dialogue. You can handle these by writing the scene as a flashback.

Trigger the memory with something in the present, then segue into the past and write a scene within the scene, dramatizing the past event, staying in the viewpoint of the character who remembers. Then segue back and continue.

Character Checklist

When you put a character on the page for the first time, you want him to make an impression.

Here's a checklist to make sure you've made that first impression count:

- ❐ Have you established the basics about the character—name and gender?
- ❐ Is the character's relationship to the narrator clear?
- ❐ Have you avoided character clichés?
- ❐ Have you given the reader enough information to visualize the character? Did you allow telling details to show?
- ❐ Have you shown your reader who this character is through his actions?
- ❐ Have you conveyed this character's mood and attitude?
- ❐ Did you suggest the character's backstory but save the details for later?

Over time, as the novel continues, you will add nuance, detail, backstory, and allow your character to show himself through his actions, thoughts, and dialogue. Short flashbacks can come after the character is fully introduced, and longer flashbacks once your story has established a good amount of forward momentum.

CHAPTER 11

Writing Dialogue

What characters say out loud—their dialogue—can serve a range of purposes. You can show a character's background and education by the words she chooses and how she puts them together. You can show the disconnect between what your character means and what she says, and between what she reveals and what she is trying to keep hidden. You can use dialogue to show how characters relate to one another. Dialogue, used well, enables you to show the reader who your characters are while moving your story forward.

Writing Believable Dialogue

Believable dialogue should sound authentic to the reader. It should have the sound and feel of real people speaking. To write believable dialogue, start listening, really listening to the people around you. Listen to your family and friends, of course. But also become an eavesdropper. Listen to teenagers talking to each other, or clerks in a convenience store passing the time of day, or people in a restaurant or casino, or construction workers on a street corner or in a bar.

In particular, try to listen carefully to people who are not like you. Notice how their speech patterns are distinct. How they use slang and tone of voice along with gestures, props, and body language to convey additional meaning. Listen, and take notes. You can learn from real speech, using the patterns and idiosyncrasies that feel authentic, then paring and editing it down so it holds the reader's interest.

QUOTE

"In its beginning, dialogue's the easiest thing in the world to write when you have a good ear, which I think I have. But as it goes on, it's the most difficult, because it has so many ways to function."—Eudora Welty

Reaching for Authenticity

Good dialogue both conveys character and feels natural. Here is an example from *Midnight in the Garden of Good and Evil*. First, read the short excerpt and think about what the dialogue shows you about who this character is.

"The thing I like best about the squares," Miss Harty said, "is that cars can't cut through the middle; they must go *around* them. So traffic is obliged to flow at a very leisurely pace. The squares are our little oases of tranquility."

As she spoke, I recognized in her voice the coastal accent described in *Gone with the Wind*—"soft and slurring, liquid of vowels, kind to consonants."

Notice that the words Miss Harty chooses: obliged, leisurely, oases, tranquility. Her word choices enable her to express herself precisely and delicately. She speaks in long, leisurely sentences. The reader knows that she is well educated and cultured. And the wish she expresses in this dialogue shows us more—her yearning to continue living in a controlled, tranquil, unchanged world. The narrator goes on to describe the way her speech sounds, quoting that lovely line from *Gone with the Wind*.

If you have read this novel, perhaps you remember that Miss Harty is a well-bred elderly woman in Savannah who wants, of course, to preserve Savannah in all its antebellum glory. Her dialogue is totally in synch with her character and her desires.

Later in the same book, Berendt introduces the reader to an entirely different kind of character. Read this excerpt and think about how different Chablis is from Miss Harty.

"Ooooo, *child*!" she said. "You are right on time honey." Her voice crackled, her hoop earrings jangled. "I am *serious*. I cannot *tell* you." She began moving slowly toward me with an undulating walk. She trailed an index finger sensuously along the fender feeling the hollow of each and every dent. "Y-e-e-e-s, child! *Yayiss* . . . *yayiss* . . . yayiss! [. . .] Tell me something, honey," she said. "How come a white boy like you is drivin' a old, broken-down jiveass bruthuh's heap like this? If you don't mind me askin'."

Notice the how colorful language (jiveass), quirky grammar (How come . . .), and dialect (drivin') work together with physical detail (jangling earrings) and action (trailing finger) to convey this character. Lady Chablis is Savannah's larger-than-life local drag queen and entertainer. Notice also the use of italics to show how the character's voice becomes more emphatic on certain syllables. She's charming, polite, in-your-face, and utterly hilarious. The net result is that the reader can literally see and hear this character.

A note of caution: A little dialect goes a long way. In that example, Berendt was introducing Chablis, and he used dialect several times to show how she pronounces words. But as the story continues and Chablis continues to talk, Berendt only occasionally spells out the dialect. That's because continuing to spell the words phonetically is tiring for readers and unnecessary. Once you establish the dialect, the reader will "hear" it whenever that character talks without it having to be rendered every time.

Making Each Character's Dialogue Unique

By the middle of your novel, your reader shouldn't need attribution (like "Bill said") in order to figure out which character said the line. Each character should sound different and distinct from the others.

Here is a list of things to think about when you are choosing the words to put into a character's mouth:

- ❏ Does she rat-a-tat short sentences or wind thoughts through long, leisurely, complex sentences?
- ❏ Does she speak in phrases and news bulletins rather than complete thoughts?
- ❏ Do her word choices reflect her cultural, educational, ethnic, or regional distinctness?
- ❏ Does she use jargon that is related to her job or expertise?
- ❏ Is her dialogue edgy and direct or placating and obtuse?

Attribution

Attributions are the words that go with the quoted dialogue that tell the reader who's talking. The main function of those attributional phrases is to keep the reader from getting confused.

While there are a host of colorful verbs that express how words might have been uttered, from argued to yammered, from chortled to ululated, most stylists advise writers to stick to "said," "asked," along with the occasional "replied."

Here's a simple back-and-forth example of dialogue.

"How are you doing?" Olive asked.

"As if you care," Brandon replied.

"How can you say that?"

There's plenty of emotion conveyed, even with these spare bits of dialogue. The emotion is in the word choice. Notice that there's no attribution with the last line of dialogue. That's because it's not necessary. It's obvious to the reader that the last line is Olive's answer. It's best to skip attribution wherever you can do so without confusing the reader. And try to avoid "colorful" attributions. It's a good idea to follow Elmore Leonard's advice:

> "Never use a verb other than 'said' to carry dialogue. The line of dialogue belongs to the character; the verb is the writer sticking his nose in. But 'said' is far less intrusive than 'grumbled,' 'gasped,' 'cautioned,' 'lied.'"

Why skip those fancy forms of attribution? Don't they economically convey the manner in which something is said? The emotion that's conveyed? Maybe, but you can do a much better job conveying how something is said, communicating the attitude and underlying emotion, by carefully choosing the words spoken and through body language, props, and the reactions of other characters.

Placement of Attribution

Attribution can be placed at the beginning, at the end, or in the middle of dialogue. For example, take this piece of dialogue: "If you're going to leave me, then I need to know now." There are at least three ways that this could be broken up with attribution.

▼ **PLACEMENT OF ATTRIBUTION**

Beginning	She said, "If you're going to leave me, then I need to know now."
Middle	"If you're going to leave me," she said, "then I need to know now."
End	"If you're going to leave me, then I need to know now," she said.

Which placement works best? That's a judgment call. There's no rule about where to put attribution, so try writing various permutations and read them aloud to yourself to see which sounds stronger. In this case, the middle example has a slight edge.

Adding Emotion to Dialogue with Word Choice

You can show the emotion underlying dialogue by carefully picking the words to be spoken. Examine these alternatives:

- "Mr. Ohrbach? What a surprise. I didn't know you were coming."
- "Mr. Ohrbach, you came! And I thought you'd forgotten."
- "Is that you, Mr. Ohrbach? Did you . . . I mean, are you sure you want to be here?"
- "Mr. Ohrbach? Who the hell invited you?"
- "Why, Mr. Ohrbach. So you decided to grace us with your presence."

The dialogue in each of these examples conveys information as well as emotion and attitude. Sometimes, the right punctuation and words are all you need.

Adding Emotion to Dialogue with Body Language

When an actor delivers a line of dialogue, he delivers it not only with his voice but with his entire body and through the thoughtful use of props. Writers can do the same, carefully pairing dialogue with actions to show emotion.

Here are two examples of how the same dialogue, paired with action and a prop, can convey an entirely different emotion.

Example 1
"Did you know him long?" I asked.

Jane stirred her drink and stared into it. "Too long, and not long enough."

Example 2
"Did you know him long?" I asked.

Jane knocked back her drink and slammed the empty glass down on the table. "Too long, and not long enough."

In the first example, Jane staring into her drink conveys sadness and perhaps regret. In the second example, her actions convey rage.

Just about any object in a scene—a cigarette, a tissue, a chair, a necktie, a belt, shirt buttons, and so on—can be used, in combination with dialogue, to show different mental states. For example, a character who allows the ash on his cigarette to remain there so long that it falls off is in an entirely different state of mind from a character who manically puffs and flicks ashes onto the floor.

In this example from Margot Livesey's *Eva Moves the Furniture*, the author uses an egg as her prop to show a husband's reaction to his wife telling him she's pregnant.

> The day after my appointment with Dr Singer, I broke the news to Matthew at breakfast. "How could you be?" he said. His hand jerked and the boiled egg I had just set before him flew to the floor.

It's so appropriate, symbolically, for Livesey to use an egg in this way since eggs represent something conceived but not yet born.

Choose the action carefully and you effectively nuance the dialogue the character delivers. Be careful not to overuse the prop or the gesture. Avoid clichéd gestures, too, such as shrugging or grinning or clenching a jaw or narrowing eyes. Try to make your version of the gesture fresh.

Showing Relationships Through Dialogue

Dialogue among characters shows the reader their relationships. Without having to explain, you can use dialogue to show that three characters are friends; two others are lovers; and another pair are complete strangers.

Here's an example from Ken Bruen's *London Boulevard*. As you read it, think about what this dialogue shows the reader about the relationship between these two characters.

> "I presume you're here for an interview. Well? Speak up. What have you to say?"

Her voice was deep, almost coarse. The timber that cigarettes and whiskey add. 'Course arrogance helps too.

I said, "I need an ashtray."

Did you notice the haughty distance conveyed by the line of dialogue that begins "I presume"? The words convey impatience and the sense that this character is addressing someone she feels is way beneath her.

The response ("I need an ashtray") is completely irrelevant to her question. The man she's talking to refuses to respond in kind, showing in just this brief, initial interaction that he's not the kind of person who can be pushed around, bullied, or easily impressed.

Here is another example from Carol Shields's *The Stone Diaries*. What does their interaction show about the relationship between these two characters?

"Have you tried," she says at last, "not being gay?"

"What?" He shakes a dangling lock of hair out of his eyes.

"You know. Finding yourself a girlfriend and seeing if—well, you might surprise yourself, you may find that you really like having a girlfriend—what I mean is, it's possible you might change your attitude."

"Being gay, Mrs. Flett, is not a question of attitude."

The dialogue between these characters reveals the tension between them and a complete lack of mutual understanding, combined with a determination to be polite.

In this final example from *Up in Honey's Room* by Elmore Leonard, one of the modern masters of dialogue, a very different kind of relationship is conveyed. As you read it, try to guess what the relationship is between these two women.

She said to Muriel, "I honestly thought I could turn him around, but the man still acts like a Nazi. I couldn't budge him."

"You walked out," Muriel said, "just like that?"

"I valked out," Honey said. "I'm free as a bird. You know what else? I won't have to do my roots every two weeks. Dumb me, I spent a whole year wanting him to think I'm a natural blonde."

"He couldn't tell other ways that you aren't?"

If you guessed these are friends or sisters, you're right—they're sisters in law. There's a familiarity between them, a raw honesty and humor that comes from intimate friendship. This bit of dialogue is particularly effective because the author doesn't explain and belabor the joke. The bada-bing is on the page, but Leonard allows the bada-boom to go off in the reader's head.

Adding Meaning with Internal Dialogue

As your viewpoint character talks and listens to others talking, you have the opportunity to weave in dialogue that shows the character's thoughts. Inner dialogue, used in this way, can add a new dimension to dialogue.

Here is an example from Chimamanda Ngozi Adichie's *Purple Hibiscus*.

I meant to say I am sorry Papa broke your figurines, but the words that came out were, "I am sorry your figurines broke, Mama."

With the combination of internal and spoken dialogue, the author is able to show both what the character *wants* to say and what she actually says.

Here is another example, this one from Margot Livesey's *Eva Moves the Furniture*. Notice how the dialogue can work with the internal dialogue to tell a more complete story.

In the waiting room, Matthew dropped the newspaper and stood to meet me. "Eva." He put his hands on my shoulders. "Are you all right?"

Through my dress I felt his touch, warm and sure and for a moment I wanted to throw myself into his arms. I had to swallow before I could repeat Sir Hamilton's verdict.

"Splendid," he said. And suddenly, seeing his face break into a smile, I understood that my uncertain health had not entirely passed him by. He bent to kiss me.

Pitfalls of Writing Dialogue

Dialogue is a powerful tool. You can use it to convey information, to show relationships between characters, to show emotion, and to move the story along. Characters use it to say what they think, to persuade others, as well as to hide the truth.

But there are pitfalls to avoid when writing dialogue.

Empty Chitchat

Take this interchange between two characters:

"Hi, Gina. Nice day today," Bill said when he ran into her in the parking lot.

Gina said, "And I thought the rain would never stop."

"Are you going to visit your Mom?"

"She's expecting me."

The author might have written this thinking: *I need to tell the reader that Gina is going to visit her mother. I know, that's boring information. Maybe it will be more interesting if I put it in dialogue.* But the result is flat, empty dialogue that conveys a bit of information that would be better simply summarized.

See what a difference it makes when the dialogue, conveying the same information, also shows a character who is off balance?

"Hi, Gina. Nice day today," Bill said when he ran into her in the parking lot.

"Is it? I hadn't noticed."

"So it's that bad is it? Your mom?"

"I'm on the way to see her right now."

If you find yourself writing empty chitchat:

- Try deleting it completely
- Try deleting it and inserting a one-sentence summary (In this case: When Gina saw Bill in the parking lot, she told him she was on the way to see her mother.)
- Try rewriting the dialogue with conflict or emotion

If dialogue doesn't move your story forward or show the reader something about your character and her relationships with others, get rid of it. It's pretty well guaranteed that readers will simply skip over a dense paragraph of dialogue that does nothing more than deliver information.

Adverbs with Attribution

Often writers want to make sure the reader gets the emotion they want the dialogue to convey, and so they gild the lily by adding an adverb to the attribution. Here are two examples.

"Mr. Ohrbach? Who the hell invited you?" Bob said *angrily*.

"Why, Mr. Ohrbach. So you decided to grace us with your presence," Mrs. Murch said *haughtily*.

The additional adverbs—angrily and haughtily—are unnecessary and redundant. The adverbs *tell* the reader what the dialogue has already *shown* to the reader. Though the average reader may not object to the use of adverbs with attribution, editors and agents will notice the clunky writing.

Occasionally, very occasionally, an adverb works well with attribution. But inspect every one you use to make sure it's really adding to your story-telling rather than just repeating something you've already shown.

Going On Too Long

Dialogue is best when it's kept relatively short. If you look at a page of your manuscript and there's a half-page chunk of a single character talking, you probably have a problem. Here are some ways to address the problem:

- Break up the dialogue with action
- Break up the dialogue with snippets of setting
- Instead of a soliloquy, have two characters talk back and forth, and add conflict to make it more interesting.
- Summarize parts of the dialogue

Very occasionally you will have a scene where it makes sense for a character to speak, uninterrupted, for a long time. But unless it's dramatically riveting, you won't want to put the entire speech into the novel. Skip over parts and summarize others or you will probably lose your readers.

Who's Talking?

Have you ever been reading along—one character says something, then another replies, then another, and somewhere along the way the writer stops telling you who's talking and you lose track and have to backtrack to figure out who said what? Here are some ways to make it clear to the reader who is talking.

▼ **MAKING IT CLEAR WHO IS TALKING**

How . . .	For example . . .
With attribution	"Go away," Linda said.
By putting the other character's name in the dialogue	"Go away, Mamie."
By adding some physical description and putting it on the same line as the dialogue	Linda bit her cuticle. "Go away."

So, whenever it might be confusing to your reader, be sure you have provided some kind of cue about who is talking, either in attribution, in accompanying action, or in the dialogue itself.

Dialogue Clichés

Like stereotypical characters, some words and phrases keep coming back and have become stale from so much use. Someone should have put them out of their misery a long time ago. But they've become so familiar that many times writers don't realize what they're saying—or worse, what their characters are saying.

Avoid clichés like the following:

- "It was blacker than pitch outside."
- "Her eyes were bluer than the sky."
- "When in Rome . . ."
- "When life gives you lemons . . ."
- "She was happy as a clam."
- "He was cool as a cucumber."

These are only a few of the many clichés that you don't want to use. It may be argued that it is okay to use clichés in dialogue because people speak that way. Readers may understand clichés and relate to them. Writers frequently use them to express comedic characters in novels. But by avoiding clichés, your work will seem less tired and your dialogue will be more unique.

Too Much Dialect

In *The Elements of Style*, Strunk and White put it this way: "Do not attempt to use dialect unless you are a devoted student of the tongue you hope to reproduce." Writing dialogue in dialect can be a useful way to show the reader your character's background. It can be quaint or romantic. It can tell the reader a great deal about the character without any narrative to describe him. Used cautiously and sparingly, it can enhance your novel.

But when it becomes overdone, dialect is tedious and boring. There's no reason to reiterate a character's dialect in every piece of dialogue. If the character is from the South, he doesn't need to end every *ing* word by cutting off the *g*. If you write it that way a few times, the reader gets the picture.

ALERT

Four-letter words pepper the dialogue that comes out of real people's mouths; even suburban housewives can get truly pissed and utter the f-word. If you do put profanity in your dialogue or internal dialogue, write it realistically.

The same thing can be said for using the Irish brogue. Once or twice is fine, even in historical novels. Continuing to use it every time the character speaks would be like repeating the character's description in each paragraph. It's unnecessary and can distract the reader from the story you are trying to tell.

CHAPTER 12

Writing Setting

Perhaps you've heard it said that setting can be like another character—that's one of the clichés of novel writing. But ideas become clichés because they are true. The same kinds of techniques that bring characters alive on the page can bring your setting to the page more vividly, too. Following are writing techniques for making sure your setting gets transmitted in all its glory from your mind, to the printed page, to your reader's mind.

Settings and Their Uses

The most basic use of setting in a novel is to answer the question: Where are we now? The settings of your novel anchor the characters (and your readers) in time and space. Establish the setting and then your readers will be able to relax as you move the characters through it.

In addition, a setting can be used to advance the plot, create tension, set a mood, or show another aspect of a character.

Every setting has, potentially at least, a nearly infinite number of details that could be conveyed to the reader. When you introduce and develop a setting, you must pick and choose what to show the reader. You want to create a sense of place but not overwhelm with details.

Omniscient Scene Setting

One way to establish setting is to take an authorial (or omniscient) viewpoint and pull the camera way back to show the setting to the reader. Here is an example from *The Amazing Adventures of Kavalier & Clay*, Michael Chabon's rich historical novel set in the early part of the 20th century in New York City.

> The offices of the Empire Novelty Company, Inc., were on the fourth floor of the Kramler Building, in a hard-luck stretch of Twenty-fifth Street near Madison Square. A fourteen-story office block faced with stone the color of a stained shirt collar, its windows bearded with soot, ornamented with a smattering of modern zigzags, the Kramler stood out as a lone gesture of commercial hopefulness . . . .

This is in New York in the 1930s, and what is so notable about this description is the freshness of its metaphors—for instance, the color of the building's stone is like a stained shirt collar, the soot around the windows resembles a beard. The reader instantly gets what the author is talking about even though most of us have never before contemplated these comparisons.

Scene Setting with a Character

Another way of setting a scene is to show it through the eyes of a viewpoint character. In this example from *Breakfast at Tiffany's*, Truman Capote shows us the interior of Holly Golightly's bedroom as seen through the eyes of her neighbor, the first person narrator

> The room in which we stood (we were standing because there was nothing to sit on) seemed as though it were just being moved into; you expected to smell wet paint. Suitcases and packing crates were the only furniture. The crates served as tables. One supported the mixings of a martini; another a lamp, a Libertyphone, Holly's red cat and a bowl of yellow roses. Bookcases, covering one wall, boasted a half-shelf of literature. I warmed to the room at once. I liked its fly-by-night look.

Notice the details Capote uses to establish the apartment—namely its emptiness. No furniture. A bookcase with just a half-shelf of books. But there are liquor, a cat, and a burst of yellow roses. All of these details reflect the quirkiness of the apartment's inhabitant, Holly Golightly, but they also tell us something about the narrator, who says he likes the place's "fly-by-night look."

Here is a second example, a scene opening that establishes a character in a setting from *How the Garcia Girls Lost Their Accents* by Julia Alvarez.

> A small village spreads out before her—ALTAMIRA, says the rippling letters on the corrugated tin roof of the first house. A little cluster of houses on either side of the road, Altamira is just the place to stretch her legs before what she has heard is a steep and slightly (her aunts warned "very") dangerous descent to the coast. Yolanda pulls up at a cantina, its thatched roof held up by several posts, its floor poured cement, and in its very center, a lone picnic table over which a swarm of flies hover.

> Tacked to one of the central posts is a yellowing poster for Palmolive soap. A creamy, blond woman luxuriates under a refreshing shower, her head thrown back in seeming ecstasy, her mouth opened in a wordless cry.

Alvarez orients the reader, introducing Altamira by first taking in the little town from a distance. Then she comes closer to a cantina, and closer still to take in a few telling details like those hovering flies over the picnic table and the poster of a glamorous, very pale-skinned woman. The woman contrasts to what the reader knows about this narrator, Yolanda, a brown-skinned Latina.

Whenever you first introduce a place to the reader, this kind of an approach—taking it in first from afar and then moving closer—is a good strategy. It helps to try to fully imagine that setting first in your head, then imagine yourself moving through it as your character would.

As your story moves forward and settings are reprised, remind the reader ever so briefly about what you established and then layer in additional details for the new scene.

Establish Details That Will Be Important Later

Be sure to establish, early on, any aspect of a setting that is going to become an important aspect of your story later. Suppose, for instance, that your character is going to rush out the bulkhead door of her home's basement to escape robbers in the final act of your novel. Long before that page, you should have established that the house has a basement bulkhead door, and have explained all the intricacies of how it opens and whether it locks.

Or suppose your character is going to throw a precious, irreplaceable crystal vase at her husband. Long before that vase takes flight, you should have established just exactly how gorgeous, precious, meaningful, and irreplaceable it is.

Or suppose your character is going to be chased along the edge of a steep precipice in the dark of night. Establish the danger earlier, perhaps by writing a scene where she walks her dog along that path and gazes down in horror at the sharp rocks and crashing waves below.

Establish, establish, establish, because the last thing you want to do is to have to slow down in an action scene and explain some aspect of the setting that plays a critical role in your plot.

Sometimes you won't know which aspects of setting will be important later. This is why writing setting is often a back-and-forth process. You will realize that you need to go back and establish details of setting in descriptions that you've already written.

Aspects of Setting

There are many aspects of a setting that you can describe. You don't want to overwhelm the reader with details, so you should pick and choose—telling details, just as with character descriptions.

Here are some of the aspects of setting available to you:

- **Lighting:** Is the light natural or artificial; is it well lit or shadowy or dark; do things stand out in sharp relief or do their edges soften and melt into one another.
- **Time of day:** Is it morning, noon or night; is the sun high or low in the sky; is the time of day reflected in the way people (or animals) are moving about?
- **Weather:** Is it sunny or snowy; hot, cool and crisp, or sultry with a thunderstorm on the horizon; is the blue sky nearly purple or slate gray?
- **Surroundings:** Is this place in a suburban neighborhood, the center of a small town, or the middle of a bustling city; are buildings squat or towering; is it densely or sparsely developed; on the deck of a ship, or in the bowels of a submarine?
- **What's nearby:** Are there fancy restaurants, a run-down bowling alley, or an empty parking lot; is there a welcoming library, a well-kept park, or the ruins of a stable?
- **Geography:** Are there mountains or water in the distance; is it a grassy valley, a verdant rain forest, or a desert?
- **Furniture:** If it's an interior, is it unfurnished and dusty, or crowded with overstuffed pieces, or sparsely furnished with aseptic chrome and glass?
- **Other people:** Is there a boisterous crowd, a silent throng, or is there just the occasional statue-like pedestrian; are there family groups or clutches of teenagers or clots of old men; are the people dressed to the nines or in tatters, in heavy coats and boots or shorts and sandals?

Just as it's a good idea to know your protagonist's backstory even if you're not going to tell it to the reader, it's a good idea to have a complete idea of each setting even though you'll only reveal the most compelling aspects, those aspects that work with your story and your characters.

Putting Setting to Work

So, no matter the setting, you have a huge number of details that you could describe in it. How do you choose? The answer is simple: Pick the aspects of setting that work with your story.

Setting can be used to advance the plot, to give the reader insight into a character, and to show time passing.

Use Setting to Advance the Plot

Suppose you are opening a book with a scene that's going to end with a tornado that destroys your protagonist's family home. You might open with your character walking through a meadow, the spring green of the trees so bright it hurts his eyes, a light breeze blowing, and then a flash of lightning on the horizon and a rumble of thunder, so far away he barely notices it.

As he returns home, establish the proportions of the house, what it's made of, the comforting odors of the place as he comes through the front door, the heirloom furniture he grew up with. Then when the tornado rips the house apart, the reader can at least begin to appreciate the protagonist's loss.

Use Setting to Show Character

Setting can also be used as a foil for your character. Here's an example from Thomas Harris's *Red Dragon* that illustrates how setting can illuminate a character, and in this instance create tension as well.

The dark came down over him as he climbed the stairs. He couldn't turn on the lights because Grandmother had cut the cords off short so only she could reach them. He did not want to get back in the wet bed. He stood in the dark holding on to the footboard for a long time. He thought she wasn't coming. The blackest corners in the room knew she wasn't coming.

The reader knows this character is a little boy (he has a grandmother, he can't reach the light cords, he's wet his bed) and he's climbing stairs in the dark, then is in a bedroom (holding on to the footboard). The main feature of this setting is darkness, the main feeling fear and foreboding.

Use Setting to Show Time Passing

Setting can also be used to show time passing. For example, suppose a character drives to work, or sits on a park bench hoping his girlfriend will walk by, or waits for a train that's late. And suppose you want to show that this driving, or sitting, or waiting takes a long time. To simply say, "It took a long time," is weak and unconvincing. But to write sentence after sentence about how he waited, and then waited some more, is as boring as the wait itself would be.

Using setting, you can finesse this problem. Here is an example from *The High Window*, a short story by Raymond Chandler.

They said my package could be sent right over. I said I would wait for it.

It was getting dark outside now. The rushing sound of the traffic had died a little and the air from the open window, not yet cool from the night, had that tired end-of-the-day smell of dust, automobile exhaust, sun-light rising from hot walls and sidewalks, the remote smell of food in a thousand restaurants, and perhaps, drifting down from the residential hills above Hollywood—if you had a nose like a hunting dog—a touch of that peculiar tomcat smell that eucalyptus trees give off in warm weather.

I sat there smoking. Ten minutes later the door was knocked on. . . .

Notice how Chandler uses a paragraph of pure atmospherics to slow down the story sufficiently to make the reader believe that ten minutes has passed between the time that Marlowe calls for package delivery and when the package arrives. Chandler makes it feel as if time really is passing without boring his readers to tears.

Use All the Senses to Write Setting

All of your senses should be called upon when you write setting. Often the first impression the author gives the reader is what a place looks like—what the narrator sees. But don't forget to include all the senses: sounds, smells, tastes, and the textures of a setting add more dimensions to the description.

QUOTE

"Fiction begins where human knowledge begins—with the senses."—Flannery O'Connor

In writing a setting, here are just a few of the ways you might use sense perceptions to create a sense of place:

- **Sound:** traffic, birds, wind, dripping water, footsteps, airplanes, buzzing lights, ticking clock, whir and clank of machinery, music, wind chimes, clicking keyboard, stillness . . .
- **Smell:** cut grass, perfume, detergent, burning wood, mildew, urine, dust, laundry detergent, food cooking, sour milk, garbage, wet wool, incense . . .
- **Taste:** salty, sweet, bitter, malty, savory, spicy, rancid, sour, nutty, astringent, fatty, oily . . .
- **Texture/feel:** metallic, rubbery, velvety, smooth, sharp, corrugated, scaly, slick, silky, grainy, gummy, powdery, squishy, hot, cool, icy . . .

Most of the time, each glimpse of setting that you give your readers is filtered through the perceptions of a single viewpoint character. That character's senses and emotions, past experiences and preconceptions affect what the reader sees.

As you read this example from Louise Ure's *The Fault Tree*, see if you can guess something special about this character from the way she describes her setting.

A lawn sprinkler ratcheted around several yards to my left—probably a last-ditch effort to save that little patch of dry grass in front of the insurance office—and a horn honked down by the Guardian Motel on the corner. Although the air was cooing, Apache cicadas still thrummed in concert from the cottonwood tree down the block. Farther away I heard the dentist's drill whine of a Japanese motorcycle revving through the intersection at Ft. Lowell.

Did you notice that nearly this entire setting is described through sounds? This provides the reader the first clue that this character, who is narrating the setting, is blind.

Though this is an extreme example, it shows how the narrator's viewpoint potentially defines how the reader experiences the setting. So, what might look to the average observer like a miserable, dirty hovel might look to the reader like a cozy, safe haven because the narrator of the scene experiences it that way.

Here's another example of a brief bit of setting from Nancy Pickard's *The Scent of Rain and Lightning*. Notice how Pickard uses the sense of smell, and what she manages to convey without actually coming out and saying it.

A hot, pollen-scented breeze blew through the open windows. She smelled honeysuckle, which wasn't blooming yet, and lilac, which had already bloomed and gone. These things were impossible, they were all in her imagination, she knew, and they were just the sort of deceptions that the smallest feeling of contentment might spring on her.

Pickard uses the hot breeze, and the phantom scent of flowers that aren't really blooming to surround a post-coital moment for a character who distrusts any good luck or happy experience she has.

Don't just write setting. Every description of setting you deliver can do double duty serving to move your story forward, in some cases, or to reveal your characters, in others.

Writing Weather

In every scene of your novel, you should know what the weather is. Whether you choose to tell the reader will depend on whether you can use it to make your storytelling stronger. If your character has just received upsetting news, then a setting with storm clouds and wind can echo her distress. If your character is having a carefree walk in the park, a biting wind which she ignores can foreshadow an impending disaster.

In this example from Hallie Ephron's *Never Tell a Lie*, Ivy Rose is a young pregnant woman whose husband has just been taken in for police questioning. In this excerpt, the weather makes her dark mood even darker.

> Blinded by tears, Ivy stumbled to her car. *Son of a bitch.* Her heels thudded on the concrete walk. Dense afternoon cloud cover made it feel like dusk, and there was a biting chill in the air.

Weather Causes Things to Happen

Weather can be much more than a foil for the actions and emotions of your character; it can drive the story by actually causing things to happen. A storm washes up a dead body. A hurricane prevents a wedding from taking place. An unremitting drought bankrupts a family farm. Fog causes a car accident. A storm on the sun causes a rocket's navigation system to malfunction, destroying power grids and melting transformers.

Weather is a great plot device, used sparingly. Use it once or twice and the reader will buy it; more than that and it starts to feel contrived.

Weather Creates a Mood

Authors use weather to create a pervasive mood. It can be as simple as storm clouds and a biting chill to create a gloomy mood, or breezy sunshine to create an upbeat cheery mood. Be careful to pick the weather so it works with the mood you are trying to create.

Sometimes an author uses weather as metaphor for the character's mood, as in the opening lines from diary entries in Chuck Palahniuk's idiosyncratic novel, *Diary* (its conceit is that this is from a diary written by a man in a coma).

Just for the record, the weather today is calm and sunny, but the air is full of bullshit.
***

Just for the record, the weather today is partly soused with occasional bursts of despair and irritation.
***

Just for the record, the weather today is calm. Calm and resigned and defeated.

Pitfalls of Setting

Here are some pitfalls to avoid when writing setting:

- **Omniscient observer tells all:** In small doses, it works to have an omniscient observer describe the setting, but it will soon start to sound like a travel brochure or a history book if it goes on for too long.
- **Over-describing:** Pick just a few telling details to describe, enough to give the reader a sense of a unique place and enough to establish the important elements of that place; avoid paragraph after paragraph of description that doesn't (yet) connect to your story or characters.
- **Under-describing:** When a setting isn't sufficiently established, it feels to the reader as if the characters are floating in space; instead of paying attention to the drama you are so brilliantly weaving, they're distracted, busy asking themselves, "Where the heck are we?"
- **Inconsistencies:** You may not remember whether the chair in your character's living room was green or yellow, or whether it was a rocker or an easy chair, but you can be guaranteed that more than a few of your readers will; keep track of the details of all the settings you write so when you set another scene there, your reader won't get distracted from the actions by inconsistencies of place.

Avoid writing setting for setting's sake. Put your setting to work moving your story forward or giving the reader insight into character.

CHAPTER 13

Writing Action

Action in a novel can be as calm as a character taking a leisurely stroll through the park, or as fast-paced as a character riding a motorcycle speeding through the streets in hot pursuit of a villain. How you write action depends on the feeling you're trying to create in the reader. This chapter discusses a variety of techniques for writing action sequences, and avoiding the associated pitfalls.

Simple Action: To'ing and Fro'ing

The most basic form of action is when your character must get from one place to another. For instance, suppose your plot requires your character to drive from work to home, take the elevator up to her apartment, pour herself a drink in the kitchen, and then get into bed. You could simply write those movements as quickly and economically as possible, skipping over some parts of the trip. For example:

> Verna drove home and parked her car in the parking garage. An hour later she was lying in bed, sipping a glass of chilled Pinot Grigio and watching *Project Runway*.

This approach is straightforward, no muss no fuss, moving the character quickly and painlessly. First she's here, then she's there. No big deal. Even though it's uninteresting, it gets the job done without being so long that it bores the reader.

Another approach is to make the trip interesting. Here are some ways:

- There's an obstacle (her car won't start, or she gets a flat tire on the way home, or she gets stuck in the elevator).
- There's a ticking clock (her headlights don't work so she has to get home before sundown, or she wants to get there in time to run into her cute single neighbor).
- There's a reason she dreads getting there (her difficult mother is at home waiting for her, or her creepy neighbor might be lurking in the garage waiting for her again, or being home reminds her of her husband who recently died).
- There's a problem she needs to puzzle out on the way home (such as how is she going to tell her husband she's leaving him, or what to make of something troubling that happened at work).

Any one or several of these options will turn a mundane trip home into a much more interesting journey.

Moving Slow, Moving Fast

A character may move slowly for a host of reasons. He's tired. He's injured. He's scared. He's being cautious. He's terrified. He's relaxed. How you describe the movement should reflect the character's physical condition and state of mind. Does he stagger? Drag himself? Limp? Inch forward? Sleepwalk? Stroll? Choose the action that conveys both the kind of movement and his emotional state.

Likewise, a character moving quickly could be terrified, angry, determined, joyful, or thrill-seeking. He may be hurrying to get somewhere or running away. Depending on why he's in such a rush, he may spring, bolt, dash, hustle, scurry, surge ahead, or jog.

Read this excerpt from *The Kite Runner* and notice the verbs that novelist Khaled Hosseini uses to show his characters in motion.

> I reached the corner and saw Hassan bolting along, his head down, not even looking at the sky, sweat soaking through the back of his shirt. I tripped over a rock and fell—I wasn't just slower than Hassan but clumsier too; I'd always envied his natural athleticism. When I staggered to my feet I caught a glimpse of Hassan disappearing around another street corner. I hobbled after him, spikes of pain battering my scraped knees.

Here are some of the verbs Hosseini uses: bolt, trip, fall, stagger, hobble. These are words that describe very specific kinds of movement. There's no need to slap on adverbs like swiftly or painstakingly. A strong, well-chosen verb is all you need to give the reader a clear idea of what kind of movement is taking place.

ESSENTIAL

Pick the verb that shows the reader how your characters are moving. Insert internal dialogue into action when you want to break the momentum. Avoid adverbs if you possibly can.

Note how Hosseini breaks the action with the following: ". . . I wasn't just slower than Hassan but clumsier too; I'd always envied his natural athleticism." Internal dialogue inserted in the middle of action breaks the flow. Use a break like this deliberately to give both your character and your readers a breather.

Lee Child is a master at writing action sequences. Read this excerpt from *The Enemy*. As you read, think about how the structure of the sentences contributes to the fast pace.

I stood up and raced the last ten feet and hauled Marshall around to the passenger side and opened the door and crammed him into the front. Then I climbed right in over him and dumped myself into the driver's seat. Hit that big red button and fired it up. Shoved it into gear and stamped on the gas so hard the acceleration slammed the door shut.

Writing like this is as spare and powerful as the action it conveys. Of course Child uses powerful verbs (raced, hauled, crammed, dumped). But he also uses a sentence structure to convey momentum:

- And, and, and: a series of short action phrases connected together by ands (. . . stood up and raced . . . and hauled . . . and opened . . .)
- Sentence fragments leading with the verb (Shoved it . . . Hit that . . .)

Choose your verbs carefully to convey exactly the kind of action you are trying to evoke in the mind of the reader. Then structure your sentences to reinforce the kind of momentum you're aiming for.

Writing Physical Fights

Among the most challenging action sequences to write well are physical fights. It's difficult to give a clear sense of what's happening without killing the excitement with a lot of clinical detail.

Here's an example of how bad it can get.

Ryzor came at Jack from the office door, fifteen feet away, closing the space in three seconds. He raised his right hand and started to bring it down, like a karate-chop, on Jack's shoulder. Jack dodged a foot to the right and caught Ryzor behind the left ankle. There was a glass coffee table adjacent to the desk and Ryzor fell into it, shattering it.

Ouch. The writer got so bogged down trying to describe the setting and action as clearly as possible that any excitement and momentum that the fight might have conveyed got buried in a jumble of words. Do we really need to know details like "fifteen feet," "three seconds," "right hand," "left ankle"? The middle of an action sequence is the wrong place to explain where the glass table is located.

ALERT

Details derail action. Anything the reader needs to know should be established earlier.

This scene from Thomas Harris's *Red Dragon* shows how to write action, in this case a fight among three characters.

He heard a low whirring sound carried on the wind and, wary of a rattler, he scanned the ground as he went into the scrub cedar.

He saw boots beneath the brush, the glint of a lens and a flash of khaki rising.

He looked into the yellow eyes of Francis Dolarhyde and fear raised the hammers of his heart.

Snick of a pistol action working an automatic coming up and Graham kicked at it, struck it as the muzzle bloomed pale yellow in the sun, and the pistol flew into the brush Graham on his back, something burning in the left side of his chest, slid headfirst down the dune onto the beach.

Dolarhyde leaped high to land on Graham's stomach with both feet and he had the knife out now and never looked up at the thin screaming from the water's edge. He pinned Graham with his knees, raised the knife high, and grunted as he brought it down. The blade missed Graham's eye and crunched deep into his cheek.

Dolarhyde rocked forward and put his weight on the handle of the knife to shove it through Graham's head.

The rod whistled as Molly swung it hard at Dolarhyde's face. The big Rapala's hooks sank solidly into his cheek and the reel screamed, paying out the line as she drew back to strike again.

Simple sentences, strong verbs, sounds, sensations—they all work to convey a fight raging. Below are some tips for writing physical fights that you can adapt from this excerpt.

- **Establish the setting in advance:** Harris shows us the cedars, the brush before Graham sees Dolarhyde waiting for him.
- **Establish the relationships among the characters in advance:** Before this scene, Harris has introduced the reader to all three of these characters and we know that Dolarhyde is a dangerous serial killer, Graham is an FBI profiler drawn from retirement to help capture Dolarhyde, and Molly is Graham's wife.
- **Harness the senses:** This passage is filled with vivid sensory detail; the reader hears the "snick" of the gun, sees "pale yellow" bloom of the gun being fired, feels Graham's heart hammering and the "burning" in his side—these sensory details put the reader right there.
- **Show action and reaction:** Action and reaction make the fight feel authentic, as when Graham kicks and then the pistol flies, or when Dolarhyde plunges in the knife and then grunts from the exertion.

A good way to prepare for writing a fight sequence like the one in *Red Dragon* is to block out the actions and reactions.

Blocking Out a Fight Before Writing

Blocking out a fight sequence before you write it enables you to write it clearly, and to anticipate opportunities to harness the senses. To block a fight scene, create a column for each of the characters. Then write out what each of them does, and in what sequence. The fight scene between Dolarhyde and Graham and Molly might have been blocked out in advance as follows:

▼ **BLOCKING OUT A FIGHT SEQUENCE**

Graham	Dolarhyde	Molly
1. Kicks the pistol	2. Pistol goes off and flies from his hand	
3. Falls, slides down the dune	4. Leaps onto Graham	5. Screams
6. Is pinned by Dolarhyde	7. Stabs Graham	8. Swings rod and hooks Dolarhyde

Once you've blocked out action like this, you will find it easier to write the sequence. Try to keep the writing spare. If you find that there are aspects of the setting or characters that should have been established, then go back and establish them in an earlier scene.

Harnessing the Senses

Because it is so important, here is one more example showing how the sensory experiences of a viewpoint character can be harnessed to make an action sequence even more visceral. This is from Ernest Hemingway's *Old Man and the Sea*. To fully appreciate the strength in this passage, read it aloud.

The shark closed fast astern and when he hit the fish the old man saw his mouth open and his strange eyes and the clicking chop of the teeth as he drove forward in the meat just above the tail. The shark's head was out of the water and his back was coming out and the old man could hear the noise of skin and flesh ripping on the big fish when he rammed the harpoon down onto the shark's head at a spot where the line between his eyes intersected with the line that ran straight back from his nose. There were no such lines. There was only the heavy sharp blue head and the big eyes and the clicking, thrusting all-swallowing jaws. But that was the location of the brain and the old man hit it. He hit it with his blood-mushed hands driving a good harpoon with all his strength. He hit it without hope but with resolution and complete malignancy.

Take a minute and reread the passage, noting the powerful verbs (hit, rammed, ripping, thrusting). Note the sensory images: the "clicking chop of the teeth," the sound of "flesh ripping." The reader feels the rage mixed with cold logic with which the old man attacks the shark.

Writing Sex

Writing a sex scene is hard for many writers. Sex seems so private, and there you go putting it on the printed page. With some genres like romance, readers expect there to be sex scenes. With other genres like mystery, readers are not expecting explicit sex. But regardless of genre, if you have two characters flirting, hot and heavy for a hundred pages and finally they do it, readers will want to know what it was like. You probably can't get away with skipping over it completely. Having said that, readers don't need a load of graphic description, either.

QUOTE

Unless you're writing pornography, the graphic description of body parts inserted into body parts is not the best way to go.—Marge Piercy

Many stories can't be told without sex, and sex is a particularly powerful lens through which to show the relationship between characters. Imagine how different the love making will be if the two characters are deeply in love or if they detest each other; or if the relationship is nothing more than a fling for him but the fulfillment of a dream for her; or if the act is consensual versus coerced?

The action between the couple can be written with a light touch, as in this example from Nancy Pickard's *Virgin of Small Plains*.

Mitch slid one hand up under Abby's sweater over her ribs under her loosened bra, then onto her left breast, and she moaned softly.

"What?" her mother called from the other side of the door.

Abby closed her eyes in bliss then opened them, and forced herself to say, "Mom?"

Mitch lifted her sweater, exposing her bare breast, and brought his mouth down onto it

"What honey?"

Abby felt as if her entire body was a single nerve cell vibrating from her left nipple.

"Is Dad here?"

Mitch's other hand began a slow descent under the waistband of her blue jeans, sliding lower, lower stopping when it reached its destination. Unable to bear the torture Abby put her hands on each of his and pressed, making him stop right where he was.

He grinned and waited.

These lovers are comfortable with each other, and the excerpt is really about desire and lust more than it is about raw sex. Putting Abby's mother outside the door adds tension.

QUOTE

"When I started my career writing romance, the expectation was that the books would contain some pretty explicit sex scenes. Initially I was incredibly embarrassed. But as time went on, I realized my readers enjoyed the action, and my husband took credit for all the research, and shopping with the money earned writing sex scenes went a long way toward making me feel comfy."—Janet Evanovich

Tips for Writing Sex

Here are some tips for writing sex:

- **Establish the relationship of characters in advance:** Are they lovers, friends, adversaries, strangers?
- **Reveal more about your couple by the way they make love:** Is he brutal and selfish or gentle and caring; is she engaged or distracted; is she comfortable or acutely self-conscious; is he in the moment or living out a fantasy in his head?
- **Harness the senses:** Is this a perfumed-sheets-and-rose-petals moment or smelly underwear and musk; is the main event surrounded by dead silence or is there a rock band pulsing; is she whispering "I love you" or cursing and screaming?
- **Don't skip over it:** Treat yourself to a glass of wine, relax and try to find a way to write it if it's essential to your story; try to get into your character's head (and body).
- **Drop the curtain:** Trust the reader to fill in some of the details. Remember, sex in fiction isn't interesting for the mechanics of the act, it's interesting for what it reveals about characters and how it moves your story forward.
- **Go easy on simile and metaphor:** You might find it easier to write about a train roaring into a tunnel than sexual intercourse, but your readers will wince.
- **Overwrite and then cut back:** You may be afraid of being too explicit and so you end up inhibited about writing anything at all; so why not get all the juicy details out on the page, let that bodice rip, and then come back to it a few days later when the heat has cooled, and edit it back.

Pitfalls in Writing Action

Action puts your characters in motion. Action sequences can be powerful, sweeping the reader along in a powerful current, or slowing things down and giving the character and the reader a chance to reflect.

But there are pitfalls:

- **Writing the slow parts too slowly:** When your characters are moving slowly, don't linger too long; you don't want to make your novel feel like an extended fugue.

- **Writing the fast parts too fast:** Fast action is interesting; although an attack or a chase would be over in ten or twenty seconds in the real world, slow it down enough when you write it that the reader isn't bewildered and confused.

- **Clinical detail:** If you find yourself talking about a character who is "eighty feet away" or who "raises her right hand" or who takes "a quarter-turn to the left," you are giving the reader an unnecessary level of detail; you want to be clear but this is fiction, not a user's manual.

- **Blah verbs:** Action is best propelled by carefully chosen verbs; avoid empty verbs like was, got, had, looked, made, moved, put, saw, took, and went; but don't fall in love with your Thesaurus and forsake a perfectly good verb like walk for ambulate.

- **Gratuitous violence:** Violence is powerful stuff, and if readers feel it's excessive, voyeuristic, or overly graphic, it will turn them off; too much violence and your reader will start to feel immune to its power.

- **Gratuitous sex:** Too much sex in your novel can get repetitive and anesthetize the reader; make sure every sex scene is unique, and be sure that the sex you write needs to be in the novel to move your story forward.

- **By the way . . . setting:** Establish the parameters of your setting before you launch an action scene; having to take a break in the middle to explain what's where will take the wind out of your sails.

Finally, be sure that your novel isn't one action scene after another after another. Modulate the pace to keep the reader engaged.

CHAPTER 14

Writing Suspense

Alfred Hitchcock was asked to define suspense. He told the interviewer to imagine two people sitting at a table at a cafe. Under the table is a bag. In the bag is a bomb. The characters don't know that the bomb is there but the viewers do. That, he said, is suspense. Here you'll learn several techniques for creating suspense in a novel.

Defining Suspense

Suspense is that itchy twitchy feeling you give a reader when they know something is going to happen. An open question hangs there: What's going to happen next? Here are some examples of situations that create suspense:

- A pistol is cocked—will it go off?
- An innocent girl climbing the shadowy stairs of an abandoned house—will the slasher jump out and grab her?
- A car breaks down on a deserted road in the middle of nowhere and another car pulls up alongside with its headlights turned off—is this a good Samaritan or a killer?
- A teenager gives herself a pregnancy test—what color will the stick turn?
- A man tells a woman he has an important question to ask her after dinner—will he ask her to marry him?
- A woman has been told by her husband, "Never open that closet door"—what will she find in that closet when she does?

The Arc of Suspense

Suspense, just like an overall plot or a scene, has an arc. You can build it gradually, teasing the reader with possibilities. The climax and resolution should feel worth the anguish of getting there.

▼ THE SUSPENSE ARC: STAGES AND EXAMPLE

Stage	Example
Establishing and foreshadowing	Dahlia learns that her husband's previous wives have all disappeared; her husband tells her that there's a room she must never go into.
Suspense begins	Dahlia's husband announces he is going away for a few days; as his departure nears, whenever she passes the door to that room she finds herself staring at it and imagining what is inside.
Tension escalates, loosens	Dahlia's husband departs; Dahlia searches for and finds the key; she's about to open the door when he returns for something he's forgotten. He leaves again.

Stage	Example
Turning point	Dahlia returns to the door and stands staring at it: Will she or won't she? She remembers her promise to her husband not to go inside; she remembers his stories about how his last wife, her sister, disappeared.
Payoff	She inserts the key. Pulls the door open, he's inside the room, waiting for her.

Finding him waiting for her dissipates the suspense, though it might begin to build again as the reader (and the character) tries to figure out what the husband is going to do, and how poor Dahlia is going to get away in one piece.

Techniques for Building Suspense

There are a range of techniques for creating suspense, and then manipulating that feeling, ratcheting it down and up, and then releasing it. The author's goal is to subtly create a feeling of unease in the reader. Suspense is about disequilibrium.

In some kinds of books—horror and thriller novels, for instance—a more heavy-handed approach to creating and sustaining suspense is expected. For others a much lighter touch is in order. There are many different ways to create suspense.

QUOTE

"The oldest and strongest emotion of mankind is fear, and the oldest and strongest kind of fear is fear of the unknown."—H. P. Lovecraft

Create a Mood of Unease

Mood is in the pit of the stomach of the beholder. In a novel, there are two beholders: the viewpoint character in a scene and the reader. If the viewpoint character feels uneasy, her thoughts and feelings should convey that unease to the reader.

For example, mood might be conveyed simply:

When Marie returned to her car, she started to turn the key and stopped. Something felt off, but she couldn't quite put her finger on what. She turned on the dome light. . . ."

Or the writing might be more explicit:

When Marie returned to where she thought she'd left her car, she was thoroughly spooked. That car that had tried to run her down had looked just like her car, right down to the dented front fender. But there her car was, parked in a shadowy corner of the parking lot right where she'd left it. She rested her hand on the hood. Did it feel warm? Maybe. A little. Or, no. Not at all. She leaned against the car and surveyed the empty parking lot around her. She was being a jerk. No one had tried to run her down. No one had stolen her car. Still, she got out her flashlight and checked out the back seat before she got in.

Remember, your viewpoint character is fallible, and you can play with that fallibility and create an "unreliable narrator." Maybe she's shown herself to be paranoid, seeing danger where there's none. Maybe she's the oblivious type, ignoring all the shadows and sounds while the reader wants to shout: Would you stop and pay attention to that thing lurking in the corner!

Harness Setting to Create Suspense

The same setting can be described so it feels bucolic and harmless or fraught with hidden danger. If you emphasize the sunlight streaming in through the windows, the smell of laundry detergent and baking cookies, and the sound of wind chimes tinkling, then a setting feels welcoming.

What if instead you create a slate gray sky, and what oozes in through the windows is frigid air and dampness, and the smells are mildew and overcooked cabbage? We get a feeling of unpleasantness and possibly impending doom.

If you're trying to create suspense, then you want to charge your setting with dark forces. You can do this by creating a slight disconnect: everything seems okay at one level, and at another everything seems increasingly fraught with peril.

When writing suspense, start slowly, subtly; give yourself somewhere to build. If you pull out all the stops at the beginning, you'll have nowhere to go; worse still, your reader will turn numb to the nuance you are trying to create.

For instance, a bookcase feels as if it's about to topple over. A dark sky looks as if it's about to explode with lightning. There's an odd smell, a layer of antiseptic over sweet, nauseating putrescence. The setting is utterly silent except for a ticking clock, or a dripping faucet, or the ever-so-faint sound of distant footsteps growing louder.

Taking it a step further, what if the sky goes black and winds howl, lightning flashes and thunder crashes, and then the lights go out? Okay, that might be a bit much. But you could write the scene full out and then dial it back to create a suspenseful mood without going quite so over-the-top.

Make the Ordinary Seem Ominous

Alfred Hitchcock was a master at endowing ordinary objects with menace. There's a famous scene in his movie *Suspicion* where Cary Grant (the husband) is bringing a glass of warm milk to Joan Fontaine (his wife). Slowly, Grant climbs the stairs and the camera focuses on the milk, and the moviegoer wonders: Is it poisoned?

The moment is full of suspense, and Hitchcock milks (ahem) the moment, slowing down time and adding some eerie music. You're not imagining it if you think that the milk itself has an eerie glow. Hitchcock rigged a light bulb in the glass of milk. As a result, this normally harmless thing, a glass or milk, feels menacing. As a writer, your job is to do the literary equivalent of putting that light bulb into that glass of milk to create a feeling of menace in ordinary objects.

J. D. Robb (Nora Roberts) does it in her novel *Salvation in Death*. It's the story of a Catholic priest killed during holy communion by poisoned wine. In one scene, the characters are in the rectory of a church—normally a place of solace and salvation. But notice how menacing the setting is made to feel in this excerpt.

"I can't decide," Peabody said as they walked around the rectory, "if the statues and candles and colored glass are really pretty or really creepy."

"Statues are too much like dolls, and dolls are creepy. You keep expecting them to blink. And the ones that smile, like this?" Eve kept her lips tight together and she curved them up. "You know they've got teeth in there. Big, sharp, shiny teeth."

"I didn't. But now I've got to worry about it."

Through dialogue, Robb plants the idea that the statues are menacing. Their closed mouths are hiding teeth, and this idea immediately conjures childhood fears of the wolf in Little Red Riding Hood.

Here's another example. Read it and think about the unsettling way in which Stephen King describes a doll in this excerpt from novel *Night Shift*.

The doll was on top. The Elizabeth doll.

She looked at it and began to shudder.

The doll was dressed in a scarf of red nylon, part of a scarf she had lost two or three months back. At a movie with Ed. The arms were pipe cleaners that had been draped in stuff that looked like blue moss. Graveyard moss, perhaps. There was hair on the doll's head, but that was wrong. It was fine white flax, taped to the doll's pink-gum eraser head. Her own hair was sandy blond and coarser than this. This was the way her hair had been—

When she was a little girl.

She swallowed and there was a clicking sound in her throat. Hadn't they all been issued scissors in the first grade, tiny scissors with rounded blade, just right for a child's hand? Had that long-ago little boy crept up behind her, perhaps at nap time, and—

King is an expert at figuring out what kinds of images creep people out. Some objects from childhood—dolls, clowns, portraits of people whose eyes seem to follow us around, costumes and masks—are particularly potent at generating this kind of uneasiness.

Use whatever makes you squirm. Chances are the image will make the reader squirm as well. Here are some tips for making ordinary objects feel menacing:

- Link the object, in the narrator's mind, to a frightening image or memory from the past
- Make the object appear to stand out from its surroundings
- Put the object in shadow
- Make the object broken or just slightly mutilated or stained
- Have a dog (or horse or cat or child or . . .) shy away from it
- Give the object an unusual smell

Another way to create suspense is to plant something that feels out of place or just slightly off. Seeing it raises a question for the readers and the viewpoint character: "What's going on here?"

Suppose, for example, that from a distance through a picture window, your character sees a crowded living room in which people are dancing. He comes closer and closer until he should be close enough to hear the music. Only there is none. "What's going on here?" the reader asks.

Here are some examples of "just off" situations that will trigger the reader to ask that question and feel a sense of unease:

- Pills spilled on a baby's blanket
- A phone that is off the hook
- A car alarm that keeps on ringing
- A broken window
- A shoe rack with only left shoes on it
- Water left running
- A broken child's swing
- An overturned chair
- Broken glass

Once again, be wary of overdoing it. You don't need to hit your readers over the head with blood-spattered towels and used condoms. More subtle touches like these can as effectively suggest menace. Trust the reader to get it.

Use Multiple Viewpoints to Create Suspense

Authors use multiple viewpoints to create suspense by allowing the reader to know more than any individual character knows. One way to do this is by allowing the villain to narrate some of the scenes.

If Maggie is walking in the park on a sunny day, there's probably no suspense. But what if the previous scene was written from the viewpoint of a man obsessed with Maggie who was stalking her, following her from her home, through the park, and now waits for her to reach a secluded spot by the lake? Maggie's walk in the park becomes shaded with menace because the reader knows something the character doesn't—that she's being stalked by someone who may want to hurt her. The closer she gets to the lake, the more tension the reader will feel, knowing that danger lies waiting for her there.

ESSENTIAL

Multiple viewpoints can create suspense, but they can rob your story of its surprises, too, because you've revealed to the reader what's coming. So choose carefully which is more important to the story you are trying to tell: surprise or suspense. Sometimes you can't have it both ways.

Romance writers often switch back and forth between the viewpoints of the hero and the heroine. This allows the reader to be in on it, for example, when one character misinterprets another character's actions, or tries to hide his true feelings, or lies. You can show the hero hurrying to meet his beloved and getting in a car accident; then show his beloved waiting and waiting, becoming angrier as she convinces herself that he's deliberately stood her up. Misunderstandings create suspense-like tension, as they cause the reader to wonder how in the world everything is going to get untangled.

Many authors feel that by adding multiple viewpoints, they add depth to their story. And it certainly creates many opportunities to create suspense. To see the technique in action, here are a few books that harness multiple viewpoints to create suspense:

- *The Da Vinci Code* by Dan Brown
- *My Sister's Keeper* by Jodi Picoult
- *The Last Spymaster* by Gayle Lynds
- *Carrie* by Stephen King
- *Lonesome Dove* by Larry McMurtry

Using multiple narrators, the author can cut away from one to the other and leave the reader hanging at a key moment. It has the added advantage of showing how one narrator might see menace in a situation where another narrator does not.

The Omniscient Tip-off Creates Suspense

Another way to create suspense—though not the most elegant solution—is to simply bring an omniscient narrator in (or let the viewpoint character take a step into the future) to tell the reader something that the characters don't yet know. For example, suppose you end a chapter with a cliffhanger moment when your character reaches for the doorknob. Instead of saying whether she opens the door, or what she finds when she does, the chapter ends with a line like this:

If Dahlia had known what lay beyond the door, she never would have opened it.

This is an omniscient narrator speaking directly to the reader from the novel's future and telegraphing that something unknown but ominous is about to happen. Is it heavy handed? Extremely. Can it work? Occasionally. Delivering a warning from the future is not a particularly elegant or literary technique, but writers have made it work.

Heightening Suspense

Suspense works best when it builds on a gradual upward trajectory. Characters who escape from one close call find themselves in even direr straits. Each release of suspense is followed by a new round with even more danger, and just when the reader thinks things can't get worse, they do.

Think of a suspenseful scene as if it were a pressure cooker. First you increase the pressure, then release it a bit, giving your readers and characters a little breathing space, then tighten again, raising the pressure even higher. Repeat until cooked.

But don't let suspense overcook your story. It is possible to tease the reader too many times. How much is too much? The answer is in the eye of the reader—this is why many writers belong to writers critique groups. It is possible to overdo suspense. If you allow it to go on too long without having it pay off or end in some way, your readers may lose interest.

Once you've got suspense going, there are many techniques for tightening the screws.

Raise the Stakes

Suspense grows when the stakes are raised. In the beginning, a character might be looking for the jerk who stole her car. By the end she's running for her life.

As the stakes grow, the suspense over whether the characters will succeed or fail is heightened. Stakes matter to readers only after you've made them care about your characters.

Add a Ticking Clock

Adding time pressure is another excellent way to increase suspense. Suddenly your character has only an hour until the bomb explodes. Or until the kidnappers fulfill their threat to kill the hostage. Or until the contest judges make their decision. Or until the deadly toxin is released into the town reservoir. Or until Mom and Dad get home.

For example, in Michael Crichton's *The Andromeda Strain*, scientists go underground to understand and neutralize a microbe that caused the death of all but two crew members on a military satellite. The microbe mutates and triggers the self-destruct sequence of an atomic bomb, and the scientists are in a deadly race against time.

As the clock in your novel ticks down, make be sure to let the reader know how much time is left. Increase the anxiety your characters and readers feel as the deadline nears.

Add Obstacles

Another way to heighten suspense is to place obstacles between your hero and the goal.

In this excerpt from Tony Hillerman's *Dance Hall of the Dead*, Detective Joe Leaphorn is pursuing a little boy who is in danger. As you read it, notice how Hillerman puts obstacles in the way of Leaphorn's pursuit.

Leaphorn began pushing his way back from the window, struggling through the packed humanity toward the passageway that ran behind the dance room to connect the two galleries. He moved as fast as he could, leaving a wake of jostled spectators, bruised feet, and curses. The passageway, too, was blocked with watchers. It took him two full minutes to fight his way through to the doorway. It was blocked as well. Finally he was in the right gallery. A Navajo woman was standing on the chair Bowlegs had used. He pushed his way through the crowd, looking frantically. The boy was nowhere.

Anything that physically slows your character down or stops him completely is an obstacle. For example, your character misses a phone call, or his car breaks down, or a storm hits and a road washes out, or a parade shuts down all routes across town. Obstacles can be internal as well. If your character is afraid of snakes, then put a snake between him and the escape route.

ALERT

Suspense grows as you peel away your character's layers of protection to make him more vulnerable and unprotected. He loses his gun. His cell phone battery dies. He runs out of ammunition. His sword breaks. Without the weapon or protection, the character becomes increasingly vulnerable and desperate. The character has to figure out how to fashion a new weapon, or find one, or find another way out through cunning and deceit.

Whatever the obstacles, they have to be logical and credible. If an obstacle feels merely convenient or coincidental, then the reader will sense the author's hand at work, and that spoils the tension.

Incapacitate Your Hero

Tension builds when a character is in heightened danger. One way to increase that danger is to weaken the character. Diminish your character's capacity. Give him a stomach bug, or a drug that makes him sleepy, or vertigo when he has to climb a tower.

For example, suppose Vincent is hiding in the basement. He knows the villain who is looking for him is going to kill him if he finds him. He hears footsteps overhead. Someone is coming down the stairs. He can even hear the person breathing. There's an open window but he can't get to it because he's broken his leg. He can barely drag himself into a corner and wait.

Depriving a character of his senses is another effective way of building tension. A character who is blindfolded, or temporarily deafened by an explosion, or unable to speak, feels even more trapped than one who is bound and gagged. For example, George hears someone coming but he can't tell if it's someone he can trust or not because it's pitch black. The longer he has to wait, the more suspense builds.

When your character is cornered, the reader is cornered with him. These are moments to elongate and heighten with sensory detail and internal dialogue.

Manipulate Chapter Endings

Strategically placed chapter breaks can affect how suspenseful your novel feels. For example, you can decide to break a chapter at a settled ending—the end of a scene when something is resolved. Or you can decide to break between chapters at an exciting, cliffhanger moment. Your decision will determine how much suspense and tension your reader will feel when he reaches that chapter break.

Take, for example, these four events that might comprise a scene:

1. Stephen arrives back at his apartment and finds the door open.
2. Cautiously he steps inside, searches the living room, bedroom, and kitchen and sees no one.

3. He's just pouring himself a drink when he hears the toilet flush.
4. An intruder emerges from the bathroom, sees him, and they fight.

Where would you break the chapter? If this is early in your novel, you might choose to put the break *after* the fight is resolved. If it is later in the novel, you might choose to put the break after the toilet flushes but before the intruder appears. This would have the effect of creating tension and forward momentum.

You can manipulate chapter breaks when you revise your manuscript, making a conscious decision where to insert the breaks between chapters in order to increase or decrease the tension in the reader's mind.

Loosening Suspense

Tension loosens its grip when something happens to defuse it. For example, a character who thinks she's being stalked reaches home safely, or encounters a friend on the way, or gets attacked. Tension releases when a character hiding from an intruder is discovered, or when the intruder leaves. Tension releases when a character who is looking for her husband discovers his dead body, or finds him dead drunk on a bar stool, or finds him slumped over the wheel of his parked car in their garage.

The release of tension might be only temporary, just enough to give the character a breather. Here are some examples of temporary tension releasers:

*   A character cracks a joke
*   Something ominous (floor boards creaking) turns out to be ordinary (a cat on the landing)
*   A change in attitude (the character flies into a rage, or bursts into song rather than being terrified)

Or, suspense might build to another level. Yes, there's a cat on the landing, but there are still footsteps. Now it sounds as if someone is coming down the attic stairs.

Or, suspense might end with action. The bomb goes off. Flirting ends in a kiss. A standoff turns into a gunfight. A stalking turns into a chase.

Create a Turning Point in a Suspense Sequence

When you write suspense, you are writing toward that critical moment, a turning point, and that turning point may be one where your character has to make a do-or-die decision. Will he open the door or walk away? Will he kiss the girl or get cold feet? Confess the truth or tell a lie? Cower in the corner or stand and fight back?

ESSENTIAL

When you write a turning point in a suspense scene, brainstorm alternatives. What your character does has to be credible, but it's even better if it surprises the reader, too.

It's in that moment that your scene is in a delicate balance. It could go one way or it could go another. Write that turning point carefully. Whatever your character does, it should be completely credible in terms of the situation and who that character is.

Here are some tips for writing those key decision points in suspense:

- **Slow down:** Turning points are written slower than they would happen in real life; give your character time to think, time to weigh options, even though it might be taking place in a split second.
- **Motivate your characters:** There should be something powerful at stake for every option.
- **Recall a trauma from the past:** This is a moment to harness your character's backstory and reprise something from his past that affects what he does now, perhaps making him determined to *get it right this time*.

Pitfalls of Writing Suspense

Suspense is a powerful tool, but it's also easy to misuse. You can overdo it or understate it, or simply have it misfire.

Here are some of the pitfalls to watch out for:

- **Releasing suspense too quickly:** Suspense takes time to build; don't release it until you've taken the time needed to create it.
- **Letting suspense go on for too long:** You can't maintain suspense, page after page, without releasing it with humor or a false payoff or two; readers will tire and tune out.
- **Making the reader feel manipulated:** Make sure that everything that happens to create suspense feels believable, not just contrived by the author in order to amp suspense.
- **Using clichéd images:** Avoid the suspense clichés like a suddenly black sky, thunder and lightning, or dense fog.
- **Characters who are too dumb to live:** Your characters shouldn't do stupid things (like run into the haunted house) just because your plot demands it; if the reader doesn't respect the character, the suspense simply won't build.

Used well, suspense is one of the most powerful tools in the writer's arsenal for making a novel a page turner. Readers who can't wait to find out what's going to happen next keep right on reading.

CHAPTER 15

Getting to "The End"

Getting to the final scene, the final paragraph, the final word, the final period for the first time is an epic, milestone moment. Getting there requires discipline and an enormous leap of faith. There are joys and potholes you should expect to encounter as you work your way to that magical moment when you get to type: *The End*.

Be Disciplined in Your Fashion

Writing a novel is a little bit like knitting a really, really, really long muffler. Keep at it, a little at a time, and you will make steady progress. Keep at it long enough and you will finish it.

Over the centuries, writers have come up with their own ways of making themselves write. Novelist John Cheever used to say that he woke up, had breakfast with his wife in their New York apartment, took an elevator to the basement, and wrote all day on a card table facing a blank wall. For years, Edith Wharton woke up each morning and wrote in bed, letting the pages fall onto the floor for her maid to pick up.

Respect your own work style and keep in mind that fiction isn't something you can produce if you're firing on just one cylinder. So, get enough sleep and work on the novel when you are sharpest. If you're a night owl, work on it at night. If you're a morning person, then block out mornings to write. If you're a binge writer, write in binges. If you're more the slow but steady type, then produce at least a minimum number of new words each day.

Some writers start their manuscript on the computer. Because they type almost as fast as they can think, the words flow. But there are plenty of other writers who prefer to write their first draft longhand. Neil Gaiman, James Patterson, Tess Gerritsen, Nelson DeMille, and many others share that vice. For some, sharpened pencils are the weapon of choice. Neal Stephenson (*Snow Crash*, *Cryptonomicon*) says he uses different colored fountain pens each day, and edits his manuscript with a different colored ink on each pass.

QUOTE

"I'm not a morning person, so I start writing about noon and can write late into the night. I don't type so I write longhand with #1 pencils on yellow legal pads. I drink lots of coffee, which stimulates the imagination (that's my secret), and too many cigarettes."—Nelson DeMille

When it comes to writing that first draft, respect your own quirks. Cater to them if it makes it easier for you to write. But if you find them getting in the way of your writing, then try another approach. The key here is consistency. Do whatever works for you, and then keep doing it.

Stay Flexible

Sometimes you will be writing along, dutifully turning your outline or synopsis into lovely drama. Then you get to the scene where your character is supposed to do something, like leap off a cliff, or take off her clothes and jump in the pool, or rob the bank. You try and you try and you try to write that scene but it's as if the character just won't go there.

This is a frustrating, but potentially wonderful and insightful moment. Instead of forcing your character off that cliff or into the water or into the bank, stop and think about why she's balking. Is it possible that what seemed like a perfectly plausible thing for her to do when you were writing your outline, weeks earlier, seems preposterous now that the character has developed into a full-fledged being on the pages of your as-yet-unfinished novel?

ESSENTIAL

Stay flexible. Allow your characters to drive your plot, don't allow your plot to herd your characters. If a character balks and won't go wherever "there" is, then there's probably a good reason.

Sometimes it seems as if a character develops a mind of her own. You write a scene that you have planned and the character does something completely different. You may be writing, but the character has taken over the keyboard. Yes, you could hit the Delete key and force her back on the beaten path. Or maybe not.

Take some time to stop and think about this fork in the road. Then continue writing, following this new track for at least a few pages more and see whether you like where it's going. If the turn of events surprised you, then it's going to surprise the reader. And that's a good thing.

Revise as You Go

Some writers just write, straight through from beginning to end with barely a look back. If that works for you, do it.

But more writers find it helpful to start each writing day by reviewing and revising the writing that they did the day or two previous. Revising can give you a running start and put you back in the groove you were in when you left off. It can also be encouraging to find that the words that yesterday might have seemed forced and lame are actually not that bad and can be salvaged with a little spit and polish.

Printed pages look and feel different than pages on your computer screen. So, from time to time, it's also useful to print out some pages and take a look back at a larger chunk. Print out the last 50 pages for example, or the entire work thus far to give you a refreshed perspective on where you are and where your novel is headed.

But don't fall into the trap of spending so much time polishing yesterday's words to lapidary perfection that you fail to move forward. Get to work writing new pages as quickly as you can.

An up-to-date outline that reflects what you've actually written will become one of your most useful tools when it comes time to revise. So as you go along, it's a good idea to create, or update, your preliminary scene-by-scene outline of the novel so it reflects what you are writing.

This can be barebones, just a time stamp with a single-sentence description of what happens in each scene. Here's an example of a scene description.

Scene 1: Tuesday, 6 p.m., Gary goes to Madison's apartment for their date; she doesn't answer the bell; he sneaks in.

An updated scene-by-scene outline allows you to see your novel's big picture rather than drowning in a sea of detail.

Getting Stuck

There are many reasons why you will find yourself writing along and then suddenly spinning your wheels, stuck and apparently unable to write the next bit.

This can happen for a number of reasons. Here are just a few:

- **Idea block:** You can't come up with a really good idea for what happens next.
- **Idea hurdle:** You know where you want to move your characters but you don't know how to get there.
- **What was I thinking?:** You know what was supposed to happen next, but as you begin to write, the idea seems farfetched or out of character.
- **Ennui:** The next scene simply isn't that interesting to you.
- **It's all terrible:** You have one of those days when everything you write seems painfully awful.
- **Performance anxiety:** This can happen if you read a particularly well-written novel while you're writing your own, and suddenly you see all the flaws in your own work.
- **Terror of the blank page:** Irrational fear incapacitates you.

It helps to know that writer's block afflicts even the most seasoned writers. All of us have that moment when we ask ourselves, in all seriousness: "What was it that made me think I could write a novel?" Then, hopefully, we ignore the gremlins in our heads, barge ahead, and write.

FACT

Writing inhibition has been documented as early as the nineteenth century. In 1804, Coleridge wrote in his notebook: "So completely has a whole year passed, with scarcely the fruits of a *month*.—O Sorrow and Shame. . . . I have done nothing!" It was the first case of writer's block recorded in English.

Getting Unstuck

It can be distressing to get stuck. Writers have come up with various solutions. Some among them—antidepressants, artificial stimulants, talk therapy, or writing secluded in a shed—may not be practical or necessary for you.

But here are some remedies and workarounds that may help you get unstuck.

- Set a timer for fifteen minutes and, for just that long, force out some words.
- Take a break, take a walk, do the laundry, read a book, take a nap; then return refreshed.
- Skip over the scene that's giving you trouble.
- Torture your writing friends. By discussing what's got you stuck you may be able find a way to get yourself unstuck.
- Update your outline. This is busy work but it might help you regain the momentum you seem to have temporarily lost.
- Brainstorm. Think of all the different things that could happen next instead of what you originally had in mind.
- Try writing somewhere new. Go to a coffee shop or the library or the backyard where the change of venue may get your productive juices flowing.
- Unplug the Internet. Cutting yourself off from the web and from e-mail might do the trick.
- Uninstall the games. If you find yourself playing Tetris or solitaire on your computer, remove the game, posthaste.
- Shake up your routine: Try writing at some other time than you normally do; try writing longhand.

The good news is that for virtually every novel that has ever been published, the author spent at least some time in anguish with some version of writer's block. It comes with the territory, and once you've been through it once, it might not get easier to get past but it will feel a whole lot more familiar.

Making Major Changes

Suppose you are writing along and you decide to make a drastic change to your story. Maybe you decide to combine two characters into one. Or you decide to add a whole new secondary plot. Or change a key plot twist, which determines the trajectory of your main plot. Or you change your main character to a man instead of a woman.

Big changes like these take courage. More than that, they require caution. To find that balance of caution and courage, you need to be able to dial it back if it doesn't work out. So use the "Save As" function in your word processor to save the manuscript, as it is, before you embark on a major change. Safely archive that older version so you can retrieve it if you need to.

Now you can continue working, fearlessly making drastic changes, knowing you can always go back to the earlier version if you need to.

Most times, you won't need to go back to that outdated version of your manuscript. Older versions will pile up and eventually you'll feel secure enough with your current draft to discard them.

Grouping Scenes into Chapters

Readers need breaks, and they expect novels to be broken up into chapters and scenes. Scenes are organic pieces of your plot that break when there's a change in the time or place or viewpoint character who is narrating. Scene breaks allow you to "jump cut" and avoid having to write too much of the boring bits of connective tissue. The term "jump cut" comes from video editing. It means jumping from one time to another without showing what happens in between. In a novel, you can jump cut by inserting a scene break right after the man she meets asks your protagonist to go home with him, and right before she wakes up in his bed the next morning.

Chapters, on the other hand, can break between scenes or in the middle of a scene. A chapter might have one or more scenes grouped together in it. A very long scene can even be broken up into two or more chapters.

Chapter breaks can be inserted at the writer's discretion. You can break your book up into chapters as you write, but be sure to revisit the placement of your chapter breaks to make sure they're all working the way you want them to.

ESSENTIAL

Manipulate the pace of your novel by the placement of chapter breaks. Break at a settled ending, a resting spot between scenes and a resting spot in your plot, and the reader will feel free to take a break from reading. Break a chapter at a cliffhanger moment and the reader will feel compelled to keep reading.

After "The End"

When you reach the end of the manuscript the first time, stop and celebrate. Break out a bottle of champagne (or sparkling apple cider) and toast yourself, because you did it. Of course, the next step is revising. Many authors will tell you that revision is where the "real" writing takes place. But don't let that minimize what you've accomplished. An unfinished draft can never be revised.

Now is the time to let your manuscript rest. You need a little distance in order to see what you have. So work on something else, take a trip, build that birdhouse you've always wanted to build—do anything at all for at least a week, preferably several.

After that, you'll be able to print it out and return to it refreshed, ready to revise your novel and take it to the next level.

CHAPTER 16

Rewrites

No one writes a publishable first draft. But, too often, writers think that after they've typed *The End*, they are ready to pick up the blue pencil and line edit their work. In reality, most manuscripts require several major revisions of the big-picture issues like plot, character, and pacing before they are ready to be line edited. Here you'll find an overview of the rewriting and revision process and some advice on determining how much revision is necessary.

Revision: An Overview

Congratulations! You finished your first draft. Please, resist the urge to start line editing. There is so much to be done before you are ready for that level of detail. Here's a step-by-step overview of what you have in store to properly address the changes needed to your manuscript.

1. Take a break while you give it to trusted readers to critique
2. Talk to your reader/critics and gather their reactions
3. Print it out after you take a break and reread from start to finish; as you read, list all of the major changes you think will be needed
4. Update your outline; analyze the pacing; scope out more changes
5. Selectively read through the manuscript, leapfrogging to sections by sub-plot, character, and setting; scope out more changes
6. Start revising, working from large to small
7. Repeat
8. Repeat
9. Repeat until you are satisfied with the overall shape of your story and the trajectory of your characters
10. Line edit only when you have addressed all of the major problems and are satisfied with the way your story is working

How long should a revision take? If it took you six months to write your first draft, it could easily take you half as long to revise it, and don't be surprised if it takes even longer. The last thing you want to do is shoot your chance with the agent of your dreams by sending out your manuscript before it's ready for prime time.

QUOTE

"The truth is that editing lines is not necessarily the same as editing a book. A book is a much more complicated entity and totality than the sum of its lines alone. Its structural integrity, the relation and proportions of its parts, and its total impact could escape even a conscientious editor exclusively intent on vetting the book line by line."—Robert Gottlieb (for many years editor-in-chief of Simon & Schuster and Alfred A. Knopf)

How do you know when a manuscript is finished? That is a hard question to answer. You might rely on another round of advance readers, folks who haven't seen an earlier draft. If they read it and think it's cooking on all cylinders, then you can assume you're good to go. Often new writers hire a freelance editor, someone outside of their circle of friends and family, to go through the manuscript. A professional editor will find things that average readers won't, and they will see more clearly what needs to be changed in order to strengthen your manuscript. In addition, they will be tuned into the issues that agents and editors have with unpublished manuscripts, and can help you overcome them.

No matter when you stop, it will always feel as if you could have done more. But is there such a thing as too much revision? It's certainly possible to revise the wrong stuff. It's just as important to figure out what's working and not spoil it, as it is to figure out what is not working and fix it.

Give It to Readers

An excellent time to send your manuscript to a few trusted advance readers is while you're waiting for your writing to "cool." The best people to critique your work are folks who love to read, read a lot, and read in the genre you are writing.

Your readers don't need to be writers, but writers who critique your work will be able to frame their comments in writerly terms. They may recognize, for instance, that a scene feels like it's floating around because you've failed to anchor the viewpoint. Non-writers, on the other hand, can usually tell you where they got confused but not why.

However, writers will be far too ready to tell you how to "fix" your book, whereas non-writers will generally leave it to you to figure out how to address the issues they raise.

You're more likely to get useful comments if you ask your readers to look at specific aspects of the novel. Stress that you are looking for big issues, not typos, and ask your readers to put comments on the manuscript itself. When they're done, ask them to jot down some high-level reactions, summarizing what they liked and what they didn't like.

Their notes will make a good starting point when you get together with them to talk about their reactions. Here's a list of topics and questions you might discuss with the folks who've read your manuscript.

- **Overall reaction:** What were the best aspects of the novel, what were the weakest?
- **Dramatic opening:** Did the opening scene hold your attention? Did it make you want to keep reading?
- **Main plot:** Is the overall story plausible? Easy to follow? Did it hold your interest? Were you satisfied with the way it ended?
- **Subplots:** Are they interesting? Plausible? Easy to follow? Do they feel as if they all belong in the novel?
- **Ending:** Is the resolution clear? Believable? Satisfying?
- **Main character:** Is the main character believable? Three-dimensional? Sympathetic? Interesting?
- **Other characters:** Do they ring true? Hold your interest?
- **Pacing:** Were there parts that felt too slow? Too fast? Did the overall novel feel well modulated?

QUESTION

How many advance readers should you ask to critique the draft of your novel?
Enough so that you will get a diversity of opinion but not so many that you are overwhelmed with suggestions. At least two; not more than five.

How to Take Criticism

Everybody finds it difficult to take criticism, especially after having labored for months and poured heart and soul into a manuscript. Most of us really, in our heart of hearts, just want to hear how wonderful it is. But this is not going to happen.

More likely you will hear criticism that you secretly suspected but didn't want to face. You'll also hear criticism that may feel off the wall. This is why you need at least two readers so you can safely ignore an issue that only one of your readers picked up.

When it comes time for your readers to tell you what they think, the most important thing for you to do is hear them. Here are some tips for listening.

- **Try not to interrupt:** If you keep interrupting, explaining what you were trying to do in a particular scene or passage, getting all worked up and defensive, you prevent yourself from hearing the criticism. Remember, listening doesn't mean you agree or have to do everything your reader suggests. It's up to you which criticisms you decide to address. But you owe it to yourself and to your readers to shut up, listen, and try your best to get what they are trying to tell you.
- **Ask clarifying questions:** If your reader says, "I loved the book," ask what the good parts were. If your reader says, "That character seemed dumb," ask for examples of where that character seemed dumb. If your reader says, "I didn't really understand the ending," ask the reader to summarize how your novel ended so you can see how it was understood.
- **Probe:** Don't settle for yes/no or short answers. Probe with follow-up questions to get specific feedback on what's working and where there are problems. The more specifics you get, the clearer it will be what needs to be revised.
- **Take notes:** You don't want to forget all the good things your readers say and get overwhelmed by the "needs work" comments. Negative comments won't seem so negative when you reread your notes twenty-four hours later. Taking notes has an added benefit: It gives you something to do while you're not interrupting.

Arguing and explaining to someone who is critiquing your manuscript will keep you from hearing what the person is trying to tell you; worse, it will discourage that person from being absolutely honest with you.

Translating Comments into Fixes

Okay, now you've heard the critique. You've got it all written down so that you can consider it rationally. How do you decide what to fix and what to ignore?

- **Look for corroboration:** If two readers identify the same problem, then it needs to be addressed.
- **Look for confirmation of your own suspicions:** When a reader picks up on something you suspected might be a problem, then it needs to be addressed.
- **If readers disagree:** Ask each one to explain his viewpoint of the issue; the more information you have, the easier it will be to decide whether to address the concern or if you can safely ignore it.
- **If it's an easy fix:** You'll probably be more inclined to go ahead and make it; if the problem affects the structure of your novel or something basic about your main character, then take your time and think about how to address it.

Next, translate problems into solutions. Carefully consider all the comments you get from readers, but a little red flag should go up whenever someone tells you *how* to fix your novel. Don't ignore the comment; try to understand where it's coming from. Ask follow-up questions so you understand the problem and can come up with your own solution. After all, it's your book.

Assessing the Scope of Changes

You've taken a break. You have a list of changes that readers have suggested. Now print out your manuscript and start to read it again yourself. Stay away from the computer so you're not tempted to jump in and make changes as you see they are needed, and read it from start to finish.

As you read, create an inventory of all the changes you think may be needed. Your list will probably include some of the same issues readers who critiqued the manuscript already picked up. Your inventory consists of specific references to chapters that need strengthening.

So, it might include items like these:

- Slow down in Chapter 7.
- Show more reaction in Chapter 9 when Vincent gets hurt.
- Boring in chapter 15—think about how to speed things up.
- Why does Miranda break the dishes? Find something in her backstory that explains this.
- Smooth the transitions in Chapter 22 flashback.
- Show how Vincent feels when Miranda fails to show up at the bar.
- Insufficient motivation for Miranda to lie in Chapter 20.

Remember, just noting a problem doesn't mean you're going to address it. If you're not sure, write it down. Later you can decide, for each item on the list, which changes you are going to make.

If you can't help yourself, correct typos and grammatical errors as you go along. But you really don't need to do that yet. What matters now is that you build a complete list of changes needed. Here are just a few of the general areas you may find you need to address.

- **Problems with Act I:** It starts off too fast, too slow, too confusing, or not sufficiently compelling; the premise seems forced, the situation not credible.
- **Problems with Act II:** It bogs down with too many subplots, too many characters; not enough focus; predictable story line or illogical plot twists.
- **Problems with Act III:** The climax feels too easy or too quick or too complex or simply false, the resolution feels unsatisfying; the ending feels contrived or unfinished.
- **Problems with characters:** Characters are not sufficiently complex or nuanced; they need more depth and emotion; too many characters blend together; they lack credibility.
- **Problems with plot:** The story feels at times confusing and overly complex or too predictable and not sufficiently complex; the plot twists lack credibility.
- **Problems with the protagonist:** The character needs a stronger goal, more motivation; the the obstacles and conflicts feel too insubstantial;

bland voice (spoken and inner dialogue); too much backstory dumped too early; implausible actions and inactions; inner journey unresolved by the end.

- **Problems with the antagonist:** Weak goal; not a formidable enough adversary; confused motivation; an evil cliché.

Update Your Outline

If you've been revising your outline as you write, then it won't take long to be sure that it reflects the novel you've written. Each scene should be described in a single line or two, including the scene number, time/date stamp, and brief description of what happens.

For example:

Scene 1: Tuesday, 6 p.m., Gary goes to Madison's apartment for their date; she doesn't answer the bell; he sneaks in.

Scene 2: Continued, Gary goes up, knocks at her door (music, shouting); the man who answers has never heard of Madison.

Scene 3: Tuesday, 8 p.m., Gary gets home, Madison is waiting for him; they argue; she leaves in a rage.

Scene 4: Continuous, Gary goes inside and finds that his house has been burgled; calls the police.

Keep your outline spare. Too much detail won't allow you to see the bones of your story. Rereading the outline will give you a sense of how those bones are fitting together.

Then, reread and analyze your outline. Here are just some of the problems you might pick up:

- **Missing pieces:** Have you failed to introduce a character or to establish some important piece of the plot, simply skipped over an important scene, or rushed through some critical transition?

- **Pacing issues:** Is there a good mix of slow scenes and fast scenes, of tense and less tense moments; does the story gather momentum as it nears the end of acts, and particularly as it nears the novel's climax; after exciting things happen, do you give your characters time to reflect?
- **Chronology issues:** Does the novel's timeline (calendar and clock) make sense; is the duration from the novel's day one to its final day correct; have you packed too much into any twenty-four hour period or simply skipped over days without accounting for them?

Selective Read-Throughs

Reading a novel through from start to finish gives you one perspective. For different angles, leapfrog through the manuscript, selectively reading related passages. This will help you tease apart more of the issues that need to be addressed so you can better focus your revision. Your scene-by-scene outline provides a useful guide for selecting scenes to reread, each time through.

Here are some ways to select sections to reread, and questions to ask yourself as you do so:

- **By subplot:** Leapfrog through the manuscript, reading each scene that develops one subplot, then jump through reading the scenes that develop another subplot until you've read them all. Ask yourself: Does each subplot have a beginning, middle, and end; if any are unresolved, is that a deliberate choice; is each subplot essential to your novel?
- **By character:** Read every scene that contains one of the characters (not the protagonist); then read all the scenes that contain another character until you've run out of major and supporting characters. Ask yourself: Is each character sufficiently introduced and developed; does each have a distinctive and consistent look and feel and voice; does each act as if what's happened in the novel has really affected them physically and/or emotionally; are any of them stereotypes; have you shown how the character changes (or doesn't change); could the character be eliminated without damaging the novel (in which case, consider deleting him from the story)?
- **By setting:** Read each scene that takes place in each particular setting until you've reviewed all the settings. Ask yourself: Has each setting

been sufficiently introduced and established; is each setting consistent each time it is reprised, and are the added details consistent; did you establish the elements of each setting that are important to your plot?

Read It Aloud

Reading your manuscript aloud to yourself is time consuming, but provides unique insights. Hearing the sentences you've written exposes all kinds of problems. Awkward phrases, clichés, repetitions, and passages that go on for too long are readily recognized when you hear them read aloud. Clumsy sentences that you might have glided right past jump out when you hear them.

Pay attention to your own response as you read. If you get bored reading the story, you can bet your readers will, too. So make a note of places where you want to cut or trim and tighten, or perhaps insert conflict or action to make it more engrossing.

Reading your manuscript aloud to yourself will also keep you from doing what all of us tend to do when we get tired—speed up and skip ahead.

Make a Revision Plan

By now your list of revisions may run to ten pages or more. Sort the items on the list, from the changes that will take the most effort and have the most far-reaching effects to those that will take the least effort and have more limited effects. Group together any revisions that you can make at the same time.

Look at the list and make sure that it makes sense to you. With this plan in hand, start rewriting. Don't forget, whenever you delete something, save it in your Out file. And hedge your bets by continuing to Save As, archiving versions of the book each time before you embark on another major change.

CHAPTER 17

Editing and Polishing

When you've made the major revisions to your novel and you are satisfied with the way the plot flows and twists, with the climax and resolution, and when the characters and settings feel as vibrant and believable as you can make them, it's time to sweat the small stuff. You'll need to polish every scene, every paragraph, and every sentence so your manuscript will be as perfect as it has to be in order to pass muster with an agent or editor.

Fine Tuning

When you've addressed all the big issues in your manuscript, given it to still another batch of advance readers to confirm that your plot and characters are working, then it's time to pull out the microscope and examine it up close.

First step: Print out the manuscript. While some final polishing can be done on-screen, reading and editing directly in the electronic file, there's no substitute for the perspective that printed pages gives you. Somehow, errors that slip past on the computer screen seem to pop off the printed page.

Expect to go through your manuscript at least three times to get the job done.

QUOTE

"What's nice about writing is that nothing's set in stone till it's finished. It's only then that you hang yourself out to dry."—Evan Hunter (Ed McBain)

Strong Starts and Finishes

First impressions and final impressions are what readers notice most. So lavish some special editing attention on all these starts and finishes in your manuscript:

- Make the first line, the first paragraph, and first scene as strong as you can make them.
- Introduce each setting vividly.
- Make each main character's first appearance memorable, establishing that character's physical presence with a few telling details as well as the character's voice.
- Pay special attention to the first and last paragraphs of each scene.
- Make the last page, the last paragraph, and the last line as strong as it can be; leave the reader with something to think about.

Tighten Each Scene

Read each scene through and assess whether it delivers everything that a scene should. A flabby beginning should be tightened. If it starts too early, cut to where things get interesting. Floating characters need to be anchored in time and place. An ending that dribbles off should be trimmed. If there's no conflict in the scene, look for opportunities to insert some.

And most of all, make sure that your novel needs every single scene that's in it. If you can cut a scene and the story won't suffer, cut it!

Here is a checklist of things to look for in each scene:

- ❐ **Strong start:** Does it engage the reader right away; are you starting it as late as possible?
- ❐ **Clear orientation:** Is it clear to the reader, within a paragraph or two, where and when the scene takes place and who is there?
- ❐ **Conflict:** Every scene should have some tension or conflict; at least one character should feel off balance.
- ❐ **Arc:** From beginning to end, something should *change* in the course of each scene, even if it's nothing more than a character's emotional state.
- ❐ **Strong finish:** Does it end strong and as early as possible, or does it just dribble off?

Tweak the Chapter Breaks

When your scenes are as tight and compelling as you can make them, then examine how you've grouped them into chapters. Chapters can be long or short. Use the placement of chapter breaks to add to the momentum you are trying to create in the story.

ALERT

Be aware that many readers like their fiction served in twenty-minute chunks. So consider breaking up a chapter that goes on longer than that.

Where you want momentum to build and the reader to keep turning pages, break a chapter in the middle of scenes at a cliffhanger moment. Where your storytelling is more leisurely, then break the chapter at natural scene breaks.

Pump Up Dialogue

One of the best ways to tell whether the dialogue in your manuscript is working is to read it aloud to yourself. The ear is much better than the eye at picking out clunky words and phrases. As you read just the bits within the quotation marks aloud, think about whether the dialogue conveys the personality and emotion of the speaker. If not, tweak the word choice and sentence structure so that it does.

Here's a simple example. Imagine all the different ways a character can greet another character, and what impact each greeting would have on the reader's understanding of the relationship between the two characters.

- "Hello."
- "How do you do?"
- "Hey, you. What's up?"
- "Yo, bro'."
- "Oh, it's you again."
- "Hey, you with that face, yeah you, I'm talkin' to you!"

Maybe the simple, "Hello," is all you need. But make that be a conscious choice.

Here are some more problems you might find with the dialogue you've written.

▼ **EDITING DIALOGUE**

If . . .	Then . . .
The dialogue sounds wooden and artificial	Revise it. Dialogue should sound like someone talking. Use sentence fragments and slang if that's how the characters would talk.
Dialogue goes on for too long	Cut it back; summarize if you need to; rarely should you let a single character go on for more than 100 words without interruption.
The characters sound alike	Revise to give each character a unique voice; insert personality and emotion into dialogue with careful choice of words, sentence structure, and content; remember, what characters choose not to say is often as interesting as what they do say.
The dialogue sounds flat and uninteresting	Pump up the vocabulary; use props and action with the dialogue to show the character's emotions.
The dialogue is unproductive	Get rid of any unnecessary chitchat (unless you're using it to show a character is nervous or hiding something); kill dialogue that doesn't serve your story and characterization.

Pump Up Verbs

Verbs are the workhorses of fiction. Throughout the manuscript pay special attention to your verb choices. Make sure you're using the best one you can to convey the action and emotion of the character and the moment.

Suppose you've written this:

Stephen got out of his car and went to the front door.

Got. Went. These are blah verbs. What if Stephen is a man on a mission? It would be much better to say:

Stephen stepped from his car and marched up the front walk.

There's nothing fancy or literary about *stepped* and *marched.* But they express determination much better than *got* and *went.*

Suppose Stephen is coming home inebriated from a debauched overnight. Just tweaking the verbs can convey that.

Stephen heaved himself from his car and stumbled up the front walk.

On the other hand, suppose Stephen's life depends on him getting into that house fast.

Stephen leapt from his car and raced up the front walk.

Only you know what you're trying to convey. Pick the verbs that show the action and attitude you're aiming for. Look out for those easy but hackneyed ways to show emotion. If your characters are constantly responding by smiling, frowning, shrugging, nodding, or shaking their heads, get in there and write it with more nuance.

Examine Distancing Verbs

There are a number of verbs that keep the reader at arm's length from the character. Sometimes that is the effect you want, as if your character is floating and not quite in the moment. Or remembering something that happened long ago. Or when the narrator is omniscient. But more often you want to go for immediacy.

Here is an example.

She felt a flash of heat sear her face.

A flash of heat seared her face.

Notice how the verb "felt" serves to distance the reader from the character's feelings. By eliminating it and writing the sentence more directly, what she is experiencing becomes more palpable and powerful to the reader.

Here's another example.

She wondered if Ralph was ever going home.

Was Ralph ever going home?

Here, the verb "wondered" distances the reader. Translating the question into a direct thought, coming from the head of the viewpoint character, makes it stronger.

Here are some distancing verbs to watch out for and consider eliminating:

- Felt
- Wondered
- Thought
- Realized

- Noticed
- Knew
- Saw
- Decided

Examine those *ing* verbs

There will be times when you want to write using what grammarians call the past progressive tense.

He *was racing* to the car . . .

But use it only when you want to show that something else was happening during the race: *He was racing to the car when he tripped over his own feet and crashed into the gutter.* In most instances, it's better to stick to the simple past tense.

He *raced* to the car.

With the active verb, *raced,* the sentence feels more direct, the action more active, the feeling more immediate.

To find the *ing* verbs in your manuscript, use the Find feature of your word processor. Enter "ing " with the trailing blank space and click Find to locate *ing* verbs in the middle of sentences. Enter "ing." with the trailing period to locate *ing* verbs at the end of sentences.

"I cut adjectives, adverbs, and every word which is there just to make an effect. Every sentence which is there just for the sentence."— Georges Simenon

You won't want to remove every *ing* verb from your manuscript. Every time you find one, ask yourself: Would this sentence be stronger using the active form of the verb? If so, revise.

Scrutinize Those *ly* Adverbs

A whole load of *ly* adverbs sneak into first drafts. Often writers use them to try to pump up bland verbs—walked (quickly), got up (jerkily), moved (painstakingly). But usually an adverb is just another form of lazy writing—a way to tell the reader something that would be much better shown.

To find *ly* adverbs in your manuscript, use the Find feature of your word processor. Enter "ly " with the trailing blank space and click Find to locate adverbs embedded in sentences. Enter "ly." with the trailing period to find adverbs at the ends of sentences. As each adverb comes up, scrutinize it (carefully). Occasionally you'll want to leave it be. But there are other times when you'll want to delete it and substitute some better writing.

When you find an adverb trying to help one of your verbs, consider taking the following actions:

- Delete the adverb and see if, just maybe, you didn't need it in the first place.
- Consider replacing the adverb/verb combo with a verb that better conveys the action being taken. For instance, *walked slowly* could be replaced by ambled, drifted, shuffled, staggered, strolled, traipsed, stumbled, or crept along, depending on what exactly you are trying to convey.
- Consider replacing the adverb with more descriptive action. For instance, instead of *He walked slowly*, you might write *He grimaced and held his side as he hunched forward and took one step, then another.* Or give the character a prop to show the feeling you are trying to convey.

Rewrite Clichéd Expressions

One man's literary flourish is another man's cliché. A manuscript full of them is the sign of an amateur. Go after them ruthlessly, these turns of phrase that have been so overused that they feel trite.

Avoid the ones below, and others like them, "like the plague."

- Batten down the hatches
- Eat like a pig
- Chomp at the bit
- Go like gangbusters

If you have a character who's a pompous windbag, then it's fine to let him spout clichés in his dialogue. But strew them in your narrative and you're the one who comes off looking like a bag of wind.

Clichés often sneak in when you're trying to be glib or smart. Sometimes, too, when you're tired and just haven't got the energy to reach beyond the cliché. Whenever you come across a clichéd expression in your manuscript, try doing one of these things:

- Replace it with your own fresh image or metaphor
- Delete the cliché and write something descriptive; for instance, instead of *Stephen ate like a pig* you could show the reader the gravy stains on his tie, his open-mouthed chewing, and how he holds his fork in a clenched fist.

Eliminate Redundant Redundancies

Maybe it's because writers don't always trust readers, but often they repeat themselves. Here are a few examples of that repetition compulsion. See if you can spot the overwriting.

- She turned white and backed away from him. "Stay away from me," she said, frightened.
- "He's so big," I said, considering the relative size of the other babies in the nursery, who were all smaller than Nathaniel.
- Linda wanted him to let her show that she could do it. "Give me a chance, would you?" she said.
- "Please stop," he begged.

In the first example, the writer showed how the character blanched and backed away. Her dialogue shows fear. So it's not necessary to add *frightened*.

You don't have to spoon-feed readers. If you show a character's desperation, anger, or confusion, you don't need to name it or add an explanation.

QUOTE

"Don't describe it, show it. That's what I try to teach all young writers—take it out! Don't describe a purple sunset, make me see that it is purple. The hardest thing in the world is simplicity. And the most fearful thing, too. You have to strip yourself of all your disguises, some of which you didn't know you had. You want to write a sentence as clean as a bone. That is the goal."—James Baldwin

Look for Inconsistencies

It's so hard to keep track of all the details in a novel. Is your protagonist's bedroom the first door off the hall or the second? Is her bathroom rug pink or blue? Does she write with her left or right hand? Does traffic on the main street around the fictional corner flow only one way or two?

You may lose track of these kinds of details, but there are plenty of readers who will not. So go through your story looking at the small stuff. Look for inconsistencies and fix them.

Here are some of the "gotchas" you might find.

- **Discontinuity:** Violet stands up and then, two paragraphs later, she stands up again; Violet and Willem toast one another but only one wine glass ends up in the sink; a coat that Violet hangs up when Willem arrives is found folded over the back of a chair the next morning.
- **Geographic inaccuracies:** A car drives the wrong way down one of Chicago's one-way streets; Violet gets a coffee at Starbucks on a corner where there's a gas station; Willem drives an hour to get somewhere that's only five minutes away. If you want to play fast and loose

with geographic details, it's best to set the novel in a fictional place, but even there readers will expect things to be consistent.

- **Time frame:** A scene takes place with a morning alarm clock going off that ends an hour later with car headlights shifting across the bedroom window; it's dark in the parking lot in Los Angeles in July before nine at night; Violet takes a three-hour drive, but there is no sense of time passing.

Character Names

Names are tricky. Suppose you have a character named Lindsay Berlinger. She's an attorney. Her sister calls her LB, her colleagues at work call her Berly, and her friends call her Lindsay. If you refer to her as Lindsay, LB, and Berly in the novel, you create a problem for the reader trying to keep your characters straight. The less attentive among them—and there are lots—will think these are three different characters.

So give your readers a break. Be as consistent as possible about what you call each character. Here are some rules of thumb to follow:

- **In the narrative:** Suppose that in scene one, you write: *Lindsay opened the door*. From then on, the narrative should refer to her as Lindsay—not LB, or Berly, or "the attractive attorney."
- **In dialogue:** In spoken dialogue you have much more flexibility. Other characters can and should refer to LB by whatever name they would, in real life. Her boss or coworker might greet her in the morning "Hey, Berlinger," her son might say "Mommy, can you come here," and her mother might say "Miss Smartypants, what on earth did you think was going to happen?"

Lock Down the Viewpoint

There are few things more distracting to readers, especially those who write or edit fiction, than a sliding viewpoint. The name for it is head hopping.

Here's an example. See if you can find the slide.

Minna was exhausted. There was her friend Samantha, just getting to the party. She waved to her. Samantha started to wave back, then hesitated, noticing the dark circles under Minna's eyes.

The first three sentences are written from Minna's viewpoint—we get her exhaustion and she sees her friend and waves. Then the viewpoint hops right over to Samantha and we discover that she's noticing Minna's dark circles. Minna wouldn't know that unless she was a mind reader.

Try to avoid allowing your own authorial viewpoint to sneak in, too, as in this example:

Minna should have been more wary of her friend, because Samantha was about to betray her trust.

Or another example:

Minna didn't realize that Randall was also watching her as she waved to her friend.

Look for point-of-view slips and clean them up. If you're telling the entire story from your protagonist's point of view, make sure every scene is written with the protagonist as the narrator. If you're telling the story from multiple points of view, the point-of-view character can shift from one scene to the next, but it should never slide around within a scene. Stick to a single narrator in each scene.

Fixing Grammar, Spelling, and Punctuation

"Don't publishers fix grammar and spelling mistakes?" an unpublished writer asks. Of course they do. But sloppy errors in your manuscript certainly won't impress agents or editors.

You're inviting that person who could help you to conclude that you can't write your way out of a paper bag. Your goal should be a manuscript that's grammatically perfect and free of errors in punctuation and spelling before you send it out into the world.

Here are some tasks to get you there:

- **Run the spell checker:** Your word processing software has a sturdy spell checker and will find and suggest fixes to misspelled words. Of course it will try to correct any dialect you've included, and it may not recognize technical terms, product names, or slang expressions, but all you have to do is reject the changes you don't want.

- **Run the grammar checker:** Grammar checkers that come with word processing software can be a pain in the behind, flagging all kinds of "problems" that you'll want to leave as is. For instance, it'll want to fix all your sentence fragments. Dialogue is full of them, as it should be. Run the grammar checker anyway, and skip over those non-problem problems. Along the way, it'll find problems you might otherwise miss—like subject-noun agreement, missing question marks, double spaces between words, or missing punctuation.

- **Read and edit:** Read through your manuscript yet again, after you check for grammar and spelling, and find all the errors your word processing software missed. For instance, it may not have caught your use of "there" instead of "their," or "its" instead of "it's." Misspelled proper nouns will have slipped by as well.

- **Have someone line edit for you:** If you're not great at catching spelling and grammatical errors, give the manuscript to someone who is, but don't give them carte blanche to make changes in the file; you should be the one to decide which changes to make.

CHAPTER 18

Reviewing Grammar and Punctuation

You didn't need to worry about grammar and punctuation as you were writing your rough draft, but now it's time to make it perfect. But are you comfortable with grammar, or are you totally lost? Many writers seem to have an almost innate sense of what to say and how to say it. If you're one of those writers, you can brush up on your basic knowledge. But if you are not so blessed, pay attention. This may be a good time to begin taking a look at your language and how you use it.

The Importance of Good Grammar

Overall, your book should adhere to the established rules of grammar, unless you're trying to make a specific point by changing them. True, you might veer off the path in your dialogue if you feel that your character speaks in a different way and you want to be able to express that. But remember this: When a reader picks up your book, you don't want your story to be hampered by unacceptable grammar. Learn the rules so you can apply them as you write, then revise carefully to catch what you missed. If you're not sure about something, look it up.

FACT

Daily Grammar, at *www.dailygrammar.com*, is an easy way to get a handle on using and recognizing good grammar. You can sign up to receive short grammar lessons five days a week. You can even take a quiz on the sixth day about what you've learned.

Learning the Rules

Even though everyone learns the rules of good writing in school, most people don't remember them by the time they graduate. They take for granted that what they say and write is correct. But like anything else you learned in school, unless you use it professionally, you've probably lost most of it.

You don't have to go back to school to learn to use grammar correctly and effectively as a writer. A short refresher course will be enough to do a good job, and then you can look up the answers to any questions you might come across as you edit your work for grammar mistakes.

Bending the Rules

Everyone has heard the phrase, "Rules were made to be broken." Writers don't break the rules of grammar; they bend them. Writing fiction is different from writing a school essay or a report for work. A fiction writer has more room to modify his or her grammar to fit with the story. Many fiction writers seem to create their own brand of grammar that suits their needs.

Once you learn the rules and know what's right, don't be afraid to bend them a little if that will help you achieve a certain effect.

Examples of bending the rules of grammar can be found in almost every contemporary fiction novel. Authors like Mickey Spillane, Nora Roberts, and Piers Anthony play with grammar usage. Hard-boiled detective novels and science fiction are famous for it. They don't so much reinvent grammar usage as enliven it.

Know Your Nouns

If you've ever listened to *Schoolhouse Rock!* you know that a noun is a person, place, or thing. That sounds pretty simple—everything you see, everything you touch is a noun. Most words are nouns: rock, tree, dog, car, elephant. Their usage depends on the sentence you put them in:

- The rock fell on the tree.
- The dog chased the car.
- The elephant sat on the dog or the car.
- Elephants can sit wherever they want.

It gets more complicated from here. But this is where you start.

Nouns are everywhere because they name everything. They can be simple or complex. They are one of the first things to change in a language. Dancehall became ballroom, ballroom became nightclub, and nightclub became disco.

Almost all sentences have a noun as a subject. These words express so much of what writers have to say that they keep up with the times better than most people. Strong, descriptive nouns that accurately portray what needs to be said are the backbone of the writer's vocabulary.

Proper Nouns

The names of certain people, places, and things are called proper nouns. These include names of people: Janice, Mike, Bill. Also names of places: Paris, Washington, New Orleans. Even some specific things like the Eiffel Tower, the Empire State Building, Buckingham Palace.

Proper nouns always refer to something in particular. They are always written with a capital letter. Whole phrases can be included under this umbrella. This can apply to book titles and specific groups such as the United Steelworkers Union.

Watch out for nouns that may seem like they should be proper nouns. The words *mother* and *father* are a good example. These words aren't capitalized, unless they're taking the place of a name.

Pronouns

A word used to substitute for a noun is a pronoun. Common pronouns (subject pronouns) include: *I, you, he, she, it, we,* and *they*. These pronouns help you refer to people without repeating their names. Instead of using your heroine's name, you can switch to *she*: "Sally went to the zoo." "She went to the zoo."

ALERT

Using and understanding pronouns is especially useful when you have long proper nouns. This means that the United Steelworkers Union may simply be referred to as *it*. By correctly placing pronouns, you can keep your readers in the loop without getting them lost in all those repetitions.

There are other pronouns as well. Pronouns like *my* and *his* are possessive pronouns, because they show possession. Instead of saying "Sally's visit to the zoo," you can say "Her visit to the zoo."

Verbs: Words of Action

Whether you choose to write mystery or romance or any other kind of fiction, you'll have to use verbs. Whether your main character puts on his socks, goes dancing, or murders his wife, you'll express everything he does with verbs. The verbs you use say something about you as a writer. They should be crisp and clear. They should tell readers exactly what they need to know. They convey the imagery from your words to your reader's imagination.

A Basic Definition

Verbs express existence, action, or occurrence. Basically, that means that verbs move your characters around in your story. "Sally walked to the mailbox." In this case, the verb *walked* moved Sally from wherever she was to the mailbox.

Subject and verb must always agree. Compare the following sentences:

- Lucy has a great idea.
- Lucy and Bill have a great idea.

The verb *to have* must change in order to agree with the subject "Lucy" and "Lucy and Bill."

A writer should always be aware of verbs. Using the right ones in the right way can make the difference between passionate prose and plain prose. Compare the following:

- She was scared.
- Terror filled her heart.

The second sentence paints a clearer picture with the verb *filled*.

Be creative. There are plenty of verbs out there waiting to be used. Your heroine doesn't just walk away after her fight with the hero. She flounces. The villain in your mystery novel doesn't just kill people. He maims and tortures them. He plays with them. Let your imagination find elegant, wonderful ways to express your characters' movements.

Plurals and Possessives

Many people have trouble keeping straight the rules for spelling plurals and possessives. Like the multiplication tables you learned as a child, the best thing to do is learn these rules by heart. You might still have some trouble remembering them from time to time, but you can correct those issues.

Plural Nouns

Most nouns have a singular and a plural form. Most commonly, the plural form is created by adding *s*:

- horse—horses
- dog—dogs
- door—doors

Some nouns that end in *f* and *fe* change these letters to *v* and add *es*:

- thief—thieves
- wife—wives

Nouns ending in *s, sh, ch, x,* and *z* take on *es* as a plural ending. For instance:

- annex—annexes
- witness—witnesses
- beach—beaches

Nouns ending in *y* preceded by a consonant, change *y* to *i* and add *es*; nouns ending in *y* preceded by a vowel simply gain an *s* ending:

- army—armies
- city—cities
- key—keys

Rules for nouns ending in *o* differ. Some form their plural by adding *s*, while others add *es*. For instance:

- hero—heroes
- radio—radios

A few nouns are the same in plural form, such as deer and sheep. Some nouns are always plural, such as acoustics and athletics. Phrases like brother-in-law are made plural by changing the first word: *brothers*-in-law.

Possessives

Noun possessives are much easier to figure out. All nouns show possession by either adding *'s* or *s'*. If the noun is singular, *'s* is used; if the noun is plural, use *s'*. For example:

- brother's wife (one brother)
- brothers' homes (more than one brother)

Additional confusion arises if the noun in the possessive form ends with *s*. For example, which is correct?

- Ross's book
- Ross' book

This depends. Some grammar manuals prefer the former and others the latter. Pick one and stick to it; if you're writing for a specific publisher, you can check with them to see which they prefer.

Active and Passive Voice

All writers have to worry about how their writing impacts their readers. Whether you're writing an insurance statement, a business proposal, or a novel, you have to write with your intended audience in mind. By thinking about your reader and how you want him to react to your work, you create more effective text.

QUESTION

What is the book most writers and editors use as a guide to editing grammar and style?
The Chicago Manual of Style is the most commonly accepted guideline by publishers and writers. It was originally published in 1906 and has been updated every few years since.

Understanding the concepts behind active and passive voice will help you become a more effective writer. While this is good practice for all writers, it's crucial for fiction writers. You have to create reality with your words. Your characters, plot, and setting are counting on you to be able to describe them in a forceful, active manner. While using the best voice is important in dialogue, even narrative descriptions can be enhanced by the right language.

Active Voice

In active voice, the verb shows the action of the subject:

- He ate his supper.
- She walked to the store.
- They drove the car off the cliff.

In these examples, the readers can easily figure out who it was that ate, walked, and drove. Active voice makes the action more direct and immediate. It can help you take your characters from place to place without slowing down the pace.

Passive Voice

There are some cases where you have to use passive voice. Usually writers do this with a form of *to be*:

- She was attacked.
- It is taken care of.
- It will be done.

Sometimes you want to avoid stating who it was that performed the action of the verb. In the first example, maybe you don't want the readers to know who it was that attacked her. But more often than not, withholding this information is not intentional. In this case, see if you can revise the passive voice sentence by figuring out what the subject is: "The killer attacked her in the dark."

Read carefully through your work when you revise. There are many ways to change passive voice to active voice. Don't forget to look for these opportunities. You don't want your readers to feel disassociated from the story.

Common Usage Problems

There are some grammar problems that continue to plague writers. They can be as small as individual words or as large as not understanding what verbs to use. All of them make a writer's job more difficult.

Most of what a writer does is a learned experience. While it's true that passion is necessary to tell the story burning in a writer's soul, all the rest is expression. Talent will take a person to great heights. But even the most talented writer has to know how to say what she wants to say. The more she writes, the better she gets because her experience in language and story-telling grows. No one remembers all the rules all of the time. Learn as many as you can and work on the rest as you edit. Don't be afraid to ask questions. It's one of the best ways to learn.

Its and It's

These two little words seem to be among the most difficult to use correctly. There is a very simple explanation that can help you avoid any confusion between them.

Its is the possessive form of the word it:

- The dog's bowl—Its bowl
- The organization's personnel—Its personnel

That's not to be confused with *it's*, a contracted form of *it is*. For example:

- It is sunny—It's sunny

There and Their

Similarly, people sometimes have trouble figuring out when to use *their* and *there*. *There* is used to show location or presence:

- She's over there.
- There are no more chips.

Their is a possessive form of *they*:

- Kenny and Joanne's home—Their home
- The students' homework—Their homework

Subjects of Confusion

Some words are easily confused with others. Here's a quick rundown of the usual suspects:

- **Affect/effect:** To *affect* something is to influence it. *Effect* is a noun that refers to the outcome of being affected.
- **Leave/let:** Don't use *leave* when you mean *let.* "Leave go of that girl" is incorrect usage.
- **Irregardless:** Although this word is beginning to make its way into English dictionaries, you should use *regardless.*
- **Nauseous/nauseated:** Use *nauseous* as a synonym for "sickening" and *nauseated* as "sickened."
- **Or/nor:** Many people overuse *nor* when *or* should be used instead. "He can't run nor jump" is incorrect. Use nor only in combination with *neither:* "He's neither tall nor short."
- **Regretful/regrettable:** *Regretful* is used to describe a person who is full of regret. *Regrettable* describes an action or circumstance that shouldn't have happened.

There are other words that can be difficult to use; you should carefully analyze them before using them in your text. Check your dictionary if you aren't sure.

Overused Phrases

There are some phrases that have been overused to the point of being comical. While some letter writers may constantly use the same phrases, fiction writers need to be aware of redundancies. Most of these phrases are too stiff and formal to use in modern fiction. Here are a few examples:

- **Due to:** "He was due to leave on the next plane." Use "had to" instead.
- **Different from/than:** "He was different from other people." Use "unlike" instead. Avoid using "different than."
- **As to whether:** "He couldn't tell as to whether she loved him." Use "whether or not" instead.
- **Each and every one:** "Each and every one of them had ice cream." Just use "all" instead.
- **He is a man who:** "He is a man who is very angry." Simply use "he" instead.
- **In terms of:** "He wasn't her type in terms of looks." Just drop the phrase altogether.

ESSENTIAL

There are many other phrases that you should avoid, including your own favorites that you'll find repeated too many times in your text. Keep a sharp eye out for them to keep your story crisp and vibrant.

If you find some of these phrases in your work, look for ways to work around them with fresh text. There's always more than one way to say something. Try to make your way exciting and interesting rather than dull and repetitive.

Rules of Punctuation

Punctuation is the glue that holds together a manuscript, or any other form of writing. Without it, many sentences would be difficult to understand. You wouldn't know where you were supposed to stop. You wouldn't be able to tell the difference between statements and questions. Needless to say, correct punctuation is very important. When you were writing your rough draft, punctuation probably fell by the wayside. Now, as you're revising, it's time to place those commas and periods where they belong.

Common Comma Problems

For one reason or another, the comma is one of the trickiest punctuation marks. There are many rules that govern its usage and placement. Punctuation specialists (English teachers) can go on for hours about the do's and don'ts of using commas.

Proper placement of commas is an art and a science. Because there are specific rules for where and when to use a comma, it's a science. But because comma usage may be subjective, it's also an art. All novel writers know that their writing has certain rhythms. Commas, as well as other punctuation, are an integral aspect of this rhythm. How you punctuate your writing makes the book easier or harder to read.

ESSENTIAL

A good place to go online for punctuation answers is Punctuation Made Simple, at *http://lilt.ilstu.edu/golson/punctuation*, put together by Gary Olson. This site gives you the rundown on major forms of punctuation and how to use them.

Because there are so many rules to using commas, here the rules are broken down to their simplest form:

- If you use a series of three or more items with a single conjunction, use a comma after each item. For instance: green, red, and blue. (Be aware, however, that in some style guides, you'll be advised to drop the final comma: green, red and blue.)
- Enclose expressions that interrupt the flow of the sentence with commas: Going to the store, unless you have a car, can be a long journey.
- Writing out the month, day, and year will require a comma: January 5, 1968.
- A comma should go before a conjunction that introduces an independent clause: The trip was bad, but the food was great.
- In dialogue, a comma separates the spoken words from the modifiers: "Mary went to school," she said. She said, "Mary went to school."
- Use a comma to add phrases to the front or back of your sentence: Surely, she'd listen to reason. She believes in Santa Claus, obviously.

ALERT

While using a conjunction with a comma to separate independent clauses is correct, most writers avoid doing this by creating two separate sentences, or fragments. Grammarians frown on the use of fragments in writing, but they can successfully be employed in novel writing.

Commas are great, but if you use too many, your readers will get thoroughly confused. A good rule of thumb is to avoid using more than three commas in a sentence. If you feel the need to do so, your sentence is too long. It would be better to rethink and revise. Remember that you're trying to create a feeling of movement. When you're writing an action scene where your hero and villain are fighting, the sentences should be even shorter, with very few commas. Here are a few examples of comma overuse:

- The swollen river, fed by streams from the mountains, fraught with ice, was dangerous, if not impossible, to pass.
- Tomorrow's stock market, reaching new highs, falling to new depths, rushing toward disaster, is nothing if not, we predict, overzealous.

One way to adjust these comma-heavy sentences would be to create more than one sentence:

The swollen river was fed by streams from the mountains. Fraught with ice, it was dangerous and difficult to pass.

The meaning remains the same, but there aren't so many commas and the reading is more casual.

Editors look for excessive comma usage as a way to tell how experienced you are as a writer. The more experienced the writer, the fewer the commas. Don't let them catch you on this. Even if you don't have tons of experience, your manuscript can read as though you do.

Quotation Marks

The most important application of quotation marks in fiction is to signal dialogue. For writers, it's not enough to hope readers realize where the dialogue is. They have to be shown. You can imagine the problems that would come up if quotation marks were gone:

> Mary said, I'm going to the house. This bucket is breaking my back. She went back to the house.

Who knows what Mary said, and what she did? Sure, if you reread the section a few times, you'll figure out that Mary said, "I'm going to the house. This bucket is breaking my back." And then she goes to the house. But if you had to read an entire novel like this, how far would you progress? It would have to be pretty interesting for the readers to continue struggling through it.

Double Quotation Marks

Double quotation marks are used for direct quotation. In fiction, this is likely a direct line of dialogue:

- "I'm going home," she said.
- She looked confused. "What about it?"

These marks are also used with the titles of short stories, magazine articles, and songs:

- Have you ever read "Indian Camp" by Ernest Hemingway?
- Is "Never Again" the name of that song?

Finally, you can sometimes use double quotation marks to denote irony, in a sense that something is "so-called."

FACT

Modern writers tend to use italics to set off words or phrases formerly set in quotation marks. For instance: She was really "messy." She was really *messy*. It makes it easier for the reader to tell when someone is speaking. Writers also use italics to denote thought.

Single Quotation Marks

Double quotation marks are used to enclose a direct quotation. But what if there is a quotation within a quotation? In this case, single quotation marks have to be used: "He read the book and said, 'That was great,' and so I gave it to him." This is the only way that single quotation marks are used in American English. On their own, the right-hand quotation mark is known as an apostrophe, and it is used in possessive forms (Mike's, students') and contractions (they're, I've).

Correct Placement

Here are basic rules for using quotation marks with other punctuation:

- Quotation marks always go outside of the comma or period: "It's time." "It's time," she said.
- With a semicolon or colon, quotation marks come first: Read the short story "Days of Our Lives"; discuss. Take a look at "The Hour": Isn't it a beautiful story?
- For question and exclamation marks, it depends on whether the mark belongs to the section inside the quotation marks: "What did she want to know?" Have you read "The Hour"?

Punctuating Clauses

Keeping sentences from running on together can be complicated. Some people feel that it's just a matter of style. They consider their short, choppy sentences or long, epic-poem sentences to be a matter of personal choice.

To a certain extent, that's true. Every novel should have a combination of short and long sentences. The short, choppy kind is good for action. The long, epic-poem kind is good for emotional difficulties. Like dialogue and narrative, these two techniques should enhance each other. No one wants to read too much of either of them.

ESSENTIAL

If you're thinking of writing like the classics, forget it. Most people wouldn't be able to get a classic novel past one of today's editors. Sentences were longer fifty years ago. So was length of narrative versus dialogue. These books, though highly prized for their literary merit, aren't good examples of how a contemporary novelist should write.

But how do you decide whether a sentence is too long or too short? How do you know if it needs breaking up or if it's best to join it with another sentence? Don't worry so much about using complete sentences. Sentence fragments can work very nicely. The most important thing is that they make sense. As far as being too long, if you read the sentence out loud and you have to pause for breath, it's too long.

Colons and Semicolons

The colon may be used to introduce a list or a long formal quotation. You can also use it after a formal salutation in a letter. Numbers used to indicate hours, minutes, and seconds—12:30:10—also use colons.

The comma has almost replaced the semicolon in contemporary writing, but there are some circumstances when only a semicolon will do. A semicolon is used between clauses in a compound sentence:

I found the evidence; you can't look the other way.

The semicolon can also be used to replace the serial comma if one or more of the terms in the series include other punctuation:

She bought plump, fragrant oranges; juicy, succulent nectarines; and ruddy apples.

Punctuation for Pauses

Creating a pause in writing is more like drawing a breath than a complete stop. It's where the hero takes time to think over the problem. It's the unspoken moment that follows a first kiss.

It's not something you'll want to use in every sentence. Too many pauses would take away the effect and make the reader feel disengaged from the story. But the right number will bring a tear or a sigh. It's the response you're looking for as you present your reader with an emotional moment.

If you think back on your life, you'll see how these poignant pauses come around. Sometimes, it can happen as you're thinking, or as you're speaking. It can happen for your characters that way too. Even the most despicable villain can take a moment to realize the completion of his terrible plan.

When a Dash Would Be Appropriate

Dashes (—) are often used in fiction to create the effect of an abrupt stop, when you need the reader to realize that something important has happened. Maybe the hero just realized that he is in love with the heroine. Maybe a conversation has ended suddenly, leaving a feeling of ill omen behind. Here's an example:

He saw her walking toward him. She looked better than he remembered. He searched for somewhere to put the mop he was holding. What an awful time for her to—

"Hi, Max. Nice mop."

When a dash is used to indicate a break, no period is needed.

FACT

Have you wondered how to type the long dash? Try typing two or three hyphens together, and see if they are auto-corrected into the long dash. Otherwise, you can do this manually. On a PC, use the keys Ctrl + Alt + hyphen. On a Mac, try Apple (command) key + Option + the number pad hyphen.

Ellipses

Another option for making a pause is to use ellipses (. . .). You may use this punctuation mark to indicate a thoughtful pause or a lingering part of speech. It's not the abrupt cutoff caused by the dash. It's something that the person has chosen not to say. Perhaps because the person he's speaking to would already know it. Perhaps because the speaker has lost his nerve.

If the ellipsis is used in the middle of a sentence, there is a space left before each dot and after the line of dots. There is also a space between each dot. Space, dot, space, dot, space, dot, space. It would look like this:

"You left me . . . what should I have done?"

When the ellipsis is used at the end of a sentence, it finishes the sentence and no other punctuation is needed. For instance:

"I looked for you . . ."

Question and Exclamation Marks

A question mark is placed at the end of a phrase to indicate that it's a question. Easy enough, right? There's not much to learn about question marks, other than the fact that novelists tend to overuse them. Try not to use an abundance of question marks. Obviously, if your characters ask questions, go ahead and use the question mark in the dialogue. But don't go overboard with question marks in the narrative.

Exclamation marks are equally overused. Many times, even though a character is very excited, a period is just as appropriate. An entire conversation filled with exclamation points will tell an editor that you haven't been writing very long.

On the other hand, if you save your exclamations for important occasions, they can really help you make your point. An exclamation point can express irony, surprise, and dissatisfaction.

"Imagine how stark that would be!"

It can also be used after a command.

"Go and get it!"

Brackets and Parentheses

Other than the physical use of brackets to hold up bookshelves, most fiction writers don't use brackets very much. But their traditional use is to enclose words and phrases that are independent of a sentence. This can include explanatory notes, omissions, and comments. For instance:

The following day [Monday] was good for her.

Note that no punctuation is needed with brackets, unless they contain an entire sentence.

For "aside" comments and other phrases that don't belong in the sentence itself, it's best to use parentheses:

She asked him for help (or so he thought).

The house payment was past due (along with everything else) but the bank wouldn't work with them.

Don't use a comma, semicolon, or colon in front of the opening parenthesis (the singular form of the upright punctuation). You can use a comma, semicolon, colon, or period after the last parenthesis.

By including subject matter in this way, the author calls attention to what is inside the parentheses. Of course, commas or long dashes may also be used to set off parenthetical text.

Showing Emphasis

There are different ways to emphasize words in your text. But before you think about how to do it, consider when to do it. Most fiction writers use emphasis in dialogue. It portrays the way something is said as well as exactly what is said. Sometimes, you'll want to use emphasis in your character's thoughts. You'll rarely use it in narrative.

Before the advent of word processing, putting emphasis in text was much different than it is today. Writers today have various options.

Capital Letters

Some writers still use capital letters to emphasize text. Most editors don't really like this. There are some cases where capital letters are used in text (besides proper nouns or the beginning of sentences). These aren't so much for emphasis as distinction: academic degrees (M.D.; Ph.D.; M.A.); initials that take the place of a proper noun (J. P. Magnus); states or countries referred to by initial (NC or USA).

Showing emphasis this way was popular when people used typewriters. But today, we have so much more.

Italics

Basically, italics is a style of type. Its *slanting letters* create emphasis by appearing different from the text around it. Most word processors do this fairly easily. Just look for the big *I* in your toolbar.

The beauty of italics is very simple. It appears to show the tone of speech, then disappears. Readers have come to know what this means. If it's in dialogue, it shows readers what words or thoughts carry particular emphasis. It's also come to represent thoughts shared with the reader directly from the point of view of the character. In science fiction or paranormal fiction, italics are frequently used to create the impression of telepathy (mental communication).

ESSENTIAL

Another type of emphasis is using bold type and underlining. Fiction writers rarely use these in text, and underlining is particularly discouraged. If you want to be sure, check the submission guidelines of the publishers you're planning to submit your work to.

Expressing Numbers

All novelists use numbers at one time or another. You have the street address where the murder took place, the amount of money stolen from the bank. Even in mainstream fiction, you could have to talk about age or how many slices of pizza your character ate. While numbers will never be as important to writers as words, it's important that they're expressed in clear ways that everyone understands.

Numbers Within a Sentence

Always spell out numbers from one through ninety-nine. Use figures to express definite amounts as well as numbers over ninety-nine:

- Eighty years
- 7,000 members
- 3.25 feet

Spell out ordinal numbers (numbers that refer to order, like first, second, third, and so on). Also note that all numbers in dialogue must be spelled out.

Time of Day and Date

When writing down the exact time, use numerals and the letters a.m., p.m. or A.M., P.M. (to create small caps, go to Format, Font, and check the box next to small caps). For instance: 1:30 a.m; 6:30 P.M. When you spell out the time, however, abbreviations should be dropped: "She left the station at one-thirty in the afternoon."

Sums of Money

Everybody likes to think about large sums of money. When writing a large sum in your text, anything over a million is spelled out. For instance: He won 12 million dollars. (Or: He won $12 million.) Don't use the dollar sign if you write out the word "dollars."

Don't use figures and words for sums of money. If you aren't sure your reader will understand what you're saying, you can use parentheses. For instance: I have forty (40) dollars.

CHAPTER 19

Avenues to Publication

There have never been so many avenues for getting a novel in print, but it remains as competitive as ever to sell a novel to one of the major publishing houses or to a prestigious small press. Still, agents and editors are eager to find the next breakthrough book by an unknown author.

Publishing: A Changing World

Titles from the "big six" and other major publishing houses still dominate *The New York Times* bestseller lists each month. But there are occasional examples of stunning success for books that take a less traditional track.

For instance, William P. Young's self-published Christian novel *The Shack* sold more than a million copies. And Lisa Genova's self-published debut novel *Still Alice* was bought by Simon & Schuster and debuted at No. 5 on the *New York Times* bestseller list. When Brunonia Barry's novel *The Lace Reader* turned into a self-published blockbuster, publishers came calling. Barry sold that book and a future one to Harper Collins for a cool $2 million.

QUOTE

> "We were emboldened by our ignorance. We knew just enough to get going, but not enough to stop us."—Brunonia Barry, on how she and her husband self published *The Lace Reader*

Industry watcher Bowker reported that in 2009, 1,052,803 books were published in the United States; 764,448 of them came from "non-traditional channels," a mix of micro-publishers, self-publishers, and reprints of public domain titles. It was in 2008 that the number of print-on-demand books exceeded books from traditional publishers for the first time.

Here are some terms you will hear for different kinds of publishers, with an overview of how they deal with authors and manuscripts.

- **Commercial publishers:** These range from large to small publishers who buy the rights to the book and pay the author a royalty on sales. They often also pay an advance against future royalties, up front. Most commercial publishers are very picky and publish only a tiny fraction of manuscripts which are typically submitted to them by literary agents. Commercial publishers edit, package, publish, distribute, and market their books, and they don't charge their authors fees.
- **Self-publishing services:** These are companies that charge the author for all costs associated with publication; they handle marketing, distribution, and warehousing. They usually offer editing services, as

well as help creating a cover and obtaining an ISBN number. Using a self-publishing service can be more economical than vanity publishing. The author retains all rights and keeps the proceeds from all sales.

- **Vanity publishers:** Typically, a vanity press publishes any book that the author is willing to pay to have published. These companies charge authors a fee to publish the book, and more to cover all the expenses associated with printing and binding. Vanity publishing is usually more costly than self-publishing. Authors retain all proceeds from sales and own the rights to their work. Vanity publishers provide a service and rarely reject manuscripts for quality.

- **Subsidy publishers:** These publishers operate with a hybrid business model. Typically they charge authors to print and bind the book but cover other expenses such as editing and distribution. They usually pay the writer a royalty for sales. Some subsidy publishers screen manuscripts; others publish virtually every manuscript submitted to them. Completed books become the property of the subsidy publisher.

QUESTION

What is a royalty?
A royalty is a share (or percentage) paid to a writer from the proceeds from the sale of a book. Royalties are calculated by multiplying the price (sometimes the full retail price, sometimes the wholesale price) of a book by the royalty percentage. So suppose you write a book that retails for $16.00 and the royalty in your contact is five percent of the retail price; you earn $.80 for each book sold.

There have never been more options for getting your book to readers. Here are some options:

- Publish it with large or medium-sized publisher
- Publish it with a small press
- Publish it as an e-book
- Publish it yourself as print on demand

- Publish it through a vanity or subsidy press
- Win a contest where the prize is a book contract

Publishing with a Traditional Publisher

Publishing your first novel with a major publishing house is every author's dream. You've labored on it, poured your heart and soul into it—there's no bigger thrill than to see your name on a hard cover and a reputable publishing house's logo on the spine.

With so many mergers in the publishing industry, by 2010 there were six large publishing houses, known as the "big six," all of which were owned by even larger media conglomerates.

The six major publishing houses that dominate the commercial publishing business publish books by brand-name authors and churn out most of the books that make their way to the bestseller lists.

Literary agents make it their business to not only know the imprints at each of the big six, but also to know the tastes and literary preferences of the acquiring editors who work there. By browsing the books listed on these big publishers' websites, you too can get a sense for where your book might find a happy home.

ESSENTIAL

Browse Publishers Marketplace regularly (*www.publishersmarketplace. com*) to get a feeling for the kinds of deals being cut by publishers who might be a good fit for your kind of novel.

Traditional publishers like those in the big six typically pay the writer an advance against sales. Royalties begin to accrue only after that advance is earned out through sales of the book.

Together, the big six publish tens of thousands of novels each year. Here is a brief introduction to the big six and an overview of their fiction imprints.

Hachette Book Group

Hachette is owned by the French Company Hachette Livre. Formerly Warner Books (when it was part of Time Warner), Hachette is the smallest of the big six. It has several imprints that publish novels.

- Little Brown & Company, which published authors like Louisa May Alcott and Emily Dickinson, today is home to blockbuster commercial authors like Stephenie Meyer and James Paterson as well as many top ranked literary authors.
- Grand Central publishes literary and commercial fiction, and it has within it several imprints including 5 Spot (fiction targeted at women), Springboard Press (fiction for Baby Boomers), and Forever (romance).
- Orbit publishes science fiction and fantasy. Established in 1974, Orbit UK was the British publisher of many of the biggest names in modern sci-fi, such as Iain M. Banks, Ken Macleod, and Charles Stross. Their fantasy authors include international bestsellers Terry Brooks and Trudi Canavan. They publish approximately eighty titles per year.

HarperCollins

HarperCollins is part of Rupert Murdoch's media holdings. Several of its imprints focus on fiction.

- William Morrow publishes commercial fiction, including authors Dennis Lehane, Neil Gaiman, Elmore Leonard, and Laura Lippman.
- Avon publishes light romance and women's fiction, and has a particularly strong stable of romance writers.
- Harper Publishing is the flagship imprint of HarperCollins; it publishes a wide range of fiction, including works by Barbara Kingsolver and Armistead Maupin.
- HarperTeen publishes novels for "teens and tweens," one of the fastest growing categories in publishing.

MacMillan Publishers

MacMillan encompasses a group of publishing houses owned by the German publishing conglomerate Holtzbrinck. Many of its imprints publish novels.

- St. Martin's Press publishes commercial fiction; its Minotaur and Thomas Dunne imprints publish more crime novels annually than any other imprint.
- Henry Holt & Company publishes many fiction authors, including Richard North Patterson, Michael Gruber, and Booker Prize winner Hilary Mantel, who wrote a historical novel set in King Henry VII's court called, *Wolf Hall.*
- Farrar, Strauss & Giroux publishes literary novels, including works by Alice McDermott, Jamaica Kincaid, and Ted Hughes.
- Picador publishes a wide range of titles, including general fiction, mysteries, and thrillers. Its authors have included Angela Carter, Thomas Pynchon, and Bret Easton Ellis.
- Tor/Forge is best known for its fantasy and science fiction novels, including series like the Conan novels; it also publishes horror, westerns, and crime fiction.

Penguin Group

The Penguin Group is a division of the British conglomerate Pearson, and has been publishing books since the late 1800s. It publishes novels under a range of imprints.

- Riverhead Books publishes literary and commercial fiction. Its authors include Anne Lamott, Walter Mosley, and Chang-rae Lee.
- Dutton, founded in Boston in 1852, originally published religious titles. Now it publishes a wide range of titles, including literary and commercial fiction. Its titles include works by Harlan Coben, Ken Follett, Jerome Dickey, and John Lescroart.
- G. P. Putnam's Sons churns out Penguin's big, bestselling novels.

- The Viking Press, founded in 1925, published John Steinbeck's *Grapes of Wrath* and the first American edition of James Joyce's *Finnegan's Wake*; Viking now publishes literary and commercial novels, including Sue Monk Kidd's *The Secret Life of Bees*, Helen Fielding's *Bridget Jones's Diary*, and Geraldine Brooks's *March*.
- Firebird, its tag line "Where fantasy takes flight," publishes fantasy novels, including many titles for young adults.
- NAL (New American Library), founded in 1948, publishes commercial fiction, and has subdivisions that publish romance and science fiction. Its science fiction list includes works by authors Jim Butcher, S. M. Stirling, and Karen Chance.
- Berkley Books, founded in 1955, publishes a wide range of fiction; it publishes paperback editions of books by bestselling authors, including Tom Clancy, Robin Cook, and Patricia Cornwell.

Random House

Random House is a subsidiary of the German media conglomerate Bertelsmann. Many of its notable imprints publish fiction.

- Knopf Doubleday Publishing Group, is known for publishing literary and commercial fiction. It publishes Dan Brown, Chuck Palahniuk, John Grisham, and Carolyn Parkhurst.
- Del Ray Books has published science fiction, fantasy, romance, and commercial fiction since 1977. It publishes books based on *Star Wars* as well as books by sci-fi greats like Isaac Asimov, Philip K. Dick, and Robert Heinlein.
- Bantam Dell, established in 1945, publishes all kinds of genre and commercial fiction for adults. Bantam Dell publishes works by Dean Koontz, Lisa Gardner, and Louis L'Amour.
- Ballantine Books was established in 1952 as primarily a publisher of paperbacks; today it publishes a wide range of commercial fiction including science fiction and fantasy in all formats. Its novelists include Suzanne Brockmann, Julie Garwood, Tess Gerritsen, Kristin Hannah, Anne Perry, and Jeff Shaara.

Simon & Schuster

Simon & Schuster is owned by the media conglomerate CBS Corporation. It releases nearly 2,000 titles a year and has a range of imprints.

- Scribner is still a revered imprint in literary publishing. Its authors have included Ernest Hemingway, Edith Wharton, F. Scott Fitzgerald, and more recently Stephen King.
- Pocket Books was the pioneer in mass market paperback publishing. Today it publishes a wide range of commercial fiction, including works by Mary Higgins Clark, Vince Flynn, Sandra Brown, and Julia London.
- Atria publishes women's fiction, commercial fiction, and a range of genre fiction. It has published works by Jennifer Weiner, Zane, and Malla Nunn.
- Touchstone/Fireside publishes a wide range of commercial fiction. Its authors include Philippa Gregory, J. A. Jance, Susan Rebecca White, Brian Gruley, Robert Dugoni, Ursula Hegi, and Joanna Trollope.

Beyond the Big Six

There are hundreds of other presses—small and medium-sized publishers, university presses, and more—that have reputations for excellence in publishing literary, commercial, and genre fiction. These presses typically enter into contracts with their authors, and pay an advance against future sales. Advances are usually far smaller than the typical advance from major publishing houses. Royalties begin to accrue only after that advance is earned out through sales of the book.

ESSENTIAL

One of the most comprehensive and up-to-date resources on publishers is the annually updated *Writer's Market* published by Writer's Digest Books. Information is also available online at *www.writersmarket.com* where, for a fee, you can research publishers and also keep track of your submissions.

There hundreds of small and medium sized independent publishers. Here are just a few:

- Harlequin publishes a hefty proportion of series romance and women's fiction. Owned by Canadian newspaper publishing company Torstar, it has many imprints specializing in romance subgenres like historical, intrigue, and romantic suspense.
- Soho Press publishes literary mysteries and fiction. Their Soho Crime imprint specializes in mysteries set in foreign countries.
- Bella Books is a good example of a small press serving a niche market; they publish a range of general fiction as well as erotica, fantasy, and romance for lesbians.
- Nightshade Books is a small press that has been publishing science fiction, fantasy, and horror since the late 1990s. It publishes between thirty and forty titles a year.
- Kensington Publishing Corp is a mid-sized independent press. It publishes a wide range of fiction, including romance and women's fiction, erotica, African-American, as well as science fiction and thrillers.
- Grove Press, which was started in the 1950s and published such literary greats as William S. Burroughs and D. H. Lawrence, is now an imprint of Grove Atlantic and publishes hardcover and paperback literary and commercial fiction.

E-Publishers

Publishers offer books in electronic format, known as e-books, which readers can purchase and download to e-readers, computers, or other devices. E-books are increasingly available through publishers' websites and at online bookstores. Some authors are being offered e-book-only contracts, and some publishers put out only e-books.

The most popular genres for the e-book format have been romance and erotica. Going straight to e-book format is appealing for authors just starting out in those genres, and for authors who see it as a first step to commercial print publication.

Some publishers specialize in publishing e-books. Many of these e-publishers don't require manuscripts to be agented, so you can submit your work directly to them. Harlequin was one of the first publishers to establish an imprint focusing only on e-books when, in 2009, it started Carina Press, publishing historical romance and historical fiction.

Increasingly there are avenues for authors to publish their books in electronic format, bypassing publishers and agents entirely. For instance, in 2010 Amazon started its e-book subsidiary, MobiPocket, through which authors can convert manuscripts, to which they own the rights, to Amazon's proprietary electronic format.

E-books are quickly increasing their market share, and the audience for this format (readers who have the appropriate technology and disposition) is growing. In 2010 Amazon reported sales of e-books exceeded sales of hard covers for the first time.

Though an e-book never gets put on a table at a big box or independent bookstore where the cover might catch the interest of an unsuspecting reader, and they are unlikely to get reviewed in mainstream media, the e-book format effectively removes the distribution barriers to self-published works. If authors can effectively spread the word about their work, then it can be quickly, easily, and inexpensively downloaded on a very popular device.

Most e-book original contracts don't include an up-front advance. The author typically receives royalties as books are sold. If you decide to publish your novel as an e-book, be sure to research the publisher and carefully examine the contract you are offered.

Self-Publishing with Print-on-Demand

Print-on-demand (POD) uses digital printing technology that enables books to be printed in minutes. They can even be printed at the point of sale. Though many small presses use POD technology to print their books, as an author you can contract directly with POD service providers to use that same technology to self-publish your book, from getting an ISBN number, to printing and binding the pages. How you distribute the book is up to you—and this is the one disadvantage of self-publishing POD. If you have a ready audience and channels for distributing your book, then this may not be an issue.

QUESTION

What is an ISBN number?
An International Standard Book Number (ISBN) is a unique thirteen digit identifier assigned to a book by the U. S. ISBN Agency; booksellers need that number in order to offer a book for sale. If you are going to distribute your book yourself you don't need an ISBN.

Most POD service providers charge a fee, some offer templates, and many provide editing, cover design, or marketing services for additional fees. This is a service business, so manuscripts usually are not screened. How much of the proceeds from the sale of each book goes to the author depends on the business model for the POD service provider. Some sell books directly to consumers and a portion of the sale price goes to the author; others sell books to the author who, in turn, sells them to consumers.

The average POD book sells fewer than 200 copies. Often bookstores will not carry self-published books because they are often not discounted and cannot be returned. Libraries will consider purchasing them if there is a demand from their patrons. Getting a book review in the mainstream press or a feature article about the book or the author in public media is especially difficult. On top of that, most POD services do not accept returns; big-box stores and independent booksellers rely on being able to return unsold books, so this can prevent them from being willing to stock your book.

But self-publishing POD is a good alternative for authors who want to avoid the time-consuming standard publishing process, do not need to sell a large number of books, or who will be distributing the book privately.

Here are some reputable POD services:

- iUniverse offers what it calls "supported self-publishing," including editorial, design, and marketing services as well as print on demand. It was founded in 1999 and, at this writing, is owned by Author Solutions, the parent company of Author House.
- Xlibris, Like iUniverse, is owned by Author Solutions, the parent company of Author House.
- Lulu.com, a popular and cost-effective service, says it "empower[s] authors to publish their work themselves for free with complete editorial and copyright control." Founded in 2002, they offer print and e-book publishing tools. At this writing it was independently owned.

If you decide to use a POD service, read your contract carefully and know what you are getting yourself into. Ideally, you should be looking at these questions:

- Does the contract enable you to keep all the rights to your book?
- Are you locked in for a period of time, or are you free to end the contract at any time without penalty?
- Do you own the files that are created to publish your book, or is there a fee you would have to pay to get them if you decide to leave the service?
- What will it cost you, at a minimum, and what will you get for that amount?
- Are there additional charges for including graphics?
- Does the cost include cover design; can you provide your own cover design if you wish?
- Does it cost additional to distribute the book through one of the standard distribution channels like Amazon or Ingram?
- What will it cost to ship books that customers purchase?
- Do you have control over the design of the book?
- Does the publisher set the retail price, or can you set it?
- Are the printing costs reasonable?
- Can you set the price so you offer a discount to booksellers?
- How much will you receive from the sale of each book?
- Does the finished book look professional?

Compare several services, get your hands on some of their titles to see their production values, and research recommendations from their customers before you decide.

QUESTION

What are vanity presses?
Vanity presses advertise their services all over the Internet and in all of the magazines for writers. Their services can be quite a bit more expensive than self-publishing, and authors should read their contracts carefully to be prepared for the charges that accrue, and also to be sure that all rights are retained. Remember, best case, you will get exactly what you pay for.

Contests

Winning a contest with your unpublished work can give you that one extra bit of cachet that will make an agent or editor give your work serious consideration. Some contests offer a prize of actually publishing your novel.

But there are contests and there are contests. Most of them charge a fee to enter, and some are scams. But others are completely on the up and up. If the first prize is a publishing contract, do your research and make sure that this is a publisher that you really want to publish your book.

Authors have launched successful careers by winning a contest. For instance, Julia Spencer-Fleming won the St. Martin's Press/Malice Domestic Best First Traditional Mystery Contest. Her debut novel *In the Bleak Midwinter* won the award and was published by St. Martin's Minotaur. It went on to win a whole batch of prestigious awards, and her subsequent novels have done quite well, with critical acclaim and multiple award nominations.

Other excellent contests include one offered by Delacorte Press. It awards as first prize a publishing contract to the winner of its First Young Adult Novel contest. Amazon Breakthrough Novel Award, offered with Penguin Group, has offered a publishing contract for a work of general fiction.

But writer beware! There are so many fake contests and awards out there, designed mainly to fleece writers. Make sure any contest you enter is legit. The Preditors and Editors website (*www.pred-ed.com/pubctst.htm*) evaluates writing contests based on a set of criteria and feedback from their users.

CHAPTER 20

Pitching, Querying, and Presenting the Final Manuscript

In order to interest an agent in representing your novel or an editor in publishing it, you need to prepare a pitch. A perfect pitch contains between one and three sentences that encapsulates the essence of your novel in such a compelling way that the listener (or reader) will ask to hear more and can hardly wait to read the manuscript.

Crafting Your Pitch

Agents and editors have notoriously short attention spans, so the perfect pitch for a novel can be delivered in less time than it takes to ride an elevator from the first floor to the sixth.

A well-crafted pitch communicates the essence of your novel. Just as the agent who listens to your pitch can judge whether or not he is interested in reading a manuscript, you use your pitch to separate the agents who resonate to the kind of novel you've written from the ones who don't. Finding *the right* agent, the one who loves your work and the kinds of books you write, is critical to your long-term career.

A pitch is not a retelling of your story. "You see, there's this woman, she's very lonely, and she lives in the desert with her pet iguana, and one day a man shows up and wants to sell her something and she knows something is up and . . . and . . . and . . . ." Keep going like that and you'll put your listener to sleep.

ESSENTIAL

A pitch is supposed to interest and intrigue, not tell the whole story of your novel. It's okay to start with the event that gets your story started, but after that stick to the high points.

A pitch has to be a grabber, a short description in just a few sentences that intrigues and engages. It should be brief, punchy, specific, and you should have more to say when you hook your listener and he says, "Boy, that sure sounds interesting. Tell me more."

Are you thinking: "But I couldn't possibly do my novel justice in a few sentences"? That may be, but if you want a top agent or editor to be interested in reading your manuscript, you need to make your best effort.

Elements of a Pitch

Beyond all the artistry in your pitch, it should also contain these basic elements:

1. The title of your novel
2. The genre (literary novel, romance, woman's fiction, etc.)

3. The name of the main character and the character's problem, desire, or goal
4. The bad guy, obstacle, or situation that stands in the way of your main character getting what she wants

Examples of Pitches

A pitch should be short, specific, and intriguing. Take this, for example: "*Going for the Jugular* is an adventure novel that tells the story of Vincent Pride, a recently divorced man who searches for adventure and finds love." This pitch is plenty short, but it's too generic. It could fit any of hundreds of books published this year, last year, and the year before.

An improved version might begin: "*Going for the Jugular* is an adventure novel that tells the story of Vincent Pride, a recently divorced linguist who travels to India seeking enlightenment and instead finds the woman of his dreams." Specifics help; be sure to include those special things that make your book unique—in this case, linguistics and travel to India.

Here are examples of pitches for some familiar novels:

- *Bridges of Madison County* is a literary romance in which Iowa housewife Francesca Johnson, stuck in her routines and a humdrum marriage, meets a handsome photographer who turns out to be her soul mate, and must choose between true love and her family's needs.
- *The Wizard of Oz* is a young adult fantasy novel in which a cyclone transports Dorothy Gale, a Kansas farm girl, to the magical land of Oz where she sets out on a dangerous journey to find a wizard with the power to send her home.
- In the thriller *The Da Vinci Code*, symbologist Robert Langdon travels across France and England in a race to decode a secret, zealously guarded by a clandestine society since the days of Christ.
- What if dinosaurs could be cloned? In *Jurassic Park*, a sci-fi adventure novel, renowned paleontologist Dr. Alan Grant journeys to a new theme park whose creators have claimed to have done just that, and gets stranded there among raptors that turn out to be as intelligent and dangerous as his theories predicted.

Tips for Writing the Perfect Pitch

Here are some tips for making your pitch as strong as it can be:

- Keep it short but specific: Remember, a six-floor ride in an imaginary elevator is all the time you have; but in that short time be as specific and as intriguing as you can.
- Highlight the elements that make your novel unique: Exotic setting? A main character with an intriguing hobby or special talent? A twist on a classic theme? Include the elements that make your novel stand out from the pack.
- Leave out most of the details: Concentrate on the main character and your main story and include only those details that make your story intriguing or unique.
- Don't try to tell the whole story: Keep your eye on the goal of getting someone interested enough in your story to ask to read the entire manuscript.
- Hold the superlatives and immodest comparisons: Avoid promising the next *New York Times* bestseller or the next *Harry Potter*.

Be Prepared to Go On

If your pitch goes well, the agent will want to know more. So be prepared to answer questions like these:

- Have you finished writing and revising the novel?
- What happens at the end?
- Fans of what current books or authors will like your novel?
- Have you workshopped this manuscript—given it to a critique group or a professional editor?
- Has this book been pitched to publishers or other agents? How did they respond?

Practice Makes Perfect

Before you go out into the world and pitch your novel, practice, and then practice some more until delivering it is as easy and automatic for you as punching a button on a jukebox and having a song come out. Commit the ideas to memory, but you want the words to feel natural, not rote.

ALERT

A pitch shouldn't feel like a sprint. We all talk too fast when we get nervous. So practice consciously slowing down. When the time comes, you'll be able to fight the urge to race to the finish line.

Practice in front of a mirror. Practice for friends. If you belong to a writing group, practice for your fellow writers and ask them to critique your performance. Pay attention to things like:

- **Eye contact.** If you find yourself staring off into space, or into your lap, or closing your eyes while you deliver your spiel, you're doing it wrong.
- **Enthusiasm.** Try to convey your own enthusiasm for your work but don't gush. A soft sell works best.
- **Relax.** Or try to. Practicing until the pitch comes out automatically will help.

From Pitch to Query

A query letter is the traditional way that authors approach agents and editors in writing. A query letter begins with a pitch that continues for two or so additional paragraphs of summary, and follows up with additional detail. Each query should be personal, addressed to a specific agent. It should include the reason why you have chosen to send this particular manuscript to this particular agent.

Parts of a Query Letter

Many writing books provide sound advice for structuring a query letter. The advice given below is fairly standard. For more detail and sample query letters, have a look at *The Writer's Digest Guide to Query Letters*, *Jeff Herman's Guide to Book Publishers, Editors, and Literary Agents*, or *The Everything® Guide to Writing a Book Proposal*.

Here are some paragraph-by-paragraph guidelines for structuring your query letter:

1. Open with the pitch discussed earlier in this chapter.
2. Continue with two or three paragraphs of synopsis that hit the high points of your plot.
3. Tell how you think this book is unique, and what you see as the potential market.
4. Insert tailored content that personalizes the query, explaining why you are pitching this manuscript to this particular agent.
5. Include, at the end, a mini-biography of yourself, highlighting the aspects that are relevant to the novel you are pitching ("Like my protagonist, I was once a cheerleader and now coach the sport nationally"); keep it short.
6. Be sure to include your full name and how to contact you.

When you're done, spell check and grammar check. Then print it out (single-spaced) and read it through to be sure it flows and makes sense, and presents your work in the best possible light. The entire query letter should fit on one printed page.

Preparing a Summary

If you do a good job presenting your pitch or query, an interested editor or agent will probably ask you to send along a summary or synopsis. They don't mean the kind of thirty-page synopsis you may have written when you started working on the book. They mean a short (two to three pages) summary.

Writers often find this short document excruciatingly difficult to write. But you probably will get asked for one, so why not prepare it in advance so you can send it right out when you're asked?

A summary should not be long. If you can do it in a page, single-spaced, that's great. Most people need two or three pages. The purpose of it is to give someone an overview of the book that is so compelling that they will want to read the whole thing. It should reveal to an agent whether this is the kind of book he likes to represent; it should show an editor whether this is the kind of book the publishing house is interested in publishing.

Your summary should tell the story of your novel, all of it, fast forward, from the beginning, hitting all the major plot points and characters and, yes, telling how it ends. Use the typical jacket copy on novels as your model, only this will be much longer and tell all of the plot, not just tease.

Synopsis: An Example

Here is an example, the start of a synopsis for *Never Tell a Lie* by Hallie Ephron. Read it to get the feel for what yours should be like.

Ivy Rose knows her husband David is indulging her when he agrees to throw a yard sale to get rid of the years of clutter left behind by the previous owner of their Victorian ark of a home. After all, she's nine months pregnant. She has suffered several miscarriages, but this time she's healthy and so is the baby.

At the yard sale, an attractive young woman who is also hugely pregnant shows up and introduces herself as Melinda White. Melinda follows Ivy around at the yard sale, reminding her that they knew each other in high school. David notices how Melinda's presence makes Ivy increasingly uncomfortable, and he offers to show Melinda the inside of the house.

A few days later, the police, responding to a missing person's report, find Melinda's car still parked a block from the Rose's home.

Of course, that synopsis went on for three pages. It revealed everything, including what really happened to Melinda White.

Did you notice that it was written in the present tense and that it was not written as scenes or as drama? A good summary does just what you've been trying *not* to do when you wrote the book—tell instead of show.

You might, for instance, focus on describing how the book opens, three or four major turning points, the exciting finish, and how the story is tied up at the end. Be sure to talk about the main character, his goal, and the obstacles that stand in his way.

If your summary is running too long, weed out the details that aren't essential. Subplots and minor characters don't need to be explained. If you've spent any time talking about the author, you can remove that, too. You're trying to reveal your novel's backbone, its essential essence, not write the *Readers Digest* condensed version.

Preparing the Final Manuscript

Your book is written and edited. For most writers, the next step is getting published. Many things change in the publishing world, and these days many agents and editors accept manuscript excerpts and manuscripts in electronic format. It's important to learn how to prepare a submission-ready manuscript.

If you never intend to submit your book to publishers, you may not want to bother with this section. On the other hand, it's always good to have the information.

Make an Impression

Perhaps you met that editor or agent at a writing conference and impressed him with your personal charm. You pitched your manuscript so eloquently that now he wants to read it. Make a good impression by sending a manuscript that makes you look like a pro.

Attention to detail includes whether you send your work electronically or in hard copy, and what format it is in. Many agents and publishing houses have manuscript format guidelines right on their website that tell you what format is correct for that agent or publisher. If so, then follow what's posted to the letter. If not, here are certain specific guidelines for submissions. Most of them follow common sense.

Document Setup

There's nothing fancy about the format of manuscript pages. Below are some simple guidelines.

- Margins: One-inch margins all around
- Font: 12-point Times New Roman or 10-point Courier is standard
- Header at the top of each page: Flush left should be your name, the title of your book, your contact information (use two lines if needed); flush right should be the page number.

Jane Smith—Manuscript Title—jsmith@email.com   1

- Number the pages.
- Footer at the bottom of each page: Normally there is none.
- Title Page: Centered in the middle of an otherwise blank and unnumbered page put the manuscript title, your name, the date, and your contact information (e-mail, phone number, address).
- Line spacing: Double space between lines.
- Chapter openings: Start each chapter on a fresh page, space down a few lines then type chapter title, then begin with the first paragraph.
- First line of the first paragraph of a chapter should be flush left.
- First line of every paragraph except for the first in a chapter should have a hanging indent of five or six spaces.
- Single space between words.
- Single space between sentences in the same paragraph; double spacing after a period went out decades ago.

- To indicate italicized or bolded text, simply italicize or bold the font (underlining and double-underlining are not necessary).
- Insert two blank lines between scenes; you may want to add a special character like an asterisk (*) to be sure that the scene breaks show up when they fall at the bottom of a page.
- The electronic file should be a .doc file (Microsoft Word); all word processing software allows you to save to or export your file to this format
- Don't worry about widowed lines; let the page breaks fall naturally where they fall.

QUESTION

Should the title page be numbered?
No. The cover sheet is outside the manuscript pagination. Start numbering on the first page of your story and continue consecutively after that, even if there are only a few words on a page. Appendices and bibliographies, if you have them, should be numbered continuously like the manuscript pages.

Front Matter and Back Matter

There are a handful of parts that come with the manuscript but aren't a part of your story. Known in the publishing world as "front matter" and "back matter" they include the title page, acknowledgments, dedication, references, and any other materials that say something about your submission. You might not include all of these components with every submission, but if you do, format them correctly so that an editor knows what they are.

Dedication

Authors have been writing dedications in their books for centuries—Horace's odes and Virgil's *Georgics* were dedicated to Maecenas, a wealthy patron. The dedication is a freeform part at the front of your book. It's where you have the opportunity to tell the world who or what inspired you to write this book. Some authors skip this part or use it to thank their agent or editor. Usually, the dedication is personal.

The dedication should be attached on a separate sheet of paper and clearly marked. The publisher will know what to do with it. Don't overextend yourself on this. Keep it short.

Acknowledgments

Acknowledgments may be placed in the front or at the back of the book. They are a brief message from the author thanking people for their help with the book. Think about the things that actors say when they win an Academy Award. That's what the acknowledgments are.

Just like the dedication, the acknowledgments are optional. Including them is completely up to you. If you do include them, do so on a separate sheet of paper that's clearly labeled.

References

References may encompass any number of things. You might want to include references for any quotes or poems you include in your novel, complete with copyright information. If you created special terminology or used words from a foreign language in your novel, you might wish to include a glossary that defines these terms.

You might choose to include a list of your characters and their specific roles in the book, or their family tree. You can also suggest further reading on historical, scientific, or other specific subjects covered briefly in the story. Maps and timelines also fall into this category. Be sure to clearly label each part in the header so that the editor knows what they are.

FACT

A dictionary or glossary of words usually accompanies a science fiction or fantasy novel that uses words that readers won't understand. This is done alphabetically or by order of appearance in the text. Writers also create glossaries if their book contains many foreign phrases or words.

Preparing Excerpts

Often agents and editors ask for "the first ten pages" or "the first thirty pages" of an unpublished manuscript before they ask to read the entire thing. So, it's a good idea to have excerpts prepared in advance.

Create one file that contains just the title page and the first ten pages, and another file that contains the title page and the first thirty pages, and you'll be ready to print out and mail or e-mail an excerpt as soon as you get the request. If a logical stopping point comes on page twenty-nine or thirty-one, then it's okay to make that the excerpt length.

The file should be saved as a .doc file, the format that virtually every word processor will be able to open. If your word processor automatically saves to some different format (like "pages" or "docx") then export the file or use the "Save As" function to create a copy that is a .doc file.

ALERT

If an agent asks to see ten pages of your manuscript, send the *first* ten pages; she will be especially interested in seeing how the novel begins. If she wants to see more, she'll ask for it.

Printing It Out

Many agents and editors today prefer to get electronic submissions. But there are still people who will want to receive a hard-copy manuscript. Here are some guidelines for printing your manuscript:

- Print single sided
- Never use any color but black ink in the printer
- Use standard white copy or multipurpose paper, not fancy bond or colored paper
- Never send manuscript pages that are stained or creased

Writing in the Margins

Once you print out your manuscript, avoid making corrections with a pen or pencil. Wite-out used to be a popular staple for writers. You could make a mistake with your typewriter, brush some Wite-out on it, and type over it. It was supposed to completely hide the error. It never did. But many writers got away with exceeding the three-errors-per-page rule by using it.

Editors just aren't that understanding anymore. They're held to a certain degree of professionalism in their own work and they expect writers to be responsible for one as well. They don't want to see white blemishes all over your manuscript. If you print out your manuscript and notice mistakes, go back to your file, make necessary corrections, and print the corrected page. It will certainly be worth the extra work.

Also avoid making notes in the margins. The only people allowed to write in the margins are editors. You can't use notes to explain your thought processes or defend your ideas. Either the writing stands on its own two legs or it doesn't.

Mailing It Out

If a hard copy is requested, send the manuscript using any of the standard mailing services (USPS, UPS, FedEx, and so on). You may want to spring for overnight delivery if the agent sounds particularly enthusiastic, but usually standard (two-day) shipping is fine. USPS "media mail" is the cheapest shipping rate, but a package shipped that way can take days or even weeks to arrive.

For your own peace of mind, you may want to get delivery confirmation. This is standard with UPS or FedEx shipping, and can be purchased for an extra fee from the USPS. Unless it's been requested that you do so, do not send the package certified.

CHAPTER 21

Working with a Literary Agent

Finding a literary agent to represent your work is the second step on the tried-and-true pathway to a contract with a commercial press. (Step one, of course, is writing a great book.) Finding the right agent for your work through the querying process can be rigorous, time consuming, and often discouraging, but it's worth the effort and will be good preparation for the final round: finding a publisher.

What Literary Agents Do

Literary agents have become the tasters and trendsetters for today's publishing industry. Editors know that the agents they work with regularly have rejected hundreds of manuscripts before picking the one to send, and that they are sending a particular manuscript not just because the quality is impeccable, but because they know that *this* editor is in the business of publishing *this* kind of manuscript.

Knowledge and taste add to that all-important business acumen. A good literary agent knows what makes a reasonable advance, knows what rights to protect, knows the ins and outs of selling subsidiary, translation, and media rights. On top of that, good agents are consummate professionals.

Here is a summary of what an agents does for an author:

- Discusses ideas for new projects and career advancement.
- Reads a manuscript and offers suggestions on how to make it saleable.
- Reads a revised manuscript and offers up even more suggestions until it meets publisher standards.
- Sends the manuscript to targeted editors; keeps the author apprised of both interest and rejections.
- Shares comments from editors who reject the manuscript; decides with the author whether to stop sending it out and go back to revising.
- Lets the author know when publishers are interested, and keeps in communications as negotiations continue.
- Negotiates a book deal, making sure that the terms are acceptable to the author; if multiple publishers are interested, conducts an auction; advises the author on which deal to accept.
- Sends the author the negotiated contract for review, and later for signature; sends the signed contract back to the publisher; sends the author a copy of the contract signed by all parties.
- Manages the advance and royalties—checks will go to the agent who, in turn, sends the author a check for the total less the agent's cut; the current industry standard is 15%.
- Negotiates (or subcontracts) media and foreign language rights.
- Discusses the author's future career, and strategizes about what to write next.

Here's what a legitimate, reputable literary agent does not do:

- Charges the author a fee—agents get paid only if and when the author gets paid.
- Writes your book—if an agent offers to doctor your book (for a fee), run the other way.

The official organization of professional literary agents is the Association of Authors' Representatives (AAR). Visit their website at *http://aaronline.org* to get answers to frequently asked questions, read their "canon of ethics," and find the list of member agents.

QUOTE

[AAR] members may not charge clients or potential clients for reading and evaluating literary works, including outlines, proposals and partial or complete manuscripts. Members may not benefit, directly or indirectly, from charges levied for such services by any other person or entity. There are two exceptions to this rule:

- Members may ask to be reimbursed for the actual cost of returning materials.
- Members may read or evaluate a writer's work at a conference or other event where writers are charged separately for individual consultations.

—From the official Canon of Ethics of the Association of Authors' Representatives (2010)

In order to become a member of AAR, an agent must have been practicing for two years and, in that time period, sold at least ten literary properties. So a brand new agent, even one who is talented and ethical and will go on to have a brilliant track record, may not yet qualify for membership. At last count, the AAR had 338 literary agents listed in its database.

You want an agent who is enthusiastic to the point of being embarrassing, someone who will be your number one booster and supporter. It should also be someone you can trust and talk to, someone who will return your phone calls. But, your agent does not have to be your friend. Remember, this is a business relationship.

Do You Need an Agent?

Whether or not you need an agent depends on your publishing goals. You need an agent if your goal is to sell your book to a major publishing house. These days most editors at major and even mid-sized publishing houses only consider manuscripts submitted to them by agents. Prestigious agents get their submissions taken more seriously and turned around more quickly. Ultimately, it's the manuscript that makes the sale but it's the agent who gets the editor to pay attention.

Many small presses consider submissions directly from the author. Check the publisher's website for their submission guidelines. So if a small press is your goal, then you may not need an agent. Your advance will be small, possibly not even worth an agent's time. But you should have an experienced attorney, one familiar with the issues of intellectual property, read through the contract before you sign it to be sure you're retaining all the rights you're entitled to.

An agent most likely will not be interested in representing you if you are self-publishing or going with a vanity press. They're in business to make money and there's usually not enough to go around if you go that route. If you have self-published a novel and it has sold well (a few thousand copies), a literary agent may be interested in representing you and helping you sell that manuscript to a traditional press.

Targeting Agents

Do your research and target agents who represent the kind of work you've written. Don't send a science fiction manuscript to an agent who represents an author whose work is on the *New York Times* bestseller list if he's not looking at science fiction.

Try to assemble a list of ten to twenty agents. Then prioritize, from your top choice on down.

ALERT

Most agents are not interested in seeing unfinished novels from unpublished writers. So wait to query agents until your novel is completed, revised, and polished so that it is as perfect and compelling as you can possibly make it.

Finding Agents That Represent Novels Like Yours

There are many sources available to you to find agents. Here are a few:

- The database of professional literary agents at *http://aaronline.org* lists its agents, the kinds of work they are looking for, and how they prefer to be queried.
- *Querytracker.net* is an interactive website and online community with a database of literary agents; just enter the kind of manuscript you are shopping, and back comes a list of literary agents and more information about them.
- *Guide to Literary Agents* is an annually updated guidebook that lists agents, how they each prefer to be contacted, and what kind of work they represent; it is also chock full of advice about selling your book.
- Preditors & Editors (*www.pred-ed.com*), a volunteer-run source for information that provides word-of-mouth feedback from writers about agents, editors, contests, conferences, and more, has been collecting information since 1997 including resources that are "not recommended."
- Writer Beware (*www.sfwa.org/for-authors/writer-beware*), a resource maintained by the Science Fiction & Fantasy Writers of America, offers excellent advice for finding a good literary agent and for avoiding scams.

Using Book Acknowledgments to Target Agents

An agent's track record is an excellent indication of whether he is likely to be interested in your manuscript. To find agents who have represented books like yours, take a field trip to a bookstore and pull off the shelf all the books that remind you of your manuscript. Look in the "Acknowledgments" sections where most authors thank their agents. Make a list—the book, the author, and the agent.

Then go to one of the databases and research the agents to find out how to contact them. Start a list!

Getting Referrals from Other Writers

Taking writing classes or going to writing conferences is an excellent way to meet published writers working in the same genre as you are. Writers you meet, especially ones who've read and enjoyed your work, may be happy to share their agent's contact information. If you make a very good impression, they may even be willing to let you use their name in your query letter. But always ask permission.

Add names to your list!

Meeting Agents at Conferences

Many writing conferences have "pitch sessions" where you can sign up to pitch your work to a literary agent. At these conferences agents often hang out between sessions in the bar. Introduce yourself, but don't make it a hard sell. On the other hand, when an agent says, "Tell me about your book," be prepared to pitch it in two pithy sentences. Research the agents who will be at the conference ahead of time so you can be sure that you are seeing an agent you would be interested in your work.

If an agent at a conference asks you to send something like thirty pages, send the *first* thirty pages of the book. And be sure, in your cover letter (or e-mail), to remind him right away: "Hello, this is Gertrude McGillicuddy. I met you at the Writers Stuff conference last week in Hoboken and you asked me to send you the opening chapter of my novel . . . ." Don't assume the agent will remember who you are. Remember, agents meet hundreds of authors.

Asking Everyone You Know

Personal referral is one of the best ways to get an agent you've never met to read and respond to your query. So ask everyone you know and use whatever contacts you have.

You may not think that you know anyone who knows an agent, but when the time comes, it doesn't hurt to ask. Someone's college roommate, or uncle, or ex-husband may now be an agent.

It's so much stronger to start off your query with, "Your sister Virginia Lockhart suggested that I contact you . . . ."

ALERT

Cold calling an agent is a no-no. Never, ever, ever call an agent you haven't met or one with whom you haven't already established a relationship. Communicate via e-mail or snail mail until you are invited to call.

Querying an Agent in Writing

Agents, like all the rest of us, have their preferences. More and more are taking query letters via e-mail, and some accept *only* e-mail queries. Others prefer snail mail. Still others are open to either e-mail or snail mail. Do your research so you approach agents based on their preference.

E-mail Query

If the agent is open to an e-mail query, then put the query letter right into the body of an e-mail message.

In the "Subject" line, make it clear that this is a query. You don't want your query to be overlooked or deleted as spam.

Subject: QUERY: SCARLET SLIPPERS

Send queries individually to each agent and personalize the body of each. Never send a query to a list of e-mail addresses. If you do, your query will probably get deleted without even being considered.

Snail Mail Query

Yes, many agents still accept queries via mail. Some prefer them, saying that it cuts down on the volume they receive and seems to generate a more serious, focused set of submissions.

Mail the agent your one-page query, single-spaced, printed on white paper, with a stamped, self-addressed envelope for response. Be sure you include your contact information; often when agents are excited about what they read, they reach for the phone.

Querying Q&A

Q. Can I include a synopsis or a chapter with my query?

A. Check the agent's preferences and only send what is requested. Some want to see a chapter (always Chapter One) and a synopsis. Others do not.

Q. What kind of response might I get?

A. "Please send a partial" means you've piqued the agent's interest and she wants you to send (typically) fifty pages or three chapters of your work.

"Please send the full manuscript" is good news and what you want to hear, and the reason why you never should start shopping your manuscript before you've finished writing it.

"Can I have an exclusive?" means the agent wants to read the manuscript and, while she's deciding, you agree to put a hold on shopping the work to other agents. You can grant the requested exclusive or not, it's up to you. It's wise, if you do grant an exclusive, to limit the time period for the agent's reply—two weeks or four weeks, for example, should be plenty of time for a highly motivated agent to get back to you with an answer.

"Thanks but no thanks" or words to that effect. If you get some substantive critique, consider it a gift and an indication that the agent thinks your writing has promise; but don't follow up with questions about why your work was rejected. It's not the agent's job to critique your manuscript.

Q. How long should I wait to hear?

A. If you've sent your query and haven't heard in six to eight weeks, move on. If a partial or full manuscript was requested, it could take one to four months before you hear. In that case, it's okay to send a quick e-mail asking for a status update after four months. You may or may not get a response.

Q. Is it okay to query multiple agents at the same time? How many?

A. While this was once considered bad form, it's perfectly acceptable these days to query multiple agents. Keep track of your submissions, and it's a good idea to send them out in batches, say five or six queries at a time. Wait three or four weeks before sending out the next batch. This makes it easier to track your queries, and also allows you to first query the agents you want most to represent you, and then agents lower down in your preferences.

Q. Is it okay to query more than one literary agent in the same agency?

A. Usually this is okay, but wait until one rejects you before you submit to the next.

Keeping Track of Your Queries

It's important to keep track of whom you've queried and the responses you've received. There's at least one website, *www.querytracker.net*, which offers a free service you can use to organize and track your query letters. Or you can create a spreadsheet and make a record whenever you send out a query, including the name and contact information of every agent and the date you sent the query.

Then keep notes. Note when you receive a response. Note whenever you send out a partial or a manuscript. You should always be able to tell, at a glance, how many balls you have in the air. And when the phone rings and an agent calls, it should be easy for you to quickly look up when you queried that agent and what you sent.

Dealing with Rejection

Some writers sell their novel through the first agent who reads it, but for others it can take years. Rejection is painful, but it comes with the turf.

Remember, agents pass on scores of manuscripts every day for reasons that have nothing to do with the quality of the writing or the potential of the author. Most agents aren't unkind so much as busy. So don't be insulted if you get what feels like a dismissive form letter.

Expecting rejection can offer some protection against its sting. But rejection can also help your writing by giving you a clue or two about what needs to be fixed.

Save your rejections. Save them all. These are your battle scars. And when you have the good fortune to receive constructive criticism about your writing, cherish it.

If your query is getting repeatedly rejected, consider revising your query letter. If agents are requesting partials and full manuscripts, and they are rejected, consider revising the manuscript. See if, among all those rejections, you can find some clues for making the work stronger.

FACT

Fantasy author James Hines surveyed nearly 250 published novelists and asked them how many years they had been writing before they made their first novel sale. Their answers ranged from one to forty-one years; the average was 11.6 years.

After the Sale

If you write a great book and get lucky too, then you'll find an agent who will find a publisher who loves your book and wants to publish it. When that happens, don't forget to celebrate! Break open the champagne. Treat yourself to a night on the town. Bake yourself a cake.

Then get ready to revise, probably several more times, working with an editor at the publishing house. As perfect as you think you've made it, there will probably be both major and minor revisions to be made.

Start thinking about marketing the book—establish a presence on Facebook if you're not already out there, create an author's website, and maybe start a blog.

Talk to your publisher about a marketing plan that might include a blog tour, or a radio tour, or visits to local bookstores to sign stock, and readings at libraries and bookstores when the book comes out. You may decide to travel more broadly, especially to places where you've lived or have a vacation home and know lots of people, or to where your book is set.

If your book has a strong nonfiction hook, then identify organizations that might be interested in having you come and speak (and sell books). For instance, if your book has a professional golfer as its hero, you could speak at golf events or country clubs. If your book is about the world of counterfeit coins, then maybe you can get yourself a speaking gig at a coin show.

You may want to do all of this yourself, or invest in an independent publicist to supplement your publisher's efforts and orchestrate your marketing campaign. All of this should begin six months before your pub date. But beware! Marketing your book can consume your time completely, but don't let it. Because the most important thing for you to be working on, after selling your first novel, is writing the next one.

Six Months to a Completed First Draft

Yes, you can complete the first draft of your first novel in just six months. You'll need discipline, a positive attitude, and a structured approach to stay on track.

Here are some basic tips to get the job done.

- **Commit!** Make a commitment to yourself to see it through, put it in writing, and stick it to your bathroom mirror or computer or office door.
- **Write regularly.** You'll be more efficient if you set aside a regular time, even if it's just two hours, to write every day. Write just 500 words a day (about a page and a half) and you could have a manuscript completed in as few as 150 days.
- **Focus on the goal.** Create a visual image that represents, for you, completing your novel. A gold pen? A bouquet of roses? A burst of confetti? The words *The End* written in glitter? Keep that image in mind every day.
- **Try not to get stuck.** There will be times when you feel as if you just can't figure out what comes next or how to write it. Refer to the advice on getting unstuck in Chapter 16, Getting to "The End."
- **Cut yourself some slack.** A first draft is just that, a *first* draft. If you try to make it perfect, you'll never get it done. So give yourself permission to just write, get the story on the page. The polishing can come later.
- **Keep track.** Whether you write in spurts or slow but steady, measure your progress; remember that successful completion comes in small increments. So before you start, get out a calendar and mark off the milestones listed below. As you reach each goal, check it off; adjust the schedule if you need to as you go along.
- **Don't forget to celebrate!** As you reach each interim milestone, celebrate. Reward yourself with a treat, toast your success, throw yourself a party—because writing a novel is challenging and you're doing it.

The Six-Month Plan: Weekly Milestones

Week 1: Set the course

- Create a premise
- Stake out a beginning, middle, and end
- Find your main character and character arc

Weeks 2–3: Research and sketch, sketch, sketch

- Research the characters, their context, the setting
- Write character sketches for the main characters
- Sketch out the main settings
- Identify the themes you are going to explore

Week 4: Outline the scenes in three acts—take a first stab

- Refine your premise
- Refine your ideas about your main character's journey: What does she want, what stands in the way
- Stake out as many plot points as you can—scenes that will take place in the novel
- Organize the plot points into scenes
- Create an outline that sorts scenes into three acts with major turning points (reversals) between each act

Week 5: Write the opening scene

- Make some basic decisions: tense (present/past), viewpoint (first-person, third-person, or multiple third-person), tone (formal/informal)
- Write the first scene
- Don't obsess over it. Move on!

Weeks 6–9: Write the rest of the scenes in "Act I"

- Start each scene as late as possible; end as early as possible
- Make sure every scene has an arc and a turning point

- Each scene should have conflict
- Slow down when you introduce a character or setting for the first time

Week 10: Between the acts: Catch your breath

- Read and revise what you've written
- Revise your outline of Act I so it reflects what you wrote
- Add as much detail as you can to your outline of Act II

Weeks 11–17: Write the scenes in "Act II"

- Continue writing scenes
- Develop the characters
- Move your story, introduce complications and raise the stakes

Week 18: Between the acts: Catch your breath

- Reread and revise what you've written
- Revise your outline of Acts I and II to reflect what you've written
- Add as much detail as you can to your outline of the scenes in Act III

Weeks 19–24: Write the scenes in "Act III"

- Continue writing scenes, raising the stakes, and bringing your main plot to its main climax
- Tie up your subplots
- Show how the conflict has been resolved and your main character has experienced a journey and a transformation
- Type *The End* for the first time.

Weeks 25–26: Read, revise, and celebrate! You've completed the first draft!

APPENDIX B

The Novelist's Resources

An Essential Library

There are loads of writing books and resources available to writers. Here are some that you might find useful:

Bell, James Scott. *Plot & Structure.* (Cincinnati, OH: Writer's Digest Books, 2004).

Benedict, Elizabeth. *The Joy of Writing Sex: A Guide for Fiction Writers.* (New York, NY: Holt Paperbacks, 2002).

Bickham, Jack M. *Scene and Structure.* (Cincinnati, OH: Writer's Digest Books, 1999).

Block, Lawrence. *Telling Lies for Fun and Profit.* (New York, NY: William Morrow: 1994).

Bradbury, Ray. *Zen in the Art of Writing.* (Santa Barbara, CA: Joshua Odell Editions, 1994).

Brande, Dorothea. *Becoming a Writer.* (New York NY: Harcourt 1934).

Brewer, Robert Lee. *Writer's Market.* (Cincinnati, OH: Writer's Digest Books, updated annually).

Brown, Renni, and Dave King. *Self-Editing for Fiction Writers.* (New York, NY: HarperCollins, 1993).

Buchman, Dian Dincin, and Seli Groves. *The Writer's Digest Guide to Manuscript Formats.* (Cincinnati, OH: Writer's Digest Books, 1987).

Chiarella, Tom. *Writing Dialogue.* (Cincinnati, OH: Writer's Digest Books, 1998).

Cowden, Tami D., Caro LaFever, and Sue Viders. *The Complete Writer's Guide to Heroes & Heroines.* (New York, NY: Lone Eagle, 2000).

Deval, Jacqueline. *Publicize Your Book! An Insider's Guide to Getting Your Book the Attention It Deserves.* (New York, NY: Berkeley, 2003).

Edelstein, Dr. Linda. *Writer's Guide to Character Traits.* (Cincinnati, OH: Writer's Digest Books, 2006).

Edgerton, Les. *Finding Your Voice: How to Put Personality in Your Writing.* (Cincinnati, OH: Writer's Digest Books, 2003).

Edgerton, Les. *Hooked: Write Fiction That Grabs the Reader at Page One and Never Lets Them Go.* (Cincinnati, OH: Writer's Digest Books, 2007).

Evanovich, Janet. *How I Write: Secrets of a Bestselling Author.* (New York, NY: St. Martin's Press, 2006).

Fulton, Robert, Jr., Ph.D. *"But . . . You Know What I Mean!" An Editor's Point of View.* (Port Orchard, WA: Tillie Ink, 2002).

Ephron, Hallie. *Writing and Selling Your Mystery Novel: How to Knock 'Em Dead with Style.* (Cincinnati, OH: Writer's Digest Books: 2000).

Gardner, John. *On Becoming a Novelist.* (New York: W. W. Norton, 1983).

Katz, Christina. *Get Known Before the Book Deal: Use Your Personal Strengths to Grow an Author Platform.* (Cincinnati, OH: Writer's Digest Books, 2008).

King, Stephen. *On Writing.* (New York, NY: Scribner, 2000).

Lamott, Anne. *Bird by Bird: Some Instructions on Writing and Life.* (New York, NY: Random House, 1994).

Larsen, Michael. *How to Get a Literary Agent.* (Naperville, IL: Sourcebooks, 2006).

Lerner, Betsy. *The Forest for the Trees: An Editor's Advice to Writers.* (New York, NY: Berkeley, 2000).

Levine, Becky. *The Writing & Critique Group Survival Guide: How to Make Revisions, Self-Edit, and Give and Receive Feedback.* (Cincinnati, OH: Writer's Digest Books, 2010)

Lukeman, Noah. *The First Five Pages: A Writer's Guide to Staying Out of the Rejection Pile.* (New York, NY: Fireside, 2000)

Lukeman, Noah T. *The Plot Thickens: 8 Ways to Bring Fiction to Life.* (New York: St. Martin's Press, 2003).

Lyon, Elizabeth. *Manuscript Makeover: Revision Techniques No Fiction Writer Can Afford to Ignore.* (New York, NY: Perigree, 2008).

Lyon, Elizabeth. *Sell Your Novel Tool Kit.* (New York: Perigee Trade, 2002).

Maass, Donald. *The Fire in Fiction.* (Cincinnati, OH: Writer's Digest Books, 2009).

Maass, Donald. *Writing the Breakout Novel: Insider Advice for Taking Your Fiction to the Next Level.* (Cincinnati, OH: Writer's Digest Books, 2001).

Marshall, Evan. *The Marshall Plan for Novel Writing*. (Cincinnati, OH: Writer's Digest Books, 2001).

McKee, Robert. *Story*. (New York, NY: HarperCollins, 1997).

Oates, Joyce Carol, ed. *Telling Stories: An Anthology for Writers*. (New York: W.W. Norton & Co., 1998).

Prose, Francine. *Reading Like a Writer: A Guide for People Who Love Books and for Those Who Want to Write Them*. (New York, NY: Harper, 2006).

Ross, Marilyn, and Sue Collier. *The Complete Guide to Self-Publishing*. (Cincinnati, OH: Writer's Digest Books, 5th edition updated in 2010).

Sambuchino, Chuck (Editor). *[Annual] Guide to Literary Agents*. (Cincinnati, OH: Writer's Digest Books, updated annually).

Sambuchino, Chuck. *Formatting & Submitting Your Manuscript*. (Cincinnati, OH: Writer's Digest Books, 2009).

Sands, Katherine (Editor). *Making the Perfect Pitch: How to Catch a Literary Agent's Eye*. (Waukesha, WI: Kalmbach, 2004).

Schmidt, Victoria Lynn. *45 Master Characters: Mythic Models for Creating Original Characters*. (Cincinnati, OH: Writer's Digest Books, 2001).

Shertzer, Margaret D. *The Elements of Grammar*. (New York: Longman Publishing Co., Inc., 1996).

Strunk, William, Jr., and E. B. White. *The Elements of Style*. 4th ed. (New York: MacMillan Publishing Co., Inc., 2000).

Vogler, Christopher. *The Writer's Journey: Mythic Structure for Writers*. (Studio City, CA: Michael Wiese Productions, 1998).

Wood, James. *How Fiction Works*. (New York, NY: Farrar, Straus and Giroux, 2008).

Zinsser, William K. *On Writing Well*. (New York, NY: HarperCollins, 1976).

Internet Resources

More and more of the resources writers used to have to purchase or borrow from the library are now readily available online. On top of that, all kinds of websites and blogs provide a rich source of inspiration and information, not to mention a supportive community for aspiring novelists.

Here's a selection of what's currently available:

AGENT QUERY
Free resource on how to target and work with agents.
www.agentquery.com

**ASSOCIATION OF AUTHORS'
REPRESENTATIVES**
This site offers lists of literary agents and their contact information.
www.aar-online.org

**THE ASSOCIATION OF WRITERS
& WRITING PROGRAMS**
This national, nonprofit literary organization serves writers, teachers, and writing programs. They publish a guide to writing programs and sponsor an annual conference and a number of annual writing competitions.
www.awpwriter.org

BARTLEBY
A reference site with dictionaries, books of quotations, books about usage and grammar, literature, history, and more.
www.bartleby.com

BOOK STATISTICS
Interesting statistics from publishing, provided by Dan Poynter and ParaPublishing.
www.bookstatistics.com

BOOKWIRE
An industry resource, powered by Bowker's Books in Print database, keeps up-to-date on books being published.
www.bookwire.com

BULWER-LYTTON CONTEST
A contest for the worst opening sentence, "where www means 'wretched writers welcome.'"
www.bulwer-lytton.com

FICTION WRITER'S CONNECTION
One of the oldest and best resources for writers who want to move to the next level. There is a fee for membership.
www.fictionwriters.com

MIDWEST BOOK REVIEW: WRITER RESOURCES
A rich list of resources for writers.
www.midwestbookreview.com/bookbiz/writers.htm

LITERARY MARKETPLACE
Offers lists of publishers and agents for your work; you can subscribe online or purchase the book.
www.literarymarketplace.com

NEWPAGES.COM
A comprehensive guide to independent publishers, university presses, and small presses primarily in the United States and Canada.
www.newpages.com

PEN AMERICAN CENTER
The U.S. branch of the world's oldest international literary and human rights organization.
www.pen.org

POETS AND WRITERS
Includes the magazine and resources for creative writers.
www.pw.org

PREDITORS & EDITORS
A guide to agents, publishers, editors, awards, etc., and alerts about what to watch out for.
www.pred-ed.com

PUBLISHER'S MARKETPLACE
The industry's go-to site for information about the latest publishing news; their daily e-mail newsletter "Publishers Lunch" is free for anyone who signs up.
www.publishersmarketplace.com

QUERY SHARK
A no-holds-barred blog where an agent critiques fiction queries; leave your ego at the door.
http://queryshark.blogspot.com

SPAWN
The Small Publishers and Writers Network (SPAWN) provides information and resources on writing, editing, and publishing books
www.spawn.org

SHAWGUIDES: GUIDE TO WRITING CONFERENCES AND WORKSHOPS
The most comprehensive list of writing conferences, workshops, and retreats worldwide.
www.shawguides.com

ULTRALINGUA
This site offers tons of information on words and language usage.
www.ultralingua.net

WRITER BEWARE
Provided by Science Fiction & Fantasy Writers of America, this is a clearinghouse for the schemes, scams, and pitfalls that threaten writers trying to get their work published.
www.sfwa.org/for-authors/writer-beware/

WRITER'S MARKET
A fee-based service from Writer's Digest with a treasure trove of information about agents of all genres.
www.writersmarket.com

WRITERS TOOLBOX
Skilled writers provide answers; offered by the Gotham Writers' Workshop.
www.writingclasses.com/WritersResources/toolbox.php

Organizations for Writers

Here are some of the best-known organizations for writers.

THE AUTHORS GUILD (FOR PUBLISHED WRITERS)
www.authorsguild.org

EROTICA READERS AND WRITERS ASSOCIATION
www.erotica-readers.com

HORROR WRITERS ASSOCIATION (HWA)
www.horror.org

MYSTERY WRITERS OF AMERICA (MWA)
www.mysterywriters.org

THE NATIONAL ASSOCIATION OF WOMEN WRITERS (NAWW)
Since 2001, providing a support and assistance network for women writers.
www.squidoo.com/naww

PEN AMERICAN CENTER
www.pen.org

ROMANCE WRITERS OF AMERICA (RWA)
www.rwanational.org

SCIENCE FICTION AND FANTASY WRITERS OF AMERICA (SFWA)
www.sfwa.org

SISTERS IN CRIME (SUPPORTING THE WORK OF WOMEN MYSTERY WRITERS) (SINC)
www.sistersincrime.org

INTERNATIONAL THRILLER WRITERS (ITW)
www.thrillerwriters.org

Conferences

Every year, writers and readers get together at conferences worldwide to talk about books and publishing. Writers come to learn how to write better and to market their manuscripts. Agents come hoping to discover the next break-out writer.

For a clearinghouse of writing conferences, workshops, and retreats worldwide, see ShawGuides (*www.shawguides.com*). Here is a list of some of the notable national conferences.

ASPEN SUMMER WORDS/WINTER WORDS
Writing workshops and presentations with some of the top literary writers.
www.aspenwritersfoundation.org

AWP ANNUAL CONFERENCE
The Annual Conference of The Association of Writers & Writing Programs features hundreds of presentations: readings, lectures, panel discussions, plus book signings, receptions, dances, and informal gatherings. The conference attracts thousands of attendees and more than 500 publishers.
www.awpwriter.org

BOOKEXPO
North America's largest publishing event; join librarians and booksellers and see what's being published in the book business.
www.bookexpoamerica.com

BOUCHERCON
The largest annual conference for readers and writers of crime fiction; location changes each year.
www.bouchercon.info

BREAD LOAF WRITERS' CONFERENCE
A venerable annual conference at Vermont's Middlebury College for serious writers; applicants are screened.
www.middlebury.edu/blwc/

LEFT COAST CRIME
The second biggest conference for readers and writers of crime fiction; location changes.
www.leftcoastcrime.org/

MALICE DOMESTIC
An annual fan conference near Washington, DC, that features traditional mysteries (aka "cozies").
www.malicedomestic.org/

MIDWEST WRITERS WORKSHOP
One of the friendlier writing conferences with lots of help for aspiring writers.
www.midwestwriters.org/

PACIFIC NORTHWEST WRITERS CONFERENCE
An annual writing conference in Seattle.
www.pnwa.org

PENNWRITERS CONFERENCE
An annual writing conference in Lancaster, PA, with workshops for writers at all levels working across the genres.
www.pennwriters.com

ROMANCE WRITERS OF AMERICA NATIONAL ANNUAL CONFERENCE
An annual conference for romance writers and readers. (Regional chapters of Romance Writers of America also sponsor excellent conferences.)
www.rwanational.org

SAN FRANCISCO WRITERS CONFERENCE
An annual West Coast conference with writing workshops and opportunities to connect with agents.
www.sfwriters.org

**SURREY INTERNATIONAL
WRITERS' CONFERENCE**
Near Vancouver in Surrey, British Colombia, this one is big and very personable; lots of workshops and agents and opportunities to get your manuscript critiqued.
www.siwc.ca

THRILLERFEST
An annual conference in New York City sponsored by the International Thriller Writers; before it, CraftFest has workshops for writers.
www.thrillerwriters.org/thrillerfest/

VIRGINIA FESTIVAL OF THE BOOK
A massive festival that brings together writers and readers to celebrate books.
www.virginiafoundation.org/vabookfest/index.html/

WILLAMETTE WRITERS
A conference for professional and aspiring writers in Portland, Oregon; a strong component here is making movie pitches.
www.willamettewriters.com/

WORLD FANTASY CONVENTION
This annual conference brings together authors, editors, publishers, and agents to celebrate fantasy.
www.worldfantasy.org/

WORLDCON
An annual international conference for readers and writers of science fiction and fantasy.
www.worldcon.org/

Index

We Have
EVERYTHING®
on Anything!

The Everything® list spans a wide range of subjects, with more than 500 titles covering 25 different categories:

Business	History	Reference
Careers	Home Improvement	Religion
Children's Storybooks	Everything Kids	Self-Help
Computers	Languages	Sports & Fitness
Cooking	Music	Travel
Crafts and Hobbies	New Age	Wedding
Education/Schools	Parenting	Writing
Games and Puzzles	Personal Finance	
Health	Pets	